Blueprint for Theocracy

Blueprint for Theocracy

The Christian Right's Vision for America

EXAMINING A RADICAL "WORLDVIEW" AND ITS ROOTS

JAMES C. SANFORD

Printed in the United States of America

First Edition, First Printing

Book and cover design by Janice Phelps Williams
Cover photograph: © Bob Daemmrich/Corbis

ISBN: 978-0-9747042-0-3 (hardcover)
ISBN: 978-0-9747042-4-1 (softcover)

LCCN: 2013915024

Metacomet Books
P.O. Box 2479
Providence, Rhode Island 02906

For Jean and Sib

CONTENTS

Preface ix

INTRODUCTION 1

PART I: MILITANT CHRISTIANITY

1 MOVEMENT ON A MISSION 13
A Sleeping Giant Awakes 13
Politics of the Righteous 20
Abortion and the Duty to Disobey 31
Reforming the Culture 37
Cosmic Dimensions 47

PART II: CHRISTIAN WORLDVIEW IN THE MAKING

2 THE ANSWER TO MODERNISM 53

3 CREDO: EVERY SQUARE INCH FOR GOD 59
John Calvin: Will over Reason 59
Abraham Kuyper: Antithesis 68
Cornelius Van Til: The Circular Defense 76

4 BLUEPRINT: GOD'S LAW 83
Christian Reconstructionism 83
R. J. Rushdoony & Co.: Apostles of a New Paradigm 87
The Enemy: Human Autonomy 97
The Antidote: Biblical Law 105
Reconstructing Society 109
Legacy of a Movement 116

5 MISSION: RECLAIMING AMERICA 121
Francis Schaeffer: A Call to Action 121
The Dominionist Urge 124
The Battle for Hearts and Minds 131

PART III: CHRISTIAN WORLDVIEW IN ACTION

6 CHRISTIAN JIHAD 141
Targeting the Enemy 141
Framing Culture War 150
7 TOTAL TRUTH 157
Theistic Facts 157
Theistic Realism vs. Science 161
Providential History vs. History 173
8 THE COMING KINGDOM 185
Christian Libertarianism and the War on Babel 185
Biblical Economics and Biblical Responsibility 191
Law and Theocracy 201
9 A PROPER DIAGNOSIS 211

Glossary 219
Endnotes 225
Index 268

Preface

The idea for this book grew out of an attempt several years ago to satisfy my curiosity. I had recently encountered certain theories on America's founding popular with the Religious Right. Key among them was the notion that the nation's laws and defining documents were rooted in Christianity. Although such theories were hardly persuasive, the odd reasoning behind them spurred my interest. It soon became evident that their formulators were dealing with a completely different body of data than was ordinarily used. Even more striking, the writers were selecting their sources and interpreting facts on the basis of a unique set of assumptions about truth and evidence, the role of the supernatural, and the meaning of history, that set them apart from other observers. Such assumptions were central to why their conclusions were so radically different from more generally accepted ones. They had as they often stated, a special "Christian Worldview" that allowed them to see *the* truth, or at least the truth as defined by their particular idea of God and the Bible.

I was soon to discover that Christian rightists were applying their special worldview to areas outside history as well. Their God-authorized approach was typical of the way they perceived virtually all matters, including culture, science, government, education, and economics. The significance of this approach for an understanding of their movement and its influence became obvious. My original endeavors thus gradually evolved into the present project, a book on the history and role of Christian rightist ideology, or Christian Worldview.

Along the way, many have laid out paths for research and provided essential assistance. In terms of previous publications, I am indebted to authors like Frederick Clarkson and Sara Diamond for their thought-provoking work on dominionism and the politics of the Religious Right. I have also benefited greatly from the work of writers at websites like *Talk to Action* and *Religion Dispatches* who have provided incisive coverage of current trends in the movement. In terms of editorial assistance, I want to give special thanks to Esther Bushman, John Carroll, Jean Doyle, and Pete McCalmont for their most generous help on the manuscript. Esther made organizational suggestions in the early going; John offered academic expertise and insight; Pete recommended changes in language, tone, and emphasis; and Jean served as a sounding board and voice of reason throughout the process, which I will always appreciate. I alone, of course, take responsibility for any and all errors in the final product.

I have many others to thank for their help as well, including P.J. Blankenhorn, Cassandra Carr, John Harkey, Ford Hill, Phil Montague, and Sibyl Sanford, all of whom were kind enough to read the manuscript in part or in whole and to provide encouragement. I am especially grateful to Sib for her unflagging support and enthusiasm. My thanks also go to Allyn Copp and Pete McCalmont for their unstinting efforts to promote the manuscript. Finally, I would like to thank Janice Phelps Williams for her fine work in designing the cover and the book's interior.

INTRODUCTION

"Ideas have consequences," intones a stocky, red-haired man with slightly baggy pants as he squeezes the edges of a lectern. Many believers, he tells his audience, are being enticed by false ideas and, as a result, falling victim to the lure of secular culture. They are abandoning the God of the Bible and worshipping modern idols in his place. Their deviation is cause for the rise of a deep "malaise" across the face of America. Today's Christians consequently face a cultural crisis of unprecedented proportions and the inevitable displeasure of an angry God.[1]

The speaker builds his case by evoking the dangers of secularism. As he sees it, secularism is a subtle, unspoken creed that fosters materialism, hedonism, and self-centeredness. It insidiously misleads the popular mind by promoting humanistic ideals and encouraging visions of self-fulfillment. This modern outlook has, over time, gained a firm grip on public consciousness. It has embedded itself in today's culture, permeating the media, arts and entertainment, education, science, and the information industry. By his reckoning, it constitutes nothing less than a substitute religion, a comprehensive "worldview" resting on deeply rooted premises that assume material things to be the primary datum of existence.

The biggest problem for Christians, in the speaker's view, is that many of them have turned a blind eye to this development. While they follow Christianity, they treat their religion as a private matter and go about their lives as if nothing were amiss. Such a passive state of mind must be drastically reversed, he insists. Traditional Christians need to confront head-on this dire threat to their religion and way of life. To resist its baleful influence, they must adopt a radical alternative, a counter-worldview with an entirely different set of premises. Such a worldview must be based on the Bible and provide a biblical approach to thinking and acting. It must offer a conservative Christian stance on public issues and provide a means of attacking false ideas. In sum, believers need to begin by embracing a "Christian Worldview." Armed with it, they will be better equipped to struggle against secular opponents and promote a distinctly Christian way of life.

The conveyer of this spirited message is the Christian lecturer, Brannon Howse, a key advocate of today's Christian Right and a leading booster of the Christian Worldview concept. Howse presides over Worldview Weekend, an organization that conducts popular conferences in over 20 states each year and boasts a roster of Christian Right celebrities to excite the crowds. In each programmed event, specialists in theology, culture, history, and science offer lectures touching on everything from orthodox doctrine to the niceties of biblical womanhood. They challenge their listeners with topics like "how biblical is your biblical worldview," "the ten most asked questions about creation and evolution," and "why being good is not good enough." No area of experience, it seems, is beyond the reach of doctrinal instruction. The knowledge imparted in such sessions is not restricted to conference attendees. Worldview Weekend disseminates its program to a wider following through books, DVD's, and other instructional materials. With its help, Christian Worldview instruction has found a key niche in today's popular culture.

Worldview Weekend is just one of many organizations on the Christian Right that are currently advancing Christian Worldview. Reinforcing its efforts are numerous fundamentalist Christian churches, homeschooling services, outreach missions, and advocacy groups, each with its own worldview offerings and seminars. Key institutional players like James Dobson and Charles Colson have invested heavily in the concept. Dobson has introduced the Truth Project, a DVD-based curriculum on the topic with its own staff and training events, as a tool of his larger Focus on the Family organization. Colson has launched the Chuck Colson Center for Christian Worldview to foster worldview-related "research, study, and networking." In the book world, conservative Christian publishers currently feature dozens of works dealing explicitly with Christian Worldview, including bestsellers like Colson's *How Now Shall We Live?*, which pleads strongly for a Christian Worldview approach. Within the Christian blogosphere, the concept has gone viral. The internet currently has so many websites featuring Christian Worldview that several yellow-pages sites have emerged to sort them all out.

While Christian Worldview has become popular in conservative evangelical circles of late, it is hardly a novel idea. The birth of the concept actually predates the rise of the Christian Right by many decades. The concept was first developed by conservative theologians in Europe who wished to restore a more doctrinaire form of Christianity to a position of dominance. After undergoing some mutations in an American context, it was ultimately adopted by militant leaders of the Religious Right, drawn to it as a means of defining their aims, strategy, and agenda. In recent times, religious rightists have given Christian Worldview special prominence as they recognized the increasing problem of retaining the loyalty of their adherents, especially young Christians. Those lost through attrition apparently were unable to withstand the pressures of secular culture. In reaction, training programs in Christian Worldview began to be instituted as a way of re-educating followers and unifying the movement.

Christian Worldview indoctrination is seen as critical in establishing a firm mental attitude on the part of adherents. One of its central purposes is to instill supreme confidence in a unique brand of Christian truth. Rooted in God's perspective as revealed in the Bible, the worldview professes to offer a "true" view of the world that serves as a kind of litmus test for correct thinking. This true view is presented as a comprehensive package. Far from being limited to morals and religion, it addresses the whole gamut of experience, including culture, society, politics, economy, science, and history. Christian Worldview, moreover, comes with powerful, self-validating arguments to back up its version of reality. It claims to endow the individual with absolute certainty because God (whose existence, it so happens, is a central premise) guarantees it.

Other worldviews are unable to provide a reliable picture of reality because they are founded on human presumptuousness and wishful thinking. With no ultimate Governor to stand behind their claims, they are awash in uncertainty and confusion.

From a position of perceived cognitive superiority, believers are able to go on the offensive against false worldviews. These they characterize as dramatic opposites of their own worldview. Indeed, they tend to picture the two kinds of belief system as entities confronting each other on a cosmic battlefield. Evangelical philosopher David Naugle asserts that "worldview warfare," i.e., the "megabattle between the forces of light and darkness over the . . . definition of the universe," is part and parcel of a Christian theory of worldview.[2] The true worldview reflects the will of God, while false worldviews represent the views of rebels and reprobates. Even so, there is a kind of irony behind this dualistic thinking. All worldviews–whether true or false–are understood to share a peculiar sort of commonality. Christian worldviewers tend to portray non-Christian worldviews as mirror images of their own worldview, endowing them with a similar scope and intensity. In this way, apparently, they are able to magnify the threat of the enemy and raise the stakes of the struggle.

Most observers would consider such notions of conflict to be a vast over-dramatization of reality. Indeed, common sense and experience would suggest that typical so-called worldviews or belief systems do not fall into any kind of rigid formula. They differ not just in their content, but in how systematically they are formulated and how rigidly they are held. A worldview can be spelled out or implicit, coherent or ad hoc, passionately believed or loosely adhered to. In American culture, many people could be said to have worldviews amounting to little more than unconscious assumptions that shape their attitudes and help in making their everyday decisions. One might call them informal sets of rules. At a somewhat higher level of definition are worldviews–one could label them "belief systems"–defined by sets of principles loosely identified with a religion or general philosophy. These are most often defined flexibly enough to overlap with other worldviews, allow for interaction with them even when they disagree, and be capable of some modification.

Finally, at the most systematic level are worldviews that assert their own unique view of reality and make forceful claims to exclusive truth. These last present themselves as comprehensive systems and have little room for toleration of other viewpoints. Rather than being typical, such worldviews are unusual in open societies.

The Christian Worldview advanced by religious rightists belongs to the third type. It is a worldview that asserts the legitimacy of its own perspective in opposition to all others, using unequivocal language. It explains the sum of experience in a uniform fashion from unshakeable (biblical) premises, adopting its own distinctive approach to facts and knowledge. And, being action-oriented, it embraces a social and political program that fits its framework. If we take ideology in its dictionary sense to denote an "integrated" package of doctrines that finds expression in "a sociopolitical program," it is in a real sense ideological.[3] Like an ideology, and unlike a religion or philosophy, Christian Worldview is at home in a secular landscape where considerations of political power are paramount. Its doctrines provide an organized framework that allows it to articulate a comprehensive agenda and adopt a disciplined approach toward other claimants in the secular sphere.

Some moderate evangelicals might offer more benign constructions of Christian Worldview and object to its being broadly characterized as an ideology with monolithic tendencies. In consideration of this objection, a qualification is in order. Christian Worldview does not have the same meaning in all contexts. Being a function of several historical components, it is subject to different shades of interpretation. A roomful of biblical Christians would probably differ about its proper usage. Some, for example, would likely defend a fairly restricted definition of Christian Worldview, using it to describe a more or less philosophical stance toward the world. Like all adherents of Christian Worldview, they would see it as describing a biblical perspective superior to all others in its ability to explain reality and enlighten minds. But their use of it would be relatively non-political. This usage of the term is often found in the pages of the evangelical journal, *Christianity Today*, or in books by academic Christian apologists like James Sire and Albert Wolters. On the other hand, Christians aligned with the Religious Right would generally defend the term's wholesale application in the secular area. They would understand it in the context of a cultural struggle against the prevailing worldview and link it to an argument for fundamental "reform" of the political, cultural, and economic spheres. While they might disagree among themselves about how closely Christian Worldview should be tied to specific programs, they would emphasize transforming the world to reflect a biblical outlook.

This book will focus on Christian Worldview in the latter sense, as it has been employed in the hands of today's Religious Right. It will be called an ideology for the reasons given. This ideology has been at least partially manifest for over three decades. Most citizens are familiar with its zealous outpourings on culture war, secular humanism, Christian nationhood, parental rights, the naked public square, and similar themes. They know it operationally because it has come to permeate the attitudes not only of the Christian Right, but also of much of the current Republican Party. But rarely do observers recognize Christian Worldview as a distinct phenomenon, with its own logical center, raison d'être, apologia, and program. Nor do they generally understand it as the molded product of historical forces from a distant and sometimes controversial past. The purpose of this book is to subject Christian Worldview to a degree of critical examination not normally given it. In our opinion, it is the best avenue to understanding not only the agenda of the Religious Right, but its psychology and mindset. If we can come to grips with the creedal assumptions of Christian Worldview, we have a better chance of assessing its impact on thought and discourse in our open society.

We have used the word "theocracy" in the title to refer to a central element of the Christian Worldview. Theocracy literally means rule by God, or government by God. It is a concept commonly associated with the Old Testament deity, who issued commands to the ancient Hebrews and expected them to comply. Today's religious rightists endorse a framework that is similar to the old biblical one, in principle at least. God for them is the definitive ruler and lawgiver whose sovereignty extends to all spheres of life and whose laws must take precedence over the human kind. To be sure, God is no longer the old tribal deity given to dictating directly to his chosen people or transmitting tablets on mountaintops. His miracle making is more subdued than in days of old, and his rule is acknowledged only indirectly through such human documents as the Declaration of Independence (so we are told). In today's modern world, he presides over a diverse and often unruly human community. But far from consigning him to irrelevance, these new circumstances make his rule more vital than ever for mankind. The reason is simple: modern government and society are currently in rebellion against God and must be brought to heel.

The chief thinkers of the Religious Right have advanced these beliefs in various forms since the late 1970s. Francis Schaeffer, a key transmitter of the Christian Worldview concept, held that God's law, biblically derived, applied to the secular realm, and he endorsed civil disobedience when human laws contradicted it.[4] "The civil government, as all of life, stands under the Law of God," he asserted in 1981. "[W]hen any office commands that which is contrary to the Word of God, those who hold that office abrogate their authority and they are not to be obeyed."[5] His recent acolytes, Charles Colson and Nancy Pearcey, have been equally adamant on the primacy of God's authority, calling for "establishing the reign of God" and "transforming the world to reflect his righteousness."[6] Today's Christian worldviewers follow in their footsteps. Believing their God to outrank all other gods and authorities, they make little, if any, concession to the principle of church-state separation or the equal treatment of different beliefs. They assert the universal scope of their God's sovereignty, holding that his law applies not just to believers but to all human beings. In our view, "theocratic" is the best term in English to describe this outlook.

The present book examines Christian Worldview by considering three general topics: first, the emergence of the movement associated with it, the Religious Right; secondly, the intellectual origins of Christian Worldview and how it developed into an ideology; and finally, the agenda of Christian Worldview in areas that have ramifications for America today. The introductory section (Chapter One) addresses the first topic by showing how the Religious Right rose to a position of influence in a few short years. We define the Christian Right (or Religious

Right) as a socio-political movement of traditionalist Christians begun in the late 1970s calling for an America based on biblical principles. Its immediate source of inspiration was the Christian philosopher, Francis Schaeffer, and its first public personality was Jerry Falwell. In the next section (Chapters Two through Five) we follow the historical rise of Christian Worldview as a puritanical, anti-modernist ideology long before the Religious Right existed. We begin with its Calvinist roots in the Protestant Reformation and consider its revival in the nineteenth and early twentieth century in the form of a militant Neo-Calvinism. We take up its adoption in the 1960s and 1970s by the Christian Reconstructionist movement, which fused it with right-wing political and economic theory. And we address Christian Worldview's eventual transformation under the current Religious Right into a platform for "reclaiming" America.

Chapters Six through Eight are attempts to examine Christian Worldview as it is expressed in three major areas: jihadism, truth and knowledge, and worldly affairs. Thus Chapter Six examines the Christian Worldview notion of "antithesis," or conflict, as it plays out in the strategy and rhetoric of the Christian Right. It focuses on how the framework of "culture war" is used to advance the movement's objectives. Chapter Seven explores the role of Christian Worldview in redefining fact and truth according to the standards of revelation. It discusses the Religious Right's rejection of empirical science and historical method in favor of so-called theistic realism and Christian revisionist history. Chapter Eight examines the use of Christian Worldview by Christian rightists to approach government, economics, and law.

While we attempt to provide a fair and accurate picture of Christian Worldview, we make no claim to neutrality. We fully acknowledge a bias in favor of pluralism, tolerance, and evidence-based thinking, and against absolutist agendas in the political sphere. In our view, Christian Worldview advocates present a direct challenge to today's open society by employing the language of non-negotiable truths. Attacking other "worldviews" for their untrustworthy assumptions, they assert that correct thinking can only be based on the direct word of God as revealed in Scripture. In the present book, we turn the tables on the advocates of religious correctness by examining the assumptions of *their* thinking. Because their assumptions are arbitrary and dogmatic in key respects, they offer a rich target for critique. Our task will be to disentangle the multiple roots of Christian Worldview and show the way it influences the mindset, agenda, and strategy of its adherents. Only by subjecting it to the light of day and spelling out its broad implications for our society and nation, can we hope to contend with its influence.

PART I:

Militant Christianity

1

MOVEMENT ON A MISSION

A Sleeping Giant Awakes

In May 1979, Robert Billings, a Washington-based lobbyist for Christian causes, arranged a meeting between several Republican political operatives and an up-and-coming Baptist televangelist by the name of Jerry Falwell. The strategy session was to take place in Falwell's hometown of Lynchburg, Virginia.[1] Falwell had made "The Old Time Gospel Hour" something of a brand name on TV stations around the country, and his emphasis on pro-family issues had made him a moral beacon for conservative evangelicals. The political trio that came to meet with him–Paul Weyrich, Howard Phillips, and Richard Viguerie–were three of the biggest "movers and shakers" of the New Right.[2] What they had in mind was a way of getting Christian evangelicals involved in the political process and bringing them under the GOP tent. Up to that time, the right wing of the Republican Party mostly consisted of Goldwater conservatives whose bread-and-butter issues were fighting communism and defending free market capitalism. Christian Protestant evangelicals represented a large demographic group that was still politically inexperienced and uncommitted (a large number of evangelicals actually voted for Jimmy Carter, the Democratic presidential candidate, in 1976).[3] If the GOP could respond to some of their concerns, they seemed a winnable constituency for the Republican cause.

When the three men, who were joined by conservative activist Ed McAteer, gathered in Lynchburg to talk to Jerry Falwell, they were armed with ideas. Convinced that Christian moral and cultural issues should be addressed in the coming election, they suggested the creation of a new organization to make the case to the Republican Party and the American electorate. Paul Weyrich came up with the phrase "moral majority," soon to become the group's official title. Falwell was to be the public face of the organization, while Robert Billings, a close associate of Weyrich, was to serve as its executive director.[4] Thus was born the organization most closely associated with the rise of the Religious Right in modern-day America. Falwell established Moral Majority Inc. on June 6, 1979, and soon turned it into a household word. After setting up 50 state chapters within months, he took to the airwaves with four priorities: to be pro-life, pro-family, pro-morality, and pro-America. When Ronald Reagan's presidential candidacy was assured in the spring of 1980, Falwell went to battle for the Republican ticket. He traveled back and forth across the country pitching his message to fellow ministers, urging them to get their pastoral flocks to the voting booths. As it turned out, his Moral Majority, by mobilizing the evangelical community, contributed substantially to Reagan's lopsided victory.

The major role played by the new Christian voting block caught many political observers off guard. The Moral Majority's organizational prowess together with its brash, confrontational style spelled the emergence of a new kind of force on the American scene. Politics in the United States would never be quite the same again. The public impact of the Christian Right in the coming years would qualify it as "one of the most successful political and social movements of modern times, arguably in American history," according to veteran journalist Frederick Clarkson.[5] The conditions behind the movement's emergence were not accidental. Although Jerry Falwell and some GOP operatives initially lit the fuse, there was flammable material in ready supply. At the center of the combustible pile was a constituency not normally prominent in national politics–Protestant evangelicals–with a long list of grievances and priorities.

Who were these evangelicals and what is remarkable, if at all, about their entry into politics? Evangelicals, by one useful definition, are those who believe in the unique authority of the Bible and the importance of a "life-transforming" faith in Jesus Christ as a way toward personal salvation.[6] They attend church faithfully, emphasize spiritual renewal, and generally hold traditional values on social issues. Within these general parameters, however, evangelicals are actually quite diverse both religiously and otherwise. Included among their ranks are traditional fundamentalists, neo-evangelicals, Reformed Christians, Pentecostals, and charismatics, to name just a few groups.[7] While all of them are faithful to the Bible, their interpretation of Scripture and general orientation can differ significantly. As in any population group, attitudes vary widely according to factors like class, education, and geography. On the other hand, there is no denying that respect for tradition and authority tends to find expression in conservative opinions. Many evangelical Christians, moreover, come from rural and small-town backgrounds and hold negative views about modern, urban life. It is thus not too remarkable that so many evangelicals identify with the traditional, moralistic message of the Religious Right and vote Republican.

While most evangelicals lean toward political conservatism, history shows that this predilection does not inevitably translate into political involvement. Until recently, in fact, evangelicals tended to be less involved in public issues than most other groups. Nineteenth century revivalism, the ancestor of today's evangelicalism, gave rise to a very personal sort of religion in which saving souls took priority over reforming the earthly kingdom. After the Civil War, premillennialism–the belief that Christ would soon return to usher in a new millennium–became popular with many believers, predisposing them to wait for the Second Coming rather than get involved in worldly affairs. These religious attitudes persevered with some vigor through the twentieth century. Evangelicals' lack of interest in taking on current issues was reinforced by their hostility towards liberal mainline Protestants, whom they condemned for making peace with the modern world. Liberal Protestants' social activism, a form of mission to the world often called the "social gospel," met with general suspicion from traditional evangelicals.

The one modern instance when many evangelicals clearly shed their reluctance to engage in national politics was the fundamentalist movement of the 1920s. World War I and its aftermath brought many cultural issues to a head and led to an anti-modernist, anti-evolutionist crusade. That movement reached a climax with the famous Scopes "Monkey Trial" of 1925, when a Tennessee teacher was tried and fined for teaching evolution in a public school. The trial captured the attention of the national media and brought unfavorable publicity and ridicule to the fundamentalist cause. The repeal in 1933 of Prohibition, a cause in which they had invested much energy, was another blow to evangelicals, leading to further disillusionment with public involvement. Accordingly, many evangelicals voluntarily withdrew from electoral politics to tend to private and spiritual concerns. Not until Communism became perceived as a threat to American society in the post-World War II era did evangelicals gradually begin to show a renewed interest in political life.

What increasingly affected evangelicals' public consciousness during the Cold War period, however, was not so much the emergence of an international enemy as the intrusion of national events into their daily lives. Nothing, for instance, made them more aware of political realities than federal policies on education. The local school was a central focus for evangelicals because they saw it as an extension of the home in inculcating moral and social values. It also stood as the guardian of a stable social order, which, at least in the South, preserved racial separation. The Supreme Court's *Brown v. Board of Education* (1954) decision outlawing school segregation shook traditional white communities like an earthquake, inaugurating a long struggle between local and federal authorities on school policy. Moreover, by the early 1960s, values issues were combining with racial issues to create further grounds for discontent. Supreme Court rulings prohibiting government-sponsored prayers and devotional Bible reading in public schools angered religious traditionalists wishing to preserve the vestiges of a Protestant Christian moral order. Such rulings often led to efforts to circumvent the public schools, notably the establishment of a large number of private Christian academies. The long-term political consequences of these educational flashpoints cannot be overestimated, especially since resentments could be ignited at any time. Paul Weyrich maintains, with some justification, that the Carter administration was responsible for "launching the Christian

Right" in 1978 by moving to revoke the tax-exempt status of Christian private schools that had not shown sufficient evidence of racial integration. Evangelicals took the IRS stance as equivalent to an attack on their way of life.[8]

Social grievances about education were augmented by a more general discontent over the state of American society. During the 1960s, American TV watchers witnessed movements of mass protest, challenges to traditional authority, and the embrace of unconventional life styles. Two political assassinations in the late 1960s were followed by the last throes of the Nixon administration, the worst economic recession since the Great Depression, and American defeat in Vietnam. Newly conscious segments of the populace seeking a voice, notably women and minority groups, alarmed traditionalists who felt threatened by changes in roles and relationships. The old Protestant establishment itself seemed to be on shaky ground. Americans were becoming more religiously diverse because of a decline in overall Christian affiliation. Popular skepticism, unfamiliar religions, and New Age beliefs were on the upswing. All of these tendencies distressed many who stood for the old Christian moral principles.

Political issues relating to gender and family also provided fuel for conservative dissatisfaction. Significantly, evangelical Protestants followed the cue of conservative Catholics on many issues. Key among them was the Equal Rights Amendment, intended to end discrimination against women, which was passed by the U.S. Senate in 1972 and sent to the state legislatures for ratification. Opponents took to the offensive, portraying the Amendment as a feminist attempt to subvert the traditional American family. Phyllis Schlafly, the Catholic head of the rightist Eagle Forum, led the campaign opposing the Amendment throughout the 1970s, shrewdly reaching out to Protestants across the country and assembling a broad coalition. It was one of the first times that conservative Catholics and Protestants were able to cooperate on an issue of national magnitude and overcome their traditional animosity.[9]

A similar pattern of Catholic initiative and Catholic-Protestant cooperation occurred on what was to become a defining issue for the Religious Right: abortion. The Supreme Court's ruling in *Roe v. Wade*

(1973), allowing abortion under certain circumstances, brought early conservative Catholic opposition. Protestant evangelicals at first were largely indifferent to the issue. Jerry Falwell, for example, never emphasized abortion in his sermons until as late as 1978. There is evidence to suggest that the initial lack of interest sprang from anti-Catholic bias. At any rate, several influential evangelicals who came to see abortion in expressly biblical terms began promoting the pro-life position in editorials and at conferences.[10] Francis Schaeffer, an evangelical preacher, and C. Everett Koop, a prominent pediatrician, contributed significantly to bringing the issue to the fore. The two collaborated on the anti-abortion book and film, *Whatever Happened to the Human Race?* (1979), which saw widespread circulation in the evangelical community. By the time of the formation of Moral Majority, abortion had become an issue that could energize evangelicals.

Throughout this period, evangelicals were clearly becoming concerned with the direction of the country. The question was whether their concern could be converted into active worldly engagement. What they still seemed to lack was the self-confidence and awareness necessary for firm political commitment. A religion-based political movement required a theology that defined dramatically what one was fighting for and against in the secular realm. To achieve cohesion and purpose, a more robust form of Christianity was needed. It just so happened that such a strain began to emerge in the late 1970s at the very time that political tensions were mounting. The agent responsible for introducing it to the evangelical world was the same pastor who helped to publicize the abortion issue: Francis Schaeffer.

Francis Schaeffer was a preacher steeped in orthodoxy, yet with a surprising maverick streak. On the one hand, his doctrinaire seminary training and fidelity to Scripture seemed to fit him for a typical fundamentalist ministry. But Schaeffer was more adventuresome than most. In the mid-1950s, he left the United States to established a Christian study center in the heart of apostate Europe at l'Abri, Switzerland, opening his doors to any wandering souls who would listen to his message. Known for his goatee and knickers, Schaeffer seemed to savor his unusual perch outside the mainstream. He made a career of listening to the young and guiding them through their spiritual troubles, bringing God's word to a generation of world-traveling American baby boomers.[11] He saw his role as introducing Christians, many of them lapsed or doctrinally naïve, to a biblical framework for interpreting the prevailing culture.

Schaeffer offered a disturbing diagnosis. American society was on a downward curve, he warned, infected by such human plagues as abortion, sexual promiscuity, drugs, relativism, secular education, judicial activism, genetic engineering, and government overreach. The great enemy was humanism, the man-oriented philosophy responsible for all that was wrong with American society. For Schaeffer, nothing short of a national campaign against humanism was needed to halt America's inexorable drift toward Gomorrah.[12] America needed to return to what he believed were its religious foundations, embodied in the values of orthodox, Protestant Christianity. Such a drastic turnaround required a strong commitment by Christians to change the culture and instill a biblical point of view.

Schaeffer did not underestimate the obstacles faced in reaching such goals. To combat secular forces, he realized that biblical Christians needed a comprehensive approach that was doctrinally consistent and uncompromising, and that could answer the enemy on every front. It needed to provide a proper basis for thought and action including a vision of what a revived Christian society should look like. It was in this context that he advanced a Christian Worldview as the answer to the so-called worldview of humanism.

Schaeffer's talk of opposing worldviews and spiritual conflict caught the attention of conservative evangelicals at a time when they were in need of a unifying theme. His message came across as combative, yet authoritative, while his willingness to discuss broader intellectual issues enhanced his reputation as a thinker with gravitas. Under his influence, a large number of apolitical evangelicals, realizing their renunciation of public involvement was getting them nowhere, began to evolve into Christian activists. By the late 1970s and early '80s, Schaeffer had become a traveling celebrity in evangelical circles, appearing frequently on Pat Robertson's 700 Club TV program and at Jerry Falwell's Thomas Road Baptist Church, among other venues. His videos on abortion and cultural crisis were widely circulated, and his book *A Christian Manifesto* (1981) was hailed by Falwell as "probably the most important piece of literature in America today."[13] Schaeffer's writings in turn inspired some of the best selling publications on the Religious Right, including Tim LaHaye's alarmist tract, *The Battle for the Mind* (1980) and John Whitehead's equally controversial *The Second American Revolution* (1982). In just a few years the groundwork had been laid for a new kind of political rhetoric and activism. A sense of mission was coming into focus for the Religious Right: a mission to transform America.

Politics of the Righteous

Ronald Reagan's triumph in 1980 provided just the sort of encouragement Schaeffer's Christian soldiers needed: it offered them the promise of political change and a central role to play. With a president who seemed to be openly sympathetic to their values, biblical Christians had real hopes of curbing so-called humanistic excesses. They now believed Schaeffer's call to "roll back" the enemy's worldview[14] to be a realizable goal. Rather than being a simple vehicle of protest, they had hopes of serving as an agent of transformation.

The realities of national politics, of course, required some getting used to. If Christian activists entered the political arena believing they could win a quick battle of worldviews, they were in for some disappointment. The terrain in Washington was more complex than the pulpit politics they were familiar with, and they now had to reckon with events and forces beyond their control. Before long, their image of their own power had to be roughly revised. It came as a rude surprise to find themselves in the role of supplicants rather than doers or facilitators. Nonetheless, the movement's leaders were motivated and willing to learn. If their experience during and after the Reagan administration turned out to be less fulfilling than frustrating, they were still able to convert their disappointments into practical knowledge. Strategic disagreements among themselves and the frictions attending them were part of that learning process. Their time in Washington is thus a tale of their gradual mastery of the system. When the winds blew strongly in their favor during the George W. Bush years, they were prepared to cash in on their years of experience.

During their first encounter with power in 1980, however, Christian rightists needed to figure out how closely to align themselves with their new allies in Washington. At the outset, the potential benefits of access and influence seemed to far outweigh the dangers of cooptation. Jerry Falwell was typical of those eager to hitch their star to Ronald Reagan. Falwell placed his firm confidence in the new president from the outset, assuming that he would "steer the nation back on a right course."[15] Leaving politics to the politicians, he generally turned his mind to other matters. He continued to raise his voice periodically, but served mostly as a cheerleader for the administration. The Reaganites returned Falwell's trust by offering access, a few appointments for evangelicals, and vocal support for Religious Right stands on abortion and prayer in public schools. But unwilling to risk political capital on socially divisive issues with little prospect of legislative success, the administration shied away from matters of central concern to moral majoritarians. It failed, for instance, to support quixotic measures like the Human Life Statute and the omnibus Family Protection Act, and gave only lukewarm support to a doomed School Prayer Amendment.[16]

Even if religious rightists had wanted to take a more assertive role, Moral Majority, Inc. was ill equipped to act as an independent power center. Like many other first efforts at organization, it had built-in problems that hampered its long-term effectiveness. While it billed itself as a "moral" rather than a sectarian organization in the hope of involving conservative Catholics and Jews, its gospel tone limited its appeal. It derived almost all of its support from the evangelical sector, primarily Baptist fundamentalists.[17] Jerry Falwell's close reliance on a network of fundamentalist pastors, who played the role of messengers and ward heelers, enabled him to gather crowds and mobilize the base in short order. He could bring in funds almost on demand through direct mail appeals and could make liberal politicians in marginal districts run scared prior to an election. But his organization had little in the way of a permanent infrastructure or any sort of local network beneath central headquarters. Most of what emanated from the organization came from the top, and much of that was rhetoric and showmanship. For all of its ability to corral and mobilize voters, Moral Majority was largely a paper affair with a good mailing list and solid pastoral contacts.[18]

By the end of the 1980s, Moral Majority seemed to be drifting toward irrelevance and eventual extinction. However, while some in the media were declaring the reign of the Religious Right to be over, they had not bargained for the rise of another personality in the movement, televangelist Pat Robertson, and the emergence of a new organization under his tutelage. Robertson's high TV profile and right-wing opinions earned him a large following among Christian rightists and the admiration of Republican bigwigs like Paul Weyrich. Nurturing ambitions to become Reagan's successor, he assembled a campaign and threw his hat in the ring as a candidate for president in the Republican primaries of 1988, attracting strong support from right-wing sources. The upshot is well-known: Robertson did surprisingly well in a few caucuses where he could rally a dedicated base, but fared poorly in large electoral settings where his ultra-conservative views were truly tested. He eventually bowed out of the primaries and backed the established candidate, George H.W. Bush, leaving disappointed Christian conservatives without a standard-bearer.[19]

But while Robertson's campaign failed in its electoral objectives, it eventually led to the formation of a permanent political organization. In the midst of defeat, Robertson found himself with a large network of experienced workers, churches, and donors drawn together through a year's worth of campaigning. The potential of such an organization, backed by the muscle of Robertson's Christian Broadcasting Network and the manpower resources of his CBN (later Regent) University, was obvious. Realizing the influence it could wield, Robertson hired a bright new talent fresh out of graduate school, Ralph Reed, to streamline it. Within a year Reed had coaxed the Christian Coalition from the ashes of Robertson's campaign machine and transformed it into the standard bearer of the Religious Right.[20]

From its inception, the Christian Coalition had little in common with the Moral Majority. By its very name it was not hesitant to declare its allegiance to the cause of Christ and base itself directly on religious loyalties. Moreover, built from the ground up, it represented a "grass roots" strategy very different from the superficial "rally" strategy followed by Jerry Falwell.[21] Robertson and Reed's aim was to develop and train a new generation of activists at the local and state level who would run for school board vacancies, legislative seats, and local government positions. They wished to establish "laboratories for testing [our] policy ideas" and to create a "farm system of future candidates."[22] Moreover, both men shared the view that the existing Republican Party could not be relied upon to embrace the Christian Right's priorities. It needed to be pressured, if not infiltrated and controlled, by Christian loyalists. Reed saw the Coalition as an ideal means of accomplishing these goals. Without delay, he set about building the organization into a force to be reckoned with, raising money, expanding the membership, hiring field directors, and funding political training. In its first two national conferences, the Coalition focused on "discussions of the mechanics of party takeover," including ways of gaining control of state GOP organizations and sending Christian delegates to the Republican Convention.[23]

Christian Coalition tactics, at least in the early years, were controversial. Reed often used the terminology of guerilla warfare to describe his approach to politics. "I want to be invisible," he asserted in 1991. "I paint my face and travel at night. You don't know it's over until you're in a body bag. You don't know until election night." A year later he defended the maneuver of putting forward "stealth candidates" for public office who did not reveal their true agenda, calling it "just good strategy." [24] Before the tactic was widely publicized and discredited, Christian Coalition commonly resorted to it in local and state elections where turnout was small and results could be swayed by a determined minority. Its use revealed Coalition leaders' obvious anxiety that public disclosure would lead to popular rejection of their point of view.[25] The Coalition exerted its power behind the scenes in other venues as well. It caught the nation, and probably the Republican old guard, by surprise when it showed up with a large contingent of delegates at the 1992

Republican National Convention. Flexing their muscles on the platform committee, Coalition delegates lobbied hard for a platform keynoted by a strict anti-abortion provision and loaded with biblical references and pro-family nostrums.

Facing media criticism for the radical image it projected at the 1992 Convention, however, the Christian Coalition began to take a more pragmatic turn. While Pat Robertson continued to issue extremist statements from time to time, he granted Reed tactical flexibility on the political front. Mainstream conservatism and even compromise became the Coalition's themes of the day. Reed made it clear that "the cluster of pro-family issues must now be expanded to attract a majority of voters."[26] In 1994 he supported Newt Gingrich's Contract with America even though it contained little red meat for cultural conservatives. The following year, the Christian Coalition came out with its own "Contract with the American Family" offering a set of ten "pro-family" legislative goals. But even these were toned down, framed to have the greatest chance of passage. Rather than insisting on an amendment prohibiting abortion, for instance, the contract called for legislation banning "partial birth abortion." Still, only two of the ten pro-family proposals ultimately passed, indicating the challenges the Coalition faced even with a Republican-controlled Congress.

At the GOP conventions of 1996 and 2000, the Christian Coalition showed increasing political sophistication. Coalition delegates strived to avoid undue controversy, avoiding embarrassment to the chosen presidential candidate. The organization had reached the point where its relationship with the Republican Party was almost proprietary. The gradual merging of the two entities is shown by a report in 2002, estimating that Christian conservatives dominated GOP committees in 18 states and held at least 25% control in all but six.[27] Having achieved much of its original purpose, the Christian Coalition gradually faded into the background. The emergence of a Bush administration bursting with Religious Right appointees in 2001 was a sign of both the organization's success and its growing redundancy. When Pat Robertson resigned as head of the Coalition in the second year of the Bush presidency, Gary Bauer, a leading Religious Right activist, gave a telling assessment of the altered state of affairs: "I think Robertson stepped down because the position has already been filled. [Bush] is that leader right now."[28]

Ironically, for all of its successes, the Christian Coalition was always a focus of controversy within Christian activist ranks. Even while it was capturing a large chunk of the Republican Party in the 1990s, it drew criticism for its strategic alliance with GOP regulars. As far back as the early Clinton years, some purists criticized the Coalition for dealing with Republicans on the party's terms rather than standing as a countervailing force. These purists developed strong organizations of their own as a way of establishing a reliable voice on the right. Prominent among them was James Dobson of Focus on the Family (FOF), whose no-nonsense approach and organizational power earned him high respect from other leaders. Starting FOF as an organization for providing Christians with family advice, Dobson expanded it over the years into a cultural media empire. He also sponsored the more politically oriented Family Research Council (FRC), which focused its attention on "pro-family" legislation in Congress. In the late 1990s, the FRC developed into the Religious Right's most aggressive lobbying operation in Washington under the stewardship of Gary Bauer. Bauer changed it from a "sleepy little think tank operation" with three staffers in 1989 to a powerhouse with a budget of $14,000,000 and a staff of 120 in 1999.[29] When the Republicans took over Congress in the mid 1990s, Dobson and Bauer were much less willing than Ralph Reed to give the party a free pass. They watched in anger as the Republican leadership soft-pedaled controversial social issues while Reed's Christian Coalition succumbed to its wishes.

While Dobson preferred to remain in the background, he decided after several years that it was time to draw a line in the sand. Threatening to desert the GOP unless the Religious Right agenda was taken seriously, he was able to transform the relationship between it and the Religious Right. The GOP House leadership convened a "values summit" in May, 1998 with Dobson and other Christian Right leaders in what one participant called "the biggest deal up until that time, a coming of age." The upshot was the deepening involvement of hard-line religious activitsts in the law-making process.[30] Groups called "Value Action Teams" (VATs), i.e. small gatherings of Religious Right leaders and Republican lawmakers, began to meet weekly in the House and Senate to evaluate legislation and coordinate strategy for the passage of bills. As active participants, religious leaders could enlist the support of their vast constituencies to exert pressure on wavering Republicans at a moment's notice. The now powerful Family Research Council, still loosely allied with Dobson, served as a control center for the VATs.[31] The Religious Right was soon able to assert a much more direct influence over the legislative process. All it seemed to lack was a friendly president who could allow laws to pass without veto threats.

That deficiency was remedied by the successful candidacy of George W. Bush, an evangelical with the right political pedigree. Bush's victory in 2000 seemed an answer to the prayers of Christian conservatives: at last, the election of one of their own. That same year they were also blessed with an ideologically friendly Congress and a Supreme Court on the verge of tipping rightward. For the first time ever, the planets seemed to be aligned in their favor.

Under the new administration, the Religious Right soon made its presence felt. The executive branch was promptly seeded with many of the movement's seasoned warriors, especially at the assistant and deputy secretary level.[32] At lower echelons, staff positions were commonly filled by a steady stream of candidates from Christian rightist institutions like Regent University, Liberty University, and Patrick Henry College.[33] Influential committees dealing with medical and scientific matters were heavily weighted with Christian conservatives to assure biblically correct conclusions.[34] These new appointments enabled Christian rightists not merely to exert pressure, but to formulate policy and steer legislation on key social, legal, medical, and educational issues.

Many areas of social and family policy in the Bush years bear the fingerprints of the Religious Right. The curtailment of embryonic stem cell research, the overruling of scientific opinion in social and environmental matters, the refusal to address abortion clinic attacks, the favoring of school voucher programs, and the funding of sex abstinence programs all provide tangible evidence of its influence. While some initiatives took the form of high profile legislation, as with the partial-birth abortion ban, others were implemented behind the scenes. For instance, the Justice Department quietly began to have its Civil Rights Division focus attention on religious cases rather than racial and gender ones, and the State Department adopted the practice of placing "family advocates" on American negotiating teams at international conferences, where they were allowed to overrule professionals on public health and other issues. In the sphere of judicial appointments, Christian Right groups had virtual veto power in the screening of nominees. Karl Rove devised a formula whereby nominees with records friendly to both corporations and the Christian Right would go to the top of the list, thus satisfying two important constituencies of the GOP.[35]

Probably the greatest success for the Religious Right, however, came with the implementation of Bush's faith-based initiative.[36] The program, aimed at shrinking government by contracting out public social obligations to private organizations, in effect gave leverage and influence to religious groups with social agendas. A huge amount of unregulated money, running possibly into the billions of dollars each year[37] found its way into the hands of such groups as a result.

On the face of it, the involvement of religious organizations in providing social services sounds innocent enough. President Bush portrayed the faith-based initiative as a means "to welcome people of faith in helping meet social objectives."[38] But the theory behind the religious approach was not quite so tenderhearted. The faith-based initiative was largely the brainchild of Marvin Olasky, a long time Christian rightist who helped coin the phrase "compassionate conservatism." The phrase is ironic because in his writings Olasky mixes "compassion" with a good dose of condemnation. Olasky believed that most candidates for public assistance suffer not so much from physical deprivation as from deficiencies of spirit. That is, recipients of job training, poverty aid, and the like lack a proper sense of sin and remorse. The ideal solution for their problems is repentance and Christian conversion.

To be sure, all sides in Washington recognized that, in theory at least, government funding for explicit religious activity was constitutionally taboo. Public funding had to occur with a line drawn between a service group's religious purpose and the legislative purpose of the program it was administering. Still, some of those distinctions were blurred when funding standards came up for discussion between Congress and the Bush administration. Bush's idea of standards, it turns out, was fuzzier than that of a majority of Congress. Unable at the end of the day to get Congress to accept his version, Bush unilaterally established his own faith-based program by executive order. He created a faith-based office in the White House and similar offices in the Departments of Education, Labor, Health and Human Services, and elsewhere. Although funds were scarce in the absence of a congressional mandate, the faith-based program was able to divert money already designated for federally run social programs into the hands of religious groups.

The ambiguous line between social services and proselytizing remained a continuing problem. Many of the groups receiving funds, such as Pat Robertson's Operation Blessing, Chuck Colson's Prison Fellowship Ministries, and the Right to Life Education Foundation, had agendas that went far beyond the furnishing of social services.[39] Knowledgeable observers were pointing out that money was being dispensed more on the basis of religious credentials and political connections than proven track records.[40] Moreover, unlike official government agencies, religious groups were able to avoid any monitoring of the effectiveness of their programs.[41] In essence, Bush's faith-based initiative evolved into a pork barrel program largely for the benefit of zealous supporters. His first appointee to head the program, John DiIulio, a conservative but idealistic Catholic who expected the program to benefit the truly needy, quit in disgust before the year was out. As he described it later, "There is no precedent in any modern White House for what is going on in this one: a complete lack of a policy apparatus. What you've got is everything–and I mean everything–being run by the political arm."[42]

While Christian rightists benefited greatly from programs like the faith-based initiative and continued to nurture their ties with the Bush administration, they still felt compelled to agitate for their own special issues in the political arena. They considered this a political necessity since elements of their social agenda were simply too bold to gain the enthusiastic support of their Republican allies. In 2003, for example,

James Dobson and other leaders committed major resources to one of their key pro-family planks: passage of a Federal Marriage Amendment that barred marriage between gay and lesbian couples. In many respects this was a quixotic quest. Given that a constitutional amendment required two-thirds majorities in the House and Senate to go forward, the strategy faced insurmountable obstacles. Still, in spite of inertia at the federal level, the Dobsonites were able to convert their efforts on the issue into political gains. Fortunately for them, the Massachusetts Supreme Judicial Court had just ordered the issuance of marriage licenses for gay couples in May of 2004, adding fresh fuel to the controversy over gay marriage. Religious Right organizations went into full alert, mobilizing their members to put anti-gay marriage propositions onto 13 state ballots in time for the presidential election of 2004. All of those initiatives passed in November and apparently drew enough evangelicals to voting booths to assure Bush's re-election.[43]

A second goal of Christian activists was curtailing the power of the federal judiciary, a branch of government that seemed fairly impervious to their influence. Several recent judicial rulings especially provoked them. Among these was the 2003 decision of the U.S. Supreme Court in *Lawrence v. Texas*, which made sodomy laws unconstitutional. The ruling collided with the movement's view that private morality could and should be legislated to conform to religious standards. The case triggered furious efforts by Religious Right groups to intimidate the courts. Pat Robertson urged his TV followers to pray for the death of targeted Supreme Court justices, while forces aligned with James Dobson conducted a national campaign of vilification that included "religious liberty" rallies and incendiary speeches.[44] But even this eruption was nothing compared to the movement's reaction to judicial involvement in the case of Terry Schiavo in 2005. At that time, a Florida state court authorized the removal of a feeding tube from Schiavo, a woman in a persistent vegetative state, after eight years of court review. Under extreme pressure from Christian Right groups, the Republican House leadership passed emergency legislation requiring federal court intervention in the case (ironically, giving jurisdiction to the hated federal judiciary over a state court on a family matter).[45] When the conservative

U.S. Court of Appeals for the Eleventh Circuit simply confirmed the Florida state court's original decision ordering the tube's removal, leading to Schiavo's death, the Religious Right went into full mobilization, treating Schiavo as a martyr who had been "killed" by the courts. Various prominent Christian rightists called the court system the "focus of evil," expressed disdain for the rule of law as then constituted, and even appeared to condone violence against federal justices.[46]

The loud posturing was not simply a stunt to score political points or help Bush fill judicial vacancies. It buttressed a strategy to pressure Congress to hamstring the federal courts in areas where the courts stood in the way of the Religious Right's pro-Christian agenda. The Republican House, more than happy to go along, passed several bills that would have narrowed the Supreme Court's jurisdiction over broad constitutional areas. The bills represented a form of legislation known as "court stripping." Two notable pieces of legislation bore directly on key First Amendment issues: these included the Pledge Protection Act, aimed at curtailing the Court's ability to rule on the constitutionality of the Pledge and its "under God" clause, and the Constitution Restoration Act, intended to limit the Court's jurisdiction in cases where state and local authorities invoked God as the source of legal authority. The latter act of Congress would virtually have allowed states to establish Christianity as a privileged religion beyond the scope of federal court review, making a mockery of the Constitution and the separation of powers.[47] Although the bills failed to pass in the Senate, they demonstrated how far a Republican Congress was willing to go in carving out a special status for God and Christianity with no constitutional basis. They were a stark reminder of the Religious Right's enhanced power.

The Christian Right's accretion of political influence and its foothold in one of the two parties remain disturbing factors in today's politics. Resolutely advancing its religious priorities, it has pushed political discourse to the right and added an extra level of fractiousness to it. But our coverage of the Religious Right cannot end with a discussion of politics. The common perception of the Religious Right as predominantly a political movement pursuing its ends through political means is in need of modification. Its power is also plainly evident in protest and resistance at the street level, where fighting for biblical principles takes volatile forms. More subtly, its influence can be seen in efforts to transform culture and delegitimize existing institutions. In the next two sections, we examine these important aspects of the movement.

Abortion and the Duty to Disobey

While a number of political issues engaged the attention of the Christian Right, none moved the movement as profoundly as that of abortion. Abortion, more than any other issue, seemed to embody modern society's waywardness. It represented a disavowal of God's authority and an endorsement of a purely human one. In a sense it transcended normal politics. So unacceptable was it in their view that many activists believed that some kind of forceful resistance was justified to defy the humanistic system that permitted it to take place.[48] Francis Schaeffer himself indicated that there was a limit to what the dutiful Christian could tolerate as a citizen. At some point one was compelled to determine a "bottom line," a point at which one had not just the "right," but the "duty," to disregard the law and disobey the state.[49] For Schaeffer, as for many others, the bottom line was abortion.

Such arguments became a powerful motivator for the Religious Right's more zealous followers once the abortion issue took hold in movement circles. As mentioned earlier, Catholics were much more engaged with the issue than Protestant evangelicals when *Roe v. Wade* broke on the scene in 1973. The reasons for this are fairly clear: unlike evangelicals, Catholics had a tradition of dealing with reproductive issues and viewing them in a philosophical context. Their means of condemning abortion was natural law. In Catholic tradition, morality is illuminated in part by what God reveals through nature and reason. Issues like birth control and abortion are seen in terms of claims about the function of the human body and its "natural" inclinations. What is not natural is considered contrary to God's purpose. By contrast, evangelicals, who look to the Bible as the preeminent source to guide them in matters of law and morality, have no strong natural law tradition to fall back on; and inconveniently, the Bible is mostly silent or ambivalent on issues like abortion.[50] The only way the Scriptures can be used to condemn it is by stretching the meaning of isolated passages. The biblical believer must essentially be persuaded that the issue is implicit in other moral commands such as the Sixth Commandment ("Thou shalt not kill"), before she can bring the full force of her religion to bear upon it. Such linkages take time to establish.

Thus when the anti-abortion movement emerged in the 1970s, it belonged almost entirely to Catholics. Traditional Catholic lobby groups like the National Right to Life Committee were created at the national level and were duplicated locally by smaller groups often staffed by "Irish Catholic housewives" and suburbanites. Eventually serious activists went beyond these polite types of organization. The movement's first important militant was a Harvard student by the name of John O'Keefe, a deeply religious Catholic who was caught up in the emotional tide of Catholic Charismatic Renewal. He had existed on the fringes of the Vietnam peace movement and had soaked up the social protest writings of Gandhi, King, and the Catholic mystic Thomas Merton. O'Keefe's protest against abortion thus had a left-wing flavor to it.[51] He was one of the first to organize sit-ins at clinics and conduct non-violent protests in conscious imitation of the civil rights movement. There was a certain irony in harking back to the memory of Martin Luther King, as many activists including even Randall Terry were inclined to do, since King during his lifetime was a firm supporter of Planned Parenthood and voiced a "striking kinship" with Margaret Sanger's birth-control movement.[52] Nonetheless, these early anti-abortion efforts readily borrowed from the model of passive resistance and tried to create public solidarity with the unborn. Indeed, as O' Keefe pointed out in his well-circulated pamphlet *A Peaceful Presence* (1978), the purpose of the sit-in was "to be defenseless, to put yourself in the same position" as the fetus.[53]

It was not long, however, before such idealistic non-resistance was superseded by a different kind of approach. A new loud and threatening style of protest came into vogue around 1980, typified by bullhorn harassment, the pestering of patients through "sidewalk counseling," and the intimidation of clinic personnel. Two Catholic organizers from the Midwest, John Ryan and especially Joseph Scheidler, became representative of the new tactics. Scheidler, unlike the intellectual O'Keefe, was a brass-knuckles scrapper ready to use whatever methods would work. His book *Closed: 99 Ways to Stop Abortion* (1985) became a popular how-to manual for fomenters of disruption. Gaining broad notoriety, he was the first to unite the abortion resistance movement under a loose national alliance, the Pro-Life Action Network. Although unwilling himself to resort to violence and apparently fearful of arrest, Scheidler refused to condemn the violent actions of others, using cleverly coded public statements that suggested support.[54]

Right-leaning Protestant evangelicals were latecomers to anti-abortion resistance, but when they arrived on the scene, they made their presence felt with a vengeance, literally. A decade of Catholic-led protest, even the kind embraced by Joe Scheidler, seems almost tepid in comparison to the apocalyptic fury that burst upon the national stage under the leadership of Randall Terry and other fundamentalists, some of whom were violence-prone. These Protestant warriors were to find their inspiration not in Catholic natural law doctrine but in the vision of a scriptural God ready to wreak punishment upon evildoers. Motivated by the desire to enforce God's will, they believed that almost any act of resistance against the discredited laws of the state was divinely justified. The protests they launched were on a truly biblical scale. Unlike former limited actions directed at single clinics, the new acts of resistance were aimed at multiple targets in urban areas like New York or Los Angeles, or at strategic locations, like the Democratic Party Convention. Such events, which often required a massive police response, were to receive wide national news coverage and have unprecedented public impact.

Randall Terry, who was to become the evangelical star of the pro-life movement, grew up in a troubled middle class family in Rochester, New York. Converting to an emotional brand of charismatic Christianity at the age of 17, he finished his education at fundamentalist Elim Bible College in Lima, New York. While there, he remembers being emotionally shaken by the Schaeffer-Koop anti-abortion film, *Whatever Happened to the Human Race?* Intellectually, he was influenced by Francis Schaeffer's works denouncing humanism and calling for Christians to rise up in opposition. Schaeffer's stress on the precedence of "God's law" over man-made law apparently made a deep impression on him.[55] After he left Elim in 1981, Terry became a leader in several fundamentalist parishes while eking out a living in odd jobs. He finally acted on his desire to take on abortion seriously in 1984 by conducting a months-long vigil with his wife in front of the Southern Tier Women's Services clinic in Binghamton, New York. Eventually convincing his fellow parishioners to join him, Terry suddenly found himself with a ready-made mobile force at his disposal. His career as an anti-abortion activist had begun.[56]

Randall Terry advanced quickly within the abortion resistance network. After receiving the blessing of Joseph Scheidler for his Binghamton efforts, he became part of Scheidler's national organization in 1986. But almost from the outset, he was advocating new and aggressive tactics that went beyond what even Scheidler had a stomach for: in particular, a willingness to endure mass arrests. Gaining the support of a majority of activists within the next year, Terry placed himself at the head of a new organization called Operation Rescue. Under Terry, Protestant fundamentalists not only ran the show, but also began to supply most of the recruits, an unprecedented situation for a national pro-life organization. This was by preference, as Terry considered the fundamentalist church unit a more dependable base of support for his campaigns than the Catholic parish. In the latter case, the priest had to answer to a cautious Church hierarchy and led parishioners who mostly deferred to its authority. The fundamentalist pastor, by contrast, was usually an independent agent, unhampered by a wider church organization, with a loyal flock often willing to do his bidding. Terry, a natural preacher of Scripture, could reach such pastors and their followers with emotional appeals to divine justice and condemnations of the sinful. His success in making abortion a national issue was a credit to his ability to energize the fundamentalist psyche.[57]

Like Joseph Scheidler, Terry was coy on the question of anti-abortion violence. As the spokesman of a national movement, he realized he could not openly condone violence even if he celebrated its results. Operation Rescue's signature slogan–"if you believe abortion is murder, then act like it"–was inflammatory but just ambiguous enough to evade responsibility for any violence it might inspire. Terry eventually straddled the issue by declaring his opposition to the killing of doctors but refusing to condemn bombings.[58] Most important to him was that his actions, and whatever occurrences came after them, were creating fear among abortion providers and raising their security costs.

Terry's movement, in fact, posed serious problems for clinics and undoubtedly resulted in diminished access in some states. Still, its overall effect on the incidence of abortion is debatable. While the number of abortions declined about 15 percent from the peak reached around 1990,[59] it is hard to know whether this trend was the consequence of protest or simply the result of demographic and other factors. The reduction of abortions, however, was never the sole focus of the resistance movement. For all their apparent zeal in behalf of the unborn, Randall Terry and his followers functioned at least as much as biblical witnesses, expressing God's condemnation of the doctors who performed the procedure, the women whose sexual freedom allegedly fed the demand for it, the churches that let it happen on their watch, the society whose laws made it legal. Their disruptive actions were a way of showing that the laws of God and man were unalterably at odds and that a good Christian had to choose between them. The humanistic legal system had to be exposed and discredited. To some extent, at least in their own eyes, their efforts bore fruit.

Meanwhile, the agents of violence who followed in Terry's wake left a path of destruction sustained by bitter rhetoric exceeding even his own. Clinic bombings and day-to-day threats increased during the tumultuous 1980s and continued unabated through the 1990s. The assassination of doctors and clinic personnel began just after Randall Terry's movement peaked, with killings carried out in 1993, 1994, and 1998, and numerous others attempted. An atmosphere of terror was created through the posting of wanted signs on the internet and the transmission of death threats to doctors in their workplaces and private homes. The zealots behind these acts subscribed to what has been called a "theology of vigilantism" and spoke openly of guerilla warfare and theocratic revolution.[60] Most of them began with an evangelical background similar to Randall Terry's.[61] They simply went farther with it.

Michael Bray, an early clinic bomber who later justified the resort to homicide in his book *A Time to Kill*, is a prime example. A Baptist seminary graduate, Bray like so many others was deeply affected by Francis Schaefer's call to protest. Increasingly militant and ostracized from his Lutheran Church as a result, he went on to become secretly involved in a series of clinic bombings. Bray was eventually caught and convicted, serving five years in prison during the late 1980s. But far from feeling chastised by his punishment, Bray afterward became a proud spokesman for the violent wing of the anti-abortion movement. He associated himself with an underground organization called the "Army of God," which modeled its views on an anonymous tract called the *Army of God Manual*. The manual states that "Amerika" is under Satan's grip and that the righteous are called to fight against "the devil and all the evil he can muster." It cites the verse from Genesis 9:6–"Whoso sheddeth man's blood, by man shall his blood be shed"–in mantra-like repetitions. Inspired by such incantations, Bray and others like him envisioned themselves as direct instruments of God's vengeance.[62]

Although the violent wing of the movement has ebbed somewhat in recent years, especially in the anti-terrorist climate following 9/11, its influence continues to linger in the form of threats on personnel, violent rhetoric, and occasional bombings.[63] The assassination of Kansas abortion provider George Tiller by a lone gunman in May, 2009 is a chilling reminder of its continued virulence in some quarters. Francis Schaeffer could not have foreseen how his condemnation of abortion would lead to a history so stained with violence. One suspects he would have been appalled by the spilling of blood, the bombings, and the tactics of intimidation. One senses little regret among anti-abortion activists, on the other hand, for the violent actions committed in behalf of their cause. By their doctrinaire logic, such actions have had at least one positive consequence: They have substantially diminished popular respect for the rule of "humanistic" law.

Reforming the Culture

When conservative evangelicals first became acquainted with national politics, they often took the attitude of a certain Washington, D.C. pastor who tried to entice a Christian lawyer from the hinterlands to the capital. He argued that the man was needed in Washington to "change the culture." The pastor's assumption was that engagement in national politics was the best way for Christians to bring about the cultural reformation they so desired. After several frustrating years in Washington, however, many disillusioned Christian rightists no longer accepted this premise. Author Nancy Pearcey conveys the new line of thinking in the words of a contemporary operative: "Politics is downstream from culture, not the other way around," he states. "Real change has to start with the culture. All we can do on Capitol Hill is try to find ways government can nurture healthy cultural trends."[64] Given the currency of this skeptical view of politics, it is not surprising that many Christian rightists have turned their attention to reforming the culture directly without taking a detour through the nation's capital.

But what actually do they mean by reforming culture? Both "culture" and "reform" are endowed, it turns out, with special meanings in a conservative theological context. "Culture" goes well beyond opera and the fine arts. Its scope, in fact, is almost infinite: culture is essentially civilization, or that which humans civilize and "cultivate." Culture building is the task that God sets out for humans in Genesis 1:26–28, when he tells them "Be fruitful, and multiply, and replenish the earth, and subdue it."[65] The command is commonly referred to as the Cultural Mandate, or Dominion Mandate. Cultural activities include the tasks people take on in their social lives, including those relating to their "families, churches, schools, neighborhoods, workplaces, professional organizations, and civic institutions."[66] The word "reform," too, is used in a distinctly theological sense. For the biblical conservative, reform connotes change that looks to a scriptural model. It represents the process of casting out existing abuses and returning to authentic principles. The phrase "reforming culture" thus suggests the ambitious task of bringing civilization in line with what God intended. Aware of the difficulties in achieving this end, orthodox believers understand that cultural reform is a gradual process. It begins in the minds of committed believers, works its way through the basic institutions–family, school, and church–and from there, radiates to the whole of society.

A program of cultural transformation is different from spreading the Gospel or winning converts. Culture reform involves not just moving minds but changing customs and institutional arrangements. It requires developing the organization and know-how to accomplish a set of long-term goals. Showing unusual aptitude in these areas, the Christian Right has spent more than three decades working toward its ideal of a biblically grounded culture. While it has yet to penetrate some regions of the country or make its mark in certain bastions of secular influence such as higher education and the corporate world, it has made its cultural imprint in sectors such as secondary education, TV and radio entertainment, publishing, and elsewhere. As one critic has observed, the Religious Right has become "institutionalized" within the fabric of the nation.[67]

The organizations that the movement has established in recent years offer some clue to its cultural ambitions. They are of several kinds: first, organizations to support biblically conservative trends in society. These offer advice, litigation services, coordination, and material aid to individuals and groups in the Christian vanguard. Second, are organizations that aim primarily to recruit and indoctrinate followers. Almost all of these employ the small interactive unit, or cell group, to evangelize and infiltrate the broader society. Finally, there are the brick-and-mortar establishments–notably, media enterprises, think tanks, and educational institutions–founded to compete with their secular counterparts and lay a permanent base for promoting the new Christian Worldview. To understand the dynamics of cultural "reform," we direct our attention to these different forms of organization.

Probably the most prominent organization of the first kind is Focus on the Family (FOF). Although its founder and leader until recently, James Dobson, has shown a tendency to stray into politics, FOF's primary role has always been cultural: namely, to advance the model of the traditional Christian family. Dobson himself remains a living legend within the organization. Starting out as a child psychologist at the University of Southern California, Dobson originally established his reputation with a best selling book on the importance of strict parenting, *Dare to Discipline* (1970). In this and later works, he took a hands-on approach to childrearing, emphasizing authority, obedience, and physical punishment when necessary. Dobson founded FOF in 1977 as a ministry committed to instilling a biblical family perspective and providing an alternative to prevailing "permissive" trends. Setting up a phone bank to provide Christian parents with free advice on family matters, he soon developed a large following among evangelicals, ensuring loyalty and a flow of contributions.[68] Today the organization oversees a sprawling operation in Colorado Springs with over a thousand employees, its own zip code, and personal links to millions of Christian families around the nation.

More typically, however, Christian "reformist" organizations are specialized and below the sweep of the radar screen. In the field of education, for example, the Home School Legal Defense Association (HSLDA) is a Christian legal organization that has fundamentally changed the way "schooling" is defined. The organization aids those Christian parents who want a home-based, biblical alternative to the public school system. Founded in the early 1980s to "advance the constitutional right of parents to direct the education of their children and protect family freedoms,"[69] the HSLDA has won a series of victories through a combination of persistence and opportunism. Christian attorney Michael Farris started the organization at a time when homeschooling parents faced legal hurdles owing to a patchwork of state requirements. Homeschooling, then in its infancy, was still a diverse and loosely organized movement. HSLDA changed the situation dramatically when it stepped in to become the national standard bearer for homeschooling reform. Taking institutional control over the movement, it adopted a socially conservative and uncompromisingly pro-family posture. Ever since, it has strongly supported parental authority when pitted against state governments, attempting to limit or terminate the states' ability to establish standards or oversee the welfare of children. On the instructional level, the HSLDA has promoted a biblical Christian curriculum through its auxiliary arm, the National Center for Home

Education (NCHE). Homeschooling families that do not buy into the conservative outlook of the HSLDA are shunned and left to fend for themselves. The organization, however, has adroitly presented itself as the representative of the entire homeschooling movement. [70]

In the sphere of religion, another little-known cultural organization, the Institute on Religion and Democracy (IRD), has taken on the goal of "reforming" institutional Christianity. Its targets are those denominations that have not conformed to the conservative biblical viewpoint. Over the years fundamentalists have made no secret of their opposition to the mainline denominations on key issues, viewing them as insufficiently faithful to Scripture. But recently the IRD has taken the fight to new levels, seeking to undermine the very institutional integrity of the major Protestant churches. In practical terms, the IRD has supported and helped to coordinate conservative factions, so-called "renewal" groups, within the Episcopal, Methodist, and Presbyterian denominations.[71] According to its web page, the IRD dispenses information and know-how to church members within these denominations in order to "mobilize grassroots support for church reform" and "restore theological integrity" to the churches.[72] While it uses the language of reform and restoration, the IRD in practice has taken on the role of a wrecking operation. An IRD document accidentally released several years ago reveals the group's ongoing strategy of fomenting dissension among the denominations it is "targeting."[73] The document speaks of the need to raise controversial issues–especially ones pertaining to gender, sexuality, and marriage–to energize traditionalists and "discredit the Religious left." It refers candidly to such tactics as engineering the installation of conservatives in staff positions, shaping debate at church conventions, and initiating legal proceedings against moderate leaders. As a result of the IRD's activities, the normal civility that has long existed in ecclesiastical circles has been replaced by dissension and recrimination. The current upheavals and splits now so common within the mainline churches should be understood as an integral part of the Christian Right's program for cultural reformation.

A second kind of organization associated with the Religious Right's cultural mission is the mass proselytizing organization. Such entities, usually purveyors of a brand of fundamentalism, generally portray themselves as simple messengers of the Gospel. Rolled into their Gospel message, however, one finds the cultural agenda of the far right. These organizations tend to have dual functions: inculcating the values of an aggressive form of religion while establishing an efficient mechanism for expansion and retention of membership. Their most distinctive tool is the "cell group."[74] The cell group, the ground-level unit assigned to convert and train individuals through intimate personal interaction, is structurally not unlike the small group in today's churches, in which congregants discuss spiritual matters. But energized by an activist worldview, the cell group becomes a far more dynamic entity. It commonly falls under the guidance of a group leader who instills the values of the parent organization and demands group discipline. Given the emphasis on cohesion and chain of command, the cell group structure is apt to become highly authoritarian.[75] Growth through recruitment is its central mission.

College campuses, the military, and the upper echelons of national government have been major targets for this aggressive type of proselytizing organization. One of the earliest organizations to make use of the cell group model was the Campus Crusade for Christ (CCC), formed by Bill Bright in 1951. Bright frankly acknowledged the authoritarian nature of his organizational structure, informing his staffers that the CCC was not a "democratic organization" and telling them that criticism of his ministry was "evidence of disloyalty to Christ."[76] Bright had his own way of describing cell group function: "Christian cells," as he put it, were a means of bringing about "spiritual multiplication." Upon reaching a certain optimum size, such cells would split and replicate the process of cell formation. Bright modeled his strategy on what he viewed as the communist method of organization. He did not shrink from using revolutionary language in justifying his methods:

> As the head of a large international movement I am involved with thousands of others in a 'conspiracy to overthrow the world.' Each year we train tens of thousands of high school and college students from more than half of the major countries of the world in the art of revolution.... [77]

Bright perfected his methods on college campuses during the 1950s and 1960s. College students, placed in an unfamiliar setting away from home, proved to be an ideal demographic for recruiting and indoctrination. Bright redoubled his efforts during the Vietnam War era, considering his legion of Christian evangelists the perfect antidote to campus radicalism. Later, allying himself with the Religious Right, Bright became a voice in advancing conservative social causes. Bolstered by its ongoing successes, the CCC has since extended its activities to non-academic venues, especially the military.[78]

The military, in fact, has become the most promising sector for cell-group recruitment and indoctrination in recent years. Like the college campus, it has a mobile population divorced from its social roots. Moreover, the type of culture nurtured within its ranks, i.e., one that is patriotic and obedient to authority, is similar to that esteemed in conservative religious milieus. Right-leaning Christian proselytizers have devoted much attention to the armed forces in the last half century, seeing its millions of young draftees as a "primary missionary target."[79] Over the years, they have come to dominate the military chaplaincy, bringing a shift toward more sectarian preaching.

The growing emphasis on proselytizing produced, as well, a climate friendly to civilian Christian organizations in and around military bases and service academies.[80] A number of large-scale evangelizers tied to the Religious Right soon availed themselves of the opportunities presented. Among them were several worldwide parachurch organizations with cell-group and "multiplier" strategies, notably the Navigators of Colorado Springs, and the Military Ministry (an affiliate of the CCC) of Newport News, Virginia. Over time, these organizations were able to establish a honeycomb of local chapters and Bible study groups at bases both in the U.S. and overseas, often with the cooperation of senior officers.[81] The overall pervasiveness of right-wing Christian influence in the military has brought increasing incidents of aggressive preaching in public settings and the inappropriate use of social pressure to encourage religious conformity.[82] The Military Religious Freedom Foundation has reported extensively on the resulting damage to morale from such activities.[83]

Movement on a Mission

While most cell-group proselytizers aim their efforts at foot soldiers, some explicitly focus on the higher echelons of the military. Christian Embassy, a fundamentalist proselytizing organization, is one of the most effective of these, committed in its own words "to helping world-changers achieve things that will outlast their lives." Established in 1976 as an offshoot of the Campus Crusade for Christ, Christian Embassy promotes "God's infallible written Word" and preaches the "everlasting condemnation" of non-believers.[84] The organization attained a foothold in high military circles in the late 1970s when Lieutenant General William Nelson agreed to establish a Christian Embassy study group for flag officers in his Pentagon office. The precedent opened the floodgates to other such groups in the years that followed.[85] One Pentagon official recently estimated that more than 350 study groups associated with Christian Embassy are now active at the Pentagon.[86]

Christian Embassy has also been active in the executive and legislative branches of government. The classic keeper of the faith in political circles, however, is an organization that has been the subject of a recent exposé by Jeff Sharlet: the Family. Founded during the Depression,[87] the Family has maintained an important foothold in power centers like Congress and the Pentagon for decades. In recent years its conservative outlook has dovetailed closely with that of the Religious Right. Seeing its role as shepherding the powerful and the well connected, the Family is highly exclusive: one estimate of its membership some years ago put it at around 20,000. Among its ranks are some of the most powerful voices in Washington, including over ten percent of the Senate, many leading congressman, and an assortment of behind-the-scenes power brokers.[88] One normally hears little of its activity because the Family carefully guards its secrecy, providing no public list of its membership. Within its ranks, the Family fosters a highly conservative and elitist ethic. The present head of the Family, Douglas Coe, encourages a mystique of power that envisions its cadres as implementers of the destiny of nations. [89] Members belong to cell groups built on covenants emphasizing strict loyalty.[90] An almost military commitment to serve in Jesus' name is the cement that unites the organization and inspires its aggressive brand of American fundamentalism.

Although the cell-group concept seems to thrive best in established settings, it has also been tried more generally with some success. One of the more dynamic organizations using cell groups has been the much-publicized Promise Keepers, founded in 1990 by University of Colorado football coach Bill McCartney. McCartney's idea was to revive the traditional family by encouraging husbands and fathers to assume their God-assigned roles as authority figures. Sponsoring gatherings of Christian men to promote biblical responsibility, the movement mushroomed into a nationwide phenomenon with stadium rallies and staged media events. In the weeks and months following these mass gatherings, participants were organized into cell groups back in their local communities, where they pledged to adhere to the movement's principles and submit to regular accountability. Although officially unaligned, Promise Keepers has long had ties with James Dobson, Bill Bright, and other Christian rightists. The movement has adopted key elements of the Religious Right's agenda and served as an effective recruiting tool for its causes.[91] While it has lost some momentum since the mid-1990s, Promise Keepers continues to exert an influence in thousands of churches through its ongoing network of cell groups.[92]

A third type of Christian rightist organization is more "institutional" in nature, demonstrating the movement's commitment to a long-term strategy of changing American society. It includes those organizations built within the fabric of American life to serve as alternatives to parallel secular ones. Such institutions serve as a kind of Christian vanguard. The enterprises and media empires of TV evangelists like Pat Robertson and D. James Kennedy, several Christian publishing houses supportive of the Religious Right, and various schools and higher educational institutions, all fall into this category.

Of particular importance to the reformers are brick-and-mortar educational establishments at the private school, college, and university level. Significantly, Christian rightists have not been content to rely simply on traditional Christian private academies or the large cluster of existing Christian colleges. These older, mostly fundamentalist institutions are deemed inadequate for expressing the proactive, society-oriented worldview of the Christian Right. Instead, the movement has made efforts to establish from scratch its own distinctive structures, often using money amassed by Christian televangelists and other religious entrepreneurs. One of the more innovative models at the primary and secondary school level is the so-called "classical and Christian" school, which loosely adheres to the curriculum of schools of the late medieval and Reformation era. The curriculum emphasizes a Christ-centered approach that takes the Bible as the ultimate reference point for all learning. At the same time, it uses a classical methodology, stressing the trivium (grammar, logic, and rhetoric) as a means of laying the basis for skills in Christian apologetics. The approach enables students to argue forcefully for the biblical Christian point of view. Model institutions include Douglas Wilson's Logos School in Moscow, Idaho and D. James Kennedy's Westminster Academy in Fort Lauderdale. Over the last decade, these schools have become more widespread and now have an advocacy organization.[93]

Religious rightists have been no less assertive at the college and university level. Pat Robertson has taken the initiative in creating a new kind of "Christian Worldview" university, hoping to make it rival more established secular institutions. Regent University, founded in 1978, offers undergraduate and graduate training in fields like communication, government, law, and leadership, all relevant to employment in influential sectors of society. Its high ambitions are voiced in its motto: "Christian leadership to change the world." The university has been able to provide Religious Right organizations and Republican politicians with a cadre of reliable staff personnel. It has been imitated by institutions like Jerry Falwell's Liberty University ("For Christ and for liberty") and Michael Farris's Patrick Henry College ("Higher education with a biblical world view"), which nurture similar aspirations.[94]

Christian reformers have also made their mark in legal education. An early milestone was Pat Robertson's founding of Regent University Law School in 1986 as part of Regent University. Herb Titus, a constitutional attorney for the Religious Right picked by Robertson to head the new school, wasted no time in developing a theologically orthodox curriculum. The approach emphasizes the alleged Christian foundation of Western law, viewing the latter as biblically based rather than the product of mere human jurisprudence. Although questions over academic freedom caused headaches for Regent in its efforts to obtain accreditation, the school managed to go through the "contortions" necessary to acquire it.[95] Other religiously orthodox schools, including Liberty University Law School in Lynchburg, Virginia and Ave Maria Law School in Ann Arbor, Michigan, soon followed suit. While one might be tempted to dismiss such schools for their relatively low academic rankings, they have gained a national reputation in areas where a background in apologetics comes in handy, such as debate and moot court competitions. Most important, these schools have served as key recruiting pools for pro-Christian non-profit law firms and, during the Bush II administration, the Department of Justice.[96]

While it has created its own islands of influence in higher education, the Religious Right has been less successful at establishing footholds within the country's existing research universities. Here it faces a bigger challenge because of the need to comply with universally recognized professional standards. The closest it came to achieving this goal was an effort in 1999 by anti-evolutionists to launch the Michael Polanyi Center (MPC), a think tank focusing on intelligent design theory, at Baylor University with the assistance of the university's president. But the Center was surrounded by controversy from the moment it became public. Faced with strong faculty opposition due to a fear that it would dilute the university's academic standing, it stalled and then eventually died a bureaucratic death by being folded into the non-scientific Baylor Institute for Faith and Learning.[97] The MPC episode underscores the current limits of the Christian Right in areas foreign to its worldview, especially when it is confronted with determined opposition. It tends to thrive primarily within controlled environments where it has a receptive audience for its biblical standards of truth.

The last example provides some perspective on the Religious Right's efforts to penetrate mainstream culture. While its accomplishments are considerable, it has had trouble advancing its agenda with equal success in all sectors of society. Especially in areas where higher education serves as the gatekeeper for admission–the professions, academia, and to a lesser extent, the corporate world, the arts, and the media–the movement has its reformist work cut out for it.

Having said this, one needs to remember that the Christian Right does not need to occupy all sectors of society to shake America's cultural foundations. It has already shaken them in a major way by fomenting an undertow of hostility to today's secular way of life. It has created bastions of support within large segments of the population, diminished the influence of its rivals, and built distinctive institutions in key areas of American society. With ready cooperation from one of the two main political parties, ample financial assets at its disposal, and a legion of activists working in its behalf, the Religious Right must be considered a potential game-changer.

Cosmic Dimensions

Our historical introduction to the Religious Right is intended to give some idea of its breadth and vitality. Unlike past movements with religious associations, e.g., the fundamentalist upsurge after World War I, it has survived public exposure over a long period and established itself as a permanent player on the American scene. Unfazed by fickle commentators who have overstated its influence at certain times and predicted its imminent demise at others, it holds an agenda that has scarcely wavered over time. It has been able to maintain broad unity as leaders have come and gone, humiliated by scandal or elevated by celebrity. By any standard, its aptitude for organization has been impressive. In the areas of recruitment, mobilization, and indoctrination, it has shown a skill that is reminiscent of disciplined revolutionary movements. In the process, it has garnered power within the Republican Party that no political observer can reasonably ignore. Overall, it has an enviable record of performance.

A list of assets, however, does not really get to the heart of the Christian Right's success. One has to ask how the movement has been able to inspire and hold the loyalty of followers, allowing it to surpass in longevity virtually all other American socio-political movements. How does one explain the certainty of its adherents and their undying commitment to the cause? What ultimately drives them? In this book we suggest the answer is to be found in the set of doctrines and assumptions that constitute its worldview. The worldview in this case provides an unequivocal explanation for how the world works, defends a return to absolute principles, and justifies worldly action by invoking transcendent authority. It offers a framework that appeals to the emotions and the intellect, serving both to motivate and guide the faithful follower.

Thus, on the emotional dimension, Christian Worldview presents a picture of Christianity under siege that taps into believers' anxieties and latent resentments. Portraying secularism as an existential threat to the Christian way of life, it justifies uncompromising struggle to counteract it. It endows the struggle with transcendent significance by stressing the "cosmic dimensions" of the battle.[98] On the other hand, the worldview appeals to believers' intellects by demonstrating its reliance on a set of consistent, absolute principles. It assures followers of the certainty of their cause and guides their thoughts and actions. As one apologist describes it, Christian Worldview is a kind of biblically informed guide, "a mental map that tells us how to navigate the world effectively."[99] The basis for that map is of course Scripture, or at least Scripture as seen through the eyes of its conservative expositors. God, as the author of Scripture, becomes the definer of meaning and purpose. Christian Worldview, by articulating God's plan for the world and its necessity in the scheme of things, prepares the believer for submission to that purpose.

Avid proponents of the Christian Worldview see it as nothing less than an inspired expression of Christianity. They would defend it as a package of truths that makes religious orthodoxy applicable to today's world. But Christian Worldview is a big step away from Christianity as normally defined. It has little to do with worship, salvation, or the teachings of Jesus, and much to do with culture, society, and politics. While advocates would see Christian Worldview as an authentic rendering of God's perspective, a sober observer would view it as a product of historical forces and earth-bound motivations. The historical record shows that Christian Worldview was formulated by doctrinaire theologians reacting with hostility to the rise of empirical science, secularism, and popular democracy. Their aim was to mount an attack on modernist trends and to reassert Christianity's ancient claims in the secular domain.

Our job in this book will be to make Christian Worldview understandable to a non-sectarian audience so that its cultural-political agenda will be more transparent. The concept of Christian Worldview, unfortunately, is not readily grasped because of the jargon that surrounds it and the various traditions out of which it springs. Christian Worldview, so named, reached a recognizable form over 100 years ago, while its theological roots go back to the Protestant Reformation and earlier. It has been through several significant modifications in the last century. Although substantially grounded in Scripture, its scriptural elements are carefully selected and distilled. In addition, it includes an assortment of extraneous ingredients, including anti-statist and anti-democratic theory, economic libertarianism, and modern conspiracy theory. The historical end product is an expansive ideology that offers the certainty of truth, an enemy to revile, and an ultra-conservative vision of the future. We move now to examine its origins, review its components, and consider it as an integrated whole.

PART II:
Christian Worldview in the Making

2

THE ANSWER TO MODERNISM

Francis Schaeffer leaves no doubt about what he considers the main intellectual problem for conservative Christians. In the first sentence of his famous call to action, *A Christian Manifesto*, he criticizes orthodox believers for perceiving things "in bits and pieces" rather than "totals." They suffer from a gap in overall perception. While they seem to recognize some of the compelling cultural issues of the day–abortion, secularism in the public schools, the breakdown of Christian morality–they are unable, he declares, to step back and see these issues as part of a larger picture. This larger reality Schaeffer summarizes in ominous terms: it is the onslaught of a materialistic, secular way of thinking responsible for a seismic shift in American culture. This "modern outlook," as he often calls it, has produced an attitude of pessimism and uncertainty with pernicious consequences not just for morality, but for art, philosophy, and law as well.[1] The failure by the faithful to understand the broad picture of change makes them impotent bystanders, in his opinion, because it prevents them from responding with their own vision of the world.

By focusing on perception and stressing the "totality" of the situation, Schaeffer is seeking to frame events in worldview terms. The cultural problems he sees are not an accidental combination of trends, but the consequence of a "worldview" aimed at the heart of Christian civilization. Tied to humanism, this worldview has been aggressively advanced after generations of declining religiosity and now apparently influences every facet of American life. As long as it holds sway, America's cultural decline is inevitable, according to Schaeffer. His response is to argue for a Christian Worldview that will counter, critique, and ultimately defeat it. Far from simply providing a moral perspective, he contends it will give Christians a broad mental framework for seeing the world in a Christian way. It will offer a conception of "final reality," a fixed idea of truth, a notion of purpose in the universe. It will place humans under the watchful eye of an all-powerful God and cast all of existence in the light of that relationship. A Christian Worldview will also provide a distinctly Christian way of approaching government and society and of articulating the meaning of life and liberty. Under its purview, no important questions will be left unanswered.

Schaeffer draws many of his ideas from a specific era of the Christian past: the Protestant Reformation. He sees the Reformation's trenchant critique of its times and its manner of appealing to believers as keys to solving the modern "problem." Historically, the Reformation was a movement intended to emphasize faith and enable Christians to appeal directly to God without going through priestly intermediaries. Under such leaders as Luther and Calvin, it aimed at casting off centuries of corrupt practices and putting Christianity on a new path. The central object of its attacks was the Christian establishment of the time, represented by the Catholic Church. In the modern context, needless to say, the target of Christian reformers is no longer a religious foe, but a secular one.

Schaeffer, although a key popularizer of Christian Worldview, was not the first to expound upon it or to present Reformation theology in worldview clothing. The concept was initially proposed in conservative Christian circles almost a century earlier, and many times thereafter. The first formulator of a "Christian view of the world" was the Scottish Presbyterian divine, James Orr (1844–1913), who published a series of lectures under the title, *The Christian View of God and the World,* in 1893.[2] Orr had studied mental philosophy at the University of Glasgow before becoming a minister and a teacher of theology at the Presbyterian Church's Theological College in Glasgow. Orr was a well-known opponent of liberal trends in Christianity, holding to the infallibility of the Bible on matters of faith and adhering to general Calvinist principles. At the close of the nineteenth century, he found himself in a historical environment not entirely different from that faced by Schaeffer a century later. James Orr was witnessing a Christianity challenged by scientific advances and modern skepticism. Although practiced by a majority of the population of Europe and North America, Christianity no longer dictated the terms of cultural debate as it had in earlier centuries. Freedom of religion was increasingly embraced in democratic societies, and the harsh memory of Christian sectarian warfare weighed against religion's involvement in the political life of nations. While agreeable to most practicing Christians, this less assertive role of religion in public life upset clerics like Orr.

Using the concept of "worldview" current in academic thinking at the time, Orr maintained that a secular "worldview" hostile to Christianity was taking over Western civilization. The problem for Christianity wasn't simply that it was vulnerable on a few points because of new findings in the natural sciences. The problem extended "to the whole manner of conceiving of the world, and of man's place in it." As Orr stated bluntly, "It is the Christian view of things in general which is attacked."[3] *The Christian View of God and the World* was Orr's answer to this trend. The book was his attempt to offer a new systematic perspective, a Christian Worldview, capable of reviving Christianity's influence and prestige. Seeking to reconstruct from Scripture a set of principles that would allow the Faith to compete with other worldviews, he presented Christianity as an ostensibly coherent philosophical system able to explain the world better than all others. It was to be a worldview in sharp contrast with the secular spirit of the age.

It should be noted that those eager to appropriate "worldview" for Christian purposes were stretching the ordinary meaning of the term. The original German word for worldview–*Weltanschaaung*–connoted an outlook influenced by the contingencies of environment and history. It had a relativistic flavor. James Orr and later followers were nonetheless determined to harness worldview for the Christian cause. They were happy to retain the term's sense of breadth and dimension, but conceived of it as signifying something far more than a subjective perspective. "Worldview" in the Christian context had to convey an absolute and unquestioned truth.[4] The question of how, given their human limitations, they could make their worldview into something eternally valid did not apparently worry them.

Orr, however, was convinced that his version of Christian Worldview was well equipped to stand the truth test. Offering it as an authoritative outlook for all who adhered to the broad tenets of biblical Christianity, i.e., most traditional Protestants, he tried to make it as ecumenical as feasible. De-emphasizing some of the harder edges of his own Calvinism, he centered his worldview on the personhood of Jesus Christ. This "christocentric" approach stressed the reality of Jesus and the truth of his message.[5] In Orr's view, these fundamental convictions logically bound the believer to a whole set of other beliefs, including a particular view of God, man, sin, Redemption, and human destiny.[6] The commitment to a Christian intellectual framework did not contradict Christianity's devotional aspects, as he saw it, but was a means of expanding religion's application to the world and addressing the "intelligence" as well as the "heart" of the believer.[7]

Although Orr receives credit for coining the term Christian Worldview, he was soon overshadowed by another theologian with a more militant worldview vision of the concept. Abraham Kuyper (1837–1920) was an unapologetic Dutch Calvinist who had committed himself to a life-long campaign against the culture of modernism. Kuyper (pronounced KOY-per) was experimenting with a contemporary formulation of Calvinism, called Neo-Calvinism, in his native Netherlands at about the time that James Orr crafted his worldview approach. When he came upon Orr's book, he readily adopted Orr's worldview concept, which he labeled a "life system," as a vehicle for expressing his own ideas.[8] However, unlike Orr, whose Calvinism played a limited role in his worldview, [9] Kuyper saw the full advantages of harnessing Calvinism's austere, single-minded outlook in a contemporary framework. Rather than emphasizing the personhood of Jesus, Kuyper placed an intrusive and all-powerful God at the center of his worldview. Like Calvin, he distilled the relationship between God and man down to its essentials and made all of human existence revolve around it.

The Calvinist prototype developed by Kuyper was eventually to become the gold standard for today's Christian Worldview. At first, however, Kuyper's ideas gained little traction outside of Holland. In 1898 he presented his stark vision of worldview to a rather startled

American theological audience in his Stone Lectures at Princeton Theological Seminary, later published as *Lectures in Calvinism.* Conservative theologians in the U.S. were not yet ready to adopt his radical new cognitive approach, which would have set them starkly at odds with America's more pragmatic intellectual traditions.[10] Still, he could take some encouragement from the fact that his ideas were politely received. His promotion of a revived Calvinism gained him some admirers and planted seeds for the future. As the twentieth century progressed, Kuyper's worldview ideas were developed further and carried to their logical conclusion by several of his followers working in seminaries and universities, notably Herman Dooyeweerd in the Netherlands and Cornelius Van Til in the United States. Both men in their own ways developed Christian Worldview into a sophisticated critique of the modern world and its assumptions. Their theories would take on significance, but only when the wider evangelical community was ready to accept and apply them.

Important breakthroughs occurred in the United States during the 1960s and early '70s, when the concept of Christian Worldview began to resonate outside of esoteric academic settings. Christian activists drawn to a social and political agenda took up the worldview theme at this time with newfound zeal. It is easy to see why. The worldview approach offered them an ideology that targeted the modernist enemy and signaled the need for social transformation. The first of these activists was R. John Rushdoony, the founder of a radical theological movement called Christian Reconstructionism. Working in isolation, Rushdoony used the framework that Kuyper and Van Til had provided as a starting point for his own right-wing Christian program. He and his followers inspired–in some cases, tutored–many members of the emerging Christian Right. Located on the radical fringe, they watched as others carried the worldview message to a nationwide audience. Francis Schaeffer amply filled this intermediary role, taking the formula of his predecessors and coming up with his own popularized version of it. Schaeffer moderated some of the worldview's Calvinistic rigor, making it more palatable to non-intellectual Christians. At the same time, he imbued it with a sense of context and urgency. The message caught on and took the evangelical world by storm.

The Christian Worldview of today's Religious Right is thus a composite product that draws ideas from each of the theologies and traditions that touched it. It combines an assortment of intellectual elements, including the idea of an intrusive and judgmental deity, a distinctive concept of truth based on biblical assumptions, a notion of "antithesis" dividing believers from non-believers, an antagonism to modernism and popular democracy, a reflexive anti-statism, and a taste for conspiracy theory. Bringing order to this patchwork of ideas and tendencies, Christian Worldview provides a well-contrived explanation of the world, an affirmation of purpose, and a recitation of socio-political goals.

We devote the next three chapters to an historical examination of Christian Worldview because there is no better way to explain its inspiration and rationale. We could begin with Abraham Kuyper since this new theology first gains traction with him. But, to provide a necessary background for Christian Worldview's contemporary face, we touch briefly on its Reformation underpinnings. Much of what the Religious Right stands for today has its roots in the thinking of John Calvin.

3

CREDO: EVERY SQUARE INCH FOR GOD

John Calvin: Will over Reason

If one were looking for a theology on which to base a compelling ideology, one could hardly do better than Calvinism. Calvinism probably comes closer than any other theology in Christendom to a rigorous system of thought based on a few simple premises. The theology has been aptly described by Dutch scholar Robert Fruin as a "logical system of divinity . . . impelled by a severely moral sense."[1] German sociologist Max Weber has emphasized its "rational" tendencies, its avoidance of magical and ritualistic elements, and its encouragement of a form of worldly asceticism. Sympathetic Calvinists like Orr and Kuyper credit it for its coherence and comprehensiveness. Orr speaks of it as having a "unity of view arising from the presence of a great central, controlling idea";[2] Kuyper refers to it as a "life-system" that is "far-reaching," with broad implications for politics, science, and the arts as well as religion.[3] Underlying all of these assessments is an understanding of the importance of God's overarching sovereignty, which illuminates the theology by infusing every activity in life with meaning. Calvinism presupposes an all-powerful God who knows all and has a far-reaching plan for his Creation.

Calvinism also has a reputation, fair or not, for a grim sort of determinism. Carried to its ultimate conclusions, the theology takes on what appear to be mechanistic features. If God is all knowing, then he is able to foresee; if all-powerful, he is able to preordain. Anything less for God puts undue power into the hands of his creatures and leads to an unpredictable and chaotic world. Such reasoning provides the basis for the doctrine of predestination, whereby God determines in advance the salvation or damnation of human souls. Predestination holds that certain humans are "elected" for divine reasons while some aren't, and that there is no ready formula for determining such election. One's ultimate fate is simply what God wills it to be. The doctrine has an important impact on the psychology of believers, because it creates an underlying anxiety and a need to be proven one of the favored. By establishing a framework of arbitrary authority combined with human insecurity, the Calvinistic system tends to lead to a religion of disciplined obedience to God. The religion leaves God in unchallenged sway, even if to sensitive minds it might cast doubt on his ultimate benevolence.

The author of this austere set of doctrines, at least in their nascent form, lived a life that mirrored its ideals. His personal seal bore the Latin inscription, *Prompte et sincere in opere Domini* ("promptly and sincerely in the work of the Lord"),[4] suggesting one who instinctively followed in God's footsteps. John Calvin (1509–1564) was born to a middle class family on the plains of northern France. A person of delicate frame, he early proved himself a devoted student and man of the mind. Though groomed for the law, he found himself drawn to the more consequential discipline of theology, a field whose controversies were beginning to alter the face of Europe. Martin Luther had begun a mini-revolution in 1517, when Calvin was a youth, by challenging the abuses of the Catholic Church in his famous Ninety-five Theses and preaching salvation by faith alone. Studying the new doctrines as he reached adulthood, Calvin became convinced that they reflected the original principles of Christianity more accurately than the syncretic teachings of the Catholic Church. In an attempt to vindicate the new thinking, which was under heavy attack by the reigning authorities, he took refuge in Switzerland to devote himself to an explication of Scripture. At the age of 26, he produced the first version of what was to be his masterpiece, *Institutes of the Christian Religion*, in an effort to systematize Christianity and put it on a new foundation. The book made his name famous throughout Europe and strengthened the movement for a "Reformed" Christianity.

As his standing grew, Calvin moved from theory to practice. Asked by the citizens of Geneva to help put their church on a Reformed footing, he spent his last 25 years helping to establish a stable ecclesiastical order in that city. His influence extended to the civil administration, which worked hand in glove with the religious bodies he controlled. Geneva became in many respects Calvin's model of the ideal Christian commonwealth.

Calvinism as a system was more than the theology of John Calvin. In the years after his death, Calvin's followers refined his original doctrines, usually emphasizing its more severe elements. Faced with doctrinal challenges from within, they saw the need to sharpen the distinctive elements of the founder's theology. Thus the emergence of Arminianism, a movement in the Reformed church aimed at asserting the principle of human free will, brought a swift reaction from orthodox forces. The upshot was the famous Synod of Dort in 1618–19, which stressed the unconditional nature of God's preordained decrees, man's total depravity, and the impossibility of salvation for much of humanity. Calvinist doctrine underwent further refinement in an English-Scottish setting with the formulation of the Westminster Confession by an assembly of Puritan divines in 1646. Both Dort and Westminster gave Calvinism a reputation for rigor and rectitude, enhancing its standing during an age of sectarian warfare. Only in more tolerant times have these tenets been relaxed by most Calvinist denominations.

Given the confined scope of our study, we will limit our discussion of Calvinism to the views of Calvin the founder. It was Calvin's writings that inspired the basic tenets of the Christian Worldview and gave it its dynamic outlook on the world. In examining those tenets, we will make no attempt to summarize the whole of Calvin's theology, which would entail a separate work. Instead, we will merely highlight a few key themes that resonated with worldview formulators. For the sake of simplicity, we group these around the topics of God, man, and the world.

The concept of God is key to an understanding of Calvin's system. His image of God is in part a reaction to the prevailing conceptions held within the Catholic Church. His God is neither as intellectualized as the deity envisioned by the scholastic philosophers, nor as surrounded by props and saintly intermediaries as the one of popular Catholic tradition.

God is more starkly conceived, more personally imposing. The Calvinist believer stands *coram deo,* "before the face of God," in all of life's circumstances. In the words of Kuyper, "The majesty of God, and the authority of God press upon the Calvinist in the whole of his human existence." God is present not only in the believer's religious life, but in "his personal, family, social, and political life."[5] God, moreover, exerts his will in a way that is immediate and dramatic. He superintends a universe where nothing happens by chance, where his personal imprint is evident everywhere, and where his governance is "watchful," "effective," "active," and "ceaseless." Far from being a simple judge of happenings on earth, God "governs all events."[6] Nothing occurs that is not foreseen, and no good act happens except through God's grace. While human responsibility is not denied, human free will is at best circumscribed in the Calvinist scheme of things.

Calvin does not stress the doctrine of predestination, but he leaves little doubt of his commitment to it. In this respect, he generally follows Augustine, who mostly draws from Paul's Epistles for hints of the doctrine.[7] Calvin fully realizes that in acknowledging God's power to pre-select winners and losers in the great salvation lottery he is affirming something that cannot be morally justified in human terms. He explicitly admits that predestination is a "dreadful" decree, guaranteed to strike terror in the hearts of those who contemplate it.[8] But Calvin adamantly rejects a human being's prerogative to question the fairness of the doctrine, citing Paul's statement that the clay lacks the credentials to quarrel with the potter. He considers such questioning a form of human insolence and a "temptation" of Satan.[9]

Most modern Christians would agree on the "dreadfulness" of predestination and hence settle on a God willing to allow the individual believer some demonstrable control of her own fate. Calvinists are able to reconcile themselves to predestination only because of their theological stress on the priority of God's will and on the necessity of obeying it without question. In philosophical terms, they put will over reason. Their view of God is voluntaristic: that is, they assume that the divine will, the defining element of God's authority, need not be defended on rational grounds. The voluntarist obeys God's command not because it represents an independent standard of goodness but because God wills it. There is, in effect, no standard of justice or morality independent of what God imposes by "arbitrary fiat."[10] Some writers on Christian morality refer to this viewpoint as "divine command theory."[11] The philosophical problem with voluntarism or command theory is that since God is all-powerful, he can in principle change the rules or seem to abandon them when he deems it appropriate. In such cases, as with certain actions taken by God in the Scriptures that appear morally inconsistent, the believer must remain content to puzzle over the mysteries of divine intent.

A Calvinist, no doubt, would chastise anyone who might delve into that matter for committing the sin of questioning divine authority. Indeed, Calvin calls those who would impute arbitrariness to the Almighty "venomous dogs." He defends God's will in absolute terms:

> God's will is so much the highest rule of righteousness that whatever he wills, by the very fact that he wills it, must be considered righteous. When, therefore, one asks why God has so done, we must reply: because he has willed it. But if you proceed further to ask why he has so willed, you are seeking something greater and higher than God's will, which cannot be found.[12]

Calvin makes clear that morality, since it is derived from divine will, is beyond the capacity of unaided human reason to fathom. His stress on will over reason shows the centrality of unquestioned authority in the Calvinist framework.

The belief in the primacy of divine will is perhaps the single most important assumption underlying the Calvinist outlook. The belief accounts for many key characteristics of the Christian Worldview, including its ready acceptance of authority endowed with arbitrary power, its tendency to associate the righteous exercise of power with anger and vengeance, its hostility to hints of resistance, and its rejection of human reason and autonomy. Supreme authority makes demands that must be obeyed at all costs, however unreasonable or unpalatable its directives may appear on their face. It is, indeed, not an adherence to consistent moral standards that sets the Christian Worldview apart from modern alternatives, as religious rightists often state. Biblical standards are not so absolute as claimed,[13] and alternative belief systems include many universal elements in their moralities. Rather, what most distinguishes the Christian Worldview from others is the stress on arbitrary will as opposed to reason.

Calvin's perception of humans and human nature is also theologically distinctive. Human beings are creatures made in God's image who have been radically corrupted through Adam's original transgression. In his portrayal of original sin, Calvin relies heavily on classic Augustinian doctrine, which asserts the total depravity of the human race. Such depravity is more insidious than a mere perversion of the will and the emotions, for it involves the perversion of human reason itself. It is sin rooted in the mind as well as the heart. Augustine's deep distrust of the human mind was not typical of Christian thinking in later years. Such distrust went out of favor during the Middle Ages, as scholastic theologians influenced by Greek philosophy tended to elevate the standing of human reason.[14] The more approving attitude toward human intellectual faculties has been inherited by the modern Catholic Church and is shared by a number of the Protestant denominations. Calvin's theology, by contrast, represents a return to Augustinian assumptions. His stress on the impairment of all human faculties, including the reasoning ones, reminds humans of their deficiencies and makes them more dependent on divine guidance.

In Calvin's view, the way out of perpetual sin for humans, mortified by their infirmities, is to come to know God. Given Calvin's interest in the cognitive aspect of sin, it is perhaps not surprising that he casts the solution in terms of acquiring a "knowledge" of God. He assigns central importance to such knowledge, devoting the first third of his *Institutes of the Christian Religion* to it.[15] But how can one hope to know God if one's intellect is fundamentally impaired in the first place? In addressing this conundrum, Calvin relies upon one important assumption: all humans have access to God because they are endowed with an innate, intuitive hint of his presence. "[T]here is . . . no nation so barbarous, no people so savage, that they have not a deep-seated conviction that there is a

God," Calvin declares near the beginning of his treatise." He adds: "Some conception of God is ever alive in all men's minds."[16] According to Calvin, God plants this awareness, or *divinitatis sensum* (literally, "awareness of the divine") like a seed in human minds to enable them to acknowledge his existence and "to prevent anyone from taking refuge in the pretense of ignorance."[17] The implanted awareness always exists in the mind as a prod and reminder.

Although it provides many with hope, Calvin's *divinitatis sensum* carries with it some problematic implications. Specifically, it results in dividing humanity into two antithetical groups based on their response to it: those who carefully heed the hint of God's presence, the faithful, and those who circumvent or dismiss it, the wicked. The latter are driven mainly by vanity and obstinacy, in Calvin's view, becoming either deluded fools or conscious rebels against God.[18] At this point we need to turn to the important biblical text cited by Calvin as the basis for his views. It is the dark passage from Romans 1:18–32, consisting of Paul's condemnation of those who yield to ungodly impulses. Paul states that since all humans have a "manifest" intuition of God, those who fail to honor him are "without excuse." Ungrateful and vain in their imaginings and "professing themselves to be wise," they are but fools, and worse yet, idolaters who turn to worship other things in God's place. These vain worshippers are abandoned by God to pursue their lusts and are denounced as "backbiters, haters of God, despiteful, proud, boasters, inventors of evil things" and "worthy of death."

Beyond its accusatory tone, the passage holds rhetorical significance for those who argue on its assumptions. First, it reinforces the notion that all thinking is explicable in religious terms. All people can be portrayed as either pro-God or anti-God according to how they respond in their minds to the *divinitatis sensum*. The framework reduces life to a simple either-or choice, fostering the idea of an existential split between the faithful and the unfaithful. It enables the Christian worldviewer to depict nonbelievers essentially as idolaters and devil-worshippers, rather than as neutrals, because they reject the true God in favor of false gods. Arguing in these terms, the zealot can more easily justify dualism, demonization, culture war, and appeals to the faithful, as will be seen in later chapters. Second, the passage stresses the idea that one's religious inclination (either for or against God) shapes one's *cognitive* view of the world. If one embraces God, then one perceives the world as God intended; if one rebels against God, one's thinking becomes clouded. The faithful see "clearly," while the unfaithful are "vain in their imagination." The disparity of perspective bolsters the Christian Worldview contention that the two groups, given their incompatible assumptions about the world, share no cognitive common ground. In effect, it renders meaningful interaction between them impossible.

The importance of the controversial Romans passage[19] for Christian worldviewers cannot be overstated. Worldview historian David Naugle calls Romans 1:18–32 the classic reference (the "locus classicus") for "matters relating to sin and the notion of worldview."[20] The verses have accordingly served as a major inspiration and philosophical prop for worldview advocates from Abraham Kuyper to today's popularizers.[21] The famous diatribe fuels the bitter and adversarial tone of Christian Worldview, even to the point of supplying its adherents with a way of heaping epithets on their opponents. [22]

Finally, Calvin's approach to the world carries important implications for Christian Worldview thinking. Calvin assumes an affirmative attitude toward the everyday world based upon his sense of God's presence in all things. Since the world is God's masterwork, Calvin believes that the fulfillment of one's earthly obligations is a means of glorifying God. Together with reformers like Martin Luther, he supports the idea of "vocation," by which individuals can follow a calling in daily life and still understand they are fulfilling their religious duties. "No task will be so sordid and base, provided you obey your calling in it," he states, "that it will not shine and be reckoned very precious in God's sight."[23] This consecration of secular activity is central to the Calvinist vision. It is reflected today in the Religious Right's commitment to worldly engagement and its blurring of sacred-secular distinctions.

One sure indication of Calvin's concern for worldly matters is his active interest in civil government. For Calvin, human civil government is decreed by God in order to limit the effects of sin and to prevent anarchy. He adheres closely to the famous words of Romans 13:1: "For there is no power but of God: the powers that be are ordained of God." God rules, even though the "powers that be" refer to all legally constituted governments, Christian or not. Paul the Apostle, who wrote these words, lived in an age when the pagan Roman Empire ruled. Obviously, he was content to regard the existing political arrangements as sanctioned by God. Not only did he identify secular authority with God's purpose, but he viewed the ministers of government as God's direct agents, delegated to dispense his justice. Calvin hewed closely to Paul on this issue.

Governments differ, of course, in how well they fulfill their obligations. Calvin's concept of ideal governance is revealed both in his writings and in the contours of his Genevan experiment. In addition to securing peace and order, he believes the ideal ruler has spiritual and instructional obligations. Key among them is the duty "to cherish and protect the outward worship of God" and "to defend sound doctrine ... and the position of the church."[24] Calvin would no doubt have denied that he was in favor of an ecclesiastical tyranny. Officially, at least, he supported the functional separation of church and civil government (noting that each was separately subject to God's authority). His actions, however, indicate he believed that punishing religious offenses like apostasy and heresy were legitimate civil functions. He is famously remembered, much to the discomfort of modern Calvinists, for condoning the execution of the theologian Michael Servetus for his heretical views. Calvin seems to hold that any ideal government committed to "civil order" and guided by communal religious principles cannot help but be involved with broad issues of religious correctness.[25] The arrangement most to his liking is an oligarchy of prominent citizens elected by the people, all committed to honoring the biblical God. There is no inconsistency in his mind between electoral government and theocracy, since, as one scholar puts it, "citizens and rulers alike were participating in what had been authorized by God."[26] The elective-government-under-God formula is similar to that fostered by today's religious rightists.

Calvin's theology, taken as a whole, provides Christian Worldview advocates with the building blocks for a compelling ideology. Not only does it expand the reach of religion and immerse it in daily life, but it also supplies the psychological motivation for committed involvement. The theology centers on the concept of a watchful, all-powerful God who requires full submission from believers. It offers a dark view of human nature, including its cognitive side, regarding it fated to err when not yoked to faith. It presents an existential choice between good and evil, stigmatizes those who act independently, and rejects the possibility of compromise with idolaters. Its view of ideal government emphasizes civil conformity and obedience to God. And its impulse to include all of life within its perimeter gives broad sanction for religious involvement in secular affairs.

Still, Calvinism has traditionally been a theology with religious applications, gaited towards believers whose ultimate goal is salvation in another world. For it to be transformed historically into an ideology able to compete in a secular environment, important changes had to occur in Calvinism's relation to the surrounding culture. For centuries there had been no major disharmony between the religion's austere religious values and the cultures where it thrived, notably England, America, and the Netherlands. It was not until more recent times that orthodox Calvinists began to feel uneasy about the direction of civilization. Believing their way of life to be threatened by the allure of modernism, they saw a need to reassert actively their religion and culture. The situation was particularly acute in late nineteenth century Netherlands, a culturally divided country where a Calvinist minority existed side by side with a modernist majority. The Dutch Calvinist theologian, Abraham Kuyper, made it his historical mission to provide Calvinism with the intellectual tools to confront the challenge. He launched a new brand of militant Calvinism that has come to be known as Neo-Calvinism. In the next two sections, we turn to him and his followers.

Abraham Kuyper: Antithesis

The era of Abraham Kuyper was far different from that of John Calvin. During the sixteenth century, Christianity was the reigning religion in

Europe. The central question was not the truth or falsity of the Christian religion but what form the religion should take. Battered, however, by later sectarian conflict, Christianity saw its prestige decline over the next few centuries. The Enlightenment and the French Revolution of 1789 represented a new trend where reliance on human reason emerged as an alternative to unquestioned belief. The revolutionary slogan "no gods, no masters" put religion on the defensive, and the call for liberty, equality, and brotherhood heralded a reordering of priorities in which human concerns took precedence over divine ones. In the nineteenth century, scientific advances, and notably the theories of Charles Darwin, gave new prominence to material factors in human life, while capitalism and its countervailing opposite, socialism, portended new tendencies toward atomization on the one hand, and collectivism on the other. All of these trends made orthodox Christians anxious about their place in the world.

It was in this context that Abraham Kuyper made his historic appearance. Kuyper was born in Holland in 1837, the son of a Dutch Reformed preacher. The Reformed (Calvinist) Church, still a powerful force in Dutch society, was the soil out of which Kuyper's ideas were to grow. Receiving a doctorate in Sacred Theology at the age of 26, Kuyper turned at first to the ministry. As a young orthodox pastor, he soon became aware of the uncertain state of the church and consequently found himself drawn to the wider world of social activism and politics. In 1872, he became editor-in-chief of the newspaper, *De Standaard*, the official mouthpiece of the conservative Anti-Revolutionary Party, whose readers were mostly orthodox Calvinists. In this post, he editorialized frequently on the plague of modernism and the threat it posed to the shrinking Calvinist culture. To preserve the identity of Reformed Christianity, Kuyper strongly advocated support for separate schools, newspapers, and institutions for religious minorities. In 1880, he was instrumental in founding the Free University of Amsterdam as a citadel of Calvinism. Politically, he attained a seat in the lower Parliament in 1874 and assumed leadership of the Anti-Revolutionary Party four years later. The Party adopted a strong nationalist program that identified Dutch constitutional traditions with the nation's Calvinist past.[27] Kuyper achieved considerable political success in his later career, rising to the position of Dutch prime minister in 1901–1905. He had a practical streak that enabled him to cooperate with opponents on discrete issues and attain much of what he wanted. Nonetheless, his lasting importance was in the realm of ideas. His key legacy was the development of a Christian ideology aimed at challenging the modernist enemy.

Kuyper's starting point was classic Calvinism: God was sovereign. Duty to God and submission to his will was an imperative for all good Christians. While Kuyper observed the devotional aspects of religion, he put special emphasis on its worldly relevance. He famously gave voice to this approach at the founding of the Free University of Amsterdam: "There is not a square inch in the whole domain of our human existence over which Christ, who is sovereign over all, does not cry: 'Mine!'"[28] Attempting to galvanize a Dutch Reformed community that stressed private worship and shunned the mainstream, he condemned what he referred to as "pietistic" attitudes. Kuyper told his followers that withdrawal from the cultural and political fray was tantamount to surrendering the world to the enemies of Christianity. The believer needed to think less of achieving personal salvation and more of saving God's Creation and restoring "the world to its original perfection."[29] Scorning the upholders of human progress, Kuyper declared that the world existed for the sake of God rather than man. Man's chief role was to enhance God's glory: "The religion of man upon this earth should consist in one echoing of God's glory, as our Creator and Inspirer. The starting-point of every motive in religion is God and not Man. Man is the instrument and means, God alone is here the goal."[30]

Kuyper was aware that most of his countrymen did not share his God-centered beliefs. The problem as he saw it was one of false consciousness. Like many of the philosophical idealists of his day including Carlyle and Hegel, he viewed life not as an expression of material forces, but of mental and spiritual ones. One's individual destiny was a reflection of one's spiritual orientation. The same was true, on a grander scale, with cultures and civilizations. Kuyper was ready and eager to use this idealistic approach to critique his times. Modern civilization was faulty because the thinking of modern man could be traced to an erroneous commitment in the depths of the heart. Its spiritual commitment to God had been replaced by a commitment to false idols.

To explain the problem fully, Kuyper employs a Calvinist framework in conjunction with a worldview perspective. Following the passage from Romans 1:18–32, he holds that humans are divided into one of two camps, either faithful or unfaithful to God. Their contrasting commitments give rise to two separate sets of assumptions or "presuppositions" about God, humanity, and the world. Such differing assumptions color attitudes toward morality, politics, science, the arts, and all areas of knowledge and endeavor. They form the basis of what Kuyper calls "life-systems," or in common parlance, "worldviews." Kuyper predictably regards orthodox Christians as holding the only legitimate worldview since it reflects a true knowledge of God and hence of the world. Conversely, he sees liberal-minded Christians and nonbelievers holding a worldview that substitutes false idols in place of God. Using this framework, Kuyper is able to direct his rhetoric against God's alleged enemies.[31]

Kuyper uses the key word "antithesis," a term already familiar in certain philosophical circles, to describe the fundamental opposition between belief and unbelief.[32] "Antithesis" connotes not only incompatibility between opposing worldviews, but spiritual warfare: "Two *life* systems are wrestling with one another, in mortal combat," he states. "If the battle is to be fought with honor and with a hope of victory, then *principle* must be arrayed against *principle*."[33] Kuyper regards traditional apologetics, i.e., the use of reasoned argument to persuade others of the truth of the faith, as generally ineffective. Neutral ground for discussion between those of different worldviews is logically unattainable because of the incompatibility of their underlying core commitments. A more aggressive approach, involving a critique of the enemy's worldview and the promotion of a distinctly Christian Worldview to replace it, becomes a necessity.

Equipped with a Christian Worldview framework, Kuyper focuses his eye on what he sees as the major threat to Christianity in the Victorian age. No longer is it Papism and heresy, as in Calvin's day, but rather modernism and its most conspicuous embodiment, the secular state. From his nineteenth century vantage point, Kuyper significantly modifies Calvin's outlook on the state and its role. While, like any good Calvinist, he accepts civil government as a necessary instrument for preserving order, he also, in keeping with his antagonism to the French Revolution and its legacy, sees government in human hands as a potential threat far beyond Calvin's imaginings.

Kuyper is able to bolster his anti-statism theologically by finding a biblical justification for it. He sees government as something "mechanical" rather than organic, an expedient introduced by God *after* the Fall to curb the sins of mankind. Being a contrivance administered by humans, it tends to overreach its proper authority and amass power. As evidence of government's tendency toward aggrandizement, Kuyper cites the biblical story of the Tower of Babel, the edifice that humans erected to unify all humanity.[34] According to Scripture, God destroyed this symbol of human pride and scattered peoples to the corners of the earth. God thereafter made sure to remind humans that all legitimate political authority originated from his sovereignty alone.[35] Kuyper continues on the same theme, stressing that human governments do not derive their legitimacy from fictitious social contracts or phantom rights. He denounces both the idea of popular sovereignty and the semi-mystical concept of the state, readily identifying the modern secular state with the demons of revolution, atomism, and collectivization.[36] As will be seen, Kuyper's anti-statism becomes a fundamental mainstay of the Christian Worldview.

In contrast to his treatment of the state, Kuyper speaks approvingly of the basic sectors or units of society, which he refers to as "social spheres." He believes that basic social functions have a special status because they originated "directly from creation." They are organic and natural to the human species by reason of God's Dominion Mandate ("be fruitful, and multiply . . . and have dominion") prior to Adam's Fall. Such human functions include familial and work responsibilities, and by analogy, economic, scientific, and artistic activities. All these functions preceded the institution of government, which, as mentioned above, came *after* the Fall. Kuyper argues that, owing to the priority that God gave to them, such spheres of activity must be responsible directly to God and be free of state interference.[37] His views on the subject form the basis of his theory of "sphere sovereignty." Originally formulated by European anti-revolutionary thinkers of the mid-19th century as an answer to state centralization, the concept envisioned the dispersal of authority to the basic social units of society and the elimination of the state's jurisdiction over them.[38] Churches, schools, corporations, welfare organizations, and voluntary associations were to be subject to private jurisdictional authority. State and society, in a sense, were to be regarded as separate. Kuyper apparently was the first to give sphere sovereignty a biblical justification and place it directly within a Christian framework.[39]

Kuyper's ideas of antithesis and sphere sovereignty were critical in shaping his political views, especially in his early years. Antithesis influenced his stance toward the secular enemy and inspired his strategy of uniting the Dutch Reformed faithful into a counterforce to be reckoned with. The idea of sphere sovereignty contributed to his program of promoting self-governing religious organizations as a means of segregating them from modern influences. His philosophy, overall, manifested itself as a rigorous and uncompromising traditionalism. Like any skillful politician, however, Kuyper was attuned to political realities. As he gained national prominence and found himself having to work more within a pluralistic framework, he realized that he had to adjust his rhetoric and somewhat modify his strategy. In the process, he developed and relied increasingly on another component of his theology that seemed on the face of it to contradict its more militant aspects: the idea of "common grace."[40]

Common grace is a concept borrowed from Calvinist theology that can be used to justify cooperation with non-believers. All humans, it is believed, are capable of good acts, regardless of their religious stance. This, however, is not because they freely will to do good but because all good acts, even acts of faith, are ultimately the work of God rather than man. The mechanism by which this happens is God's gift of grace. God offers grace in two forms, "saving grace" and "common grace." Of the two, "saving grace" is of far more importance to believers since it enables the recipient to achieve salvation. "Common grace," on the other hand, has no bearing on one's eternal destination and is dispensed by God at his discretion to all humans, Christian and non-Christian alike. Common grace has the limited purpose of arresting the worst effects of sin in the world and preventing "the complete annihilation" of God's divine handiwork.[41] It offers an explanation for the virtues and obvious accomplishments of the "heathen" and enables people of different religious commitments to work together for the betterment of society as a whole. In Kuyper's theology common grace provides a safety valve for real world practitioners of the Christian Worldview, preventing antithesis from being taken to nonsensical extremes. It allowed Kuyper the politician to pursue compromise and form alliances with his enemies when necessary to pass legislation. Significantly, it is the element of Kuyper's legacy that has been most neglected by contemporary Christian worldviewers.

Historically, Kuyper will be remembered most for casting Calvinism in a new mold. Rejecting the notion of religion as insular and strictly devotional, he was convinced that Calvin's God-centric theology could be the basis for cultural and social renewal. But to further his cause, he understood he had to put the prevailing secular order on the defensive. Accordingly, he elevated Calvin's stern rhetoric to a new level and gave Calvinism a strongly anti-statist coloration, transforming Calvinist theology into a muscular ideology well equipped to compete with the secular alternative. Kuyper's radical approach, which blossomed into a movement with numerous followers, has since been dubbed Neo-Calvinism.

Neo-Calvinism continued as an active movement well beyond Kuyper's death in 1920. Others took up the banner and, through scholarship, attempted to give it philosophical reinforcement. Key among them was the Dutch theologian and philosopher, Herman Dooyeweerd (1894–1977), who developed a broad historical critique of "apostate" worldviews. Not one to think in small terms, Dooyeweerd wished to show conclusively that 2,500 years of mainstream Western thinking and philosophy were hopelessly defective. A master of the complexities of theological discourse, Dooyeweerd invented his own unique vocabulary and was renowned for his lack of transparency. But his sweeping generalizations were music to the ears of Christian worldviewers, who were looking for scholarly justifications for their position.

Dooyeweerd's main thesis, simply stated, is that non-Christian worldviews offer a fragmented depiction of the world, leading to inconsistent thinking. They portray the world in the form of cognitive dualities: for example, distinctions between mind and matter or reason and nature.[42] The result of such dualism is allegedly a form of split consciousness or, in the modern context, alienation and ennui. For a Calvinist like Dooyeweerd, an element common to this way of thinking is the prideful tendency of human reason to objectify the world and make it amenable to control. His overall argument thus becomes a tool in the Christian Worldview kit to stigmatize false worldviews. Meanwhile, Dooyeweerd offers a theological solution to the problem of dualistic thinking. He argues that if human reason can be subordinated to God's perspective as revealed in the Bible, the dualities will evaporate. Problems of split perception can be overcome when one acknowledges God's creative role in all things and accepts the reality of God's unifying purpose. A reconciliation of dualistic tendencies occurs when a "higher standpoint," i.e., God, is found that can transcend them.[43] For the believer, this requires "total self-surrender" to the ultimate source of unity, God.[44] Any human thinking that goes counter to this self-surrender is destined to be flawed and inconsistent.

While Dooyeweerd's ambitious attempt to dethrone traditional worldviews caused scarcely a ripple among mainstream philosophers, it found favor with many Christian Worldview partisans. His dense argumentation gave Christian Worldview a patina of intellectual respectability, even though his crude reductionism was criticized in some Reformed circles.[45] His theories were refashioned by Francis Schaeffer and given new life by current apologists like Nancy Pearcey.[46] However, the boldest attempt to boost the Christian Worldview approach came from another philosophical direction, where the aim was not simply to defend it, but to make it impregnable. This effort was embodied in the concept of presuppositionalism as articulated by the Neo-Calvinist theologian Cornelius Van Til. Because of its importance for worldview thinking, we deal with presuppositionalism under a separate heading.

Cornelius Van Til: The Circular Defense

Abraham Kuyper prepared the way for presuppositionalism with his conviction that all intellectual activity is colored by one's "religious" commitment, either to God or to some substitute. Human thought is the "servant of the heart," meaning that it begins from a core attitude or disposition. No thinking, accordingly, can be "impartial" or "value-free."[47] Followers of the true Christian God form their view of the world on the basis of one set of premises, while followers of false idols do so according to an entirely different set. This creates an antithesis of true and false worldviews, each presenting a different take on reality.

Presuppositionalism is an epistemology (theory of knowledge) based upon this concept of knowledge arising out of a set of core premises. Cornelius Van Til (1895–1987) is the thinker most responsible for developing the theory into a weapon of Christian apologetics. Van Til maintains that a fully accurate worldview must be based upon the recognition of God's true word as revealed in the Bible. To be fully correct, the worldview must presuppose the content of Scripture. False worldviews, founded on a commitment to "the creature more than the Creator,"[48] necessarily presuppose an incoherent set of assumptions about the world. As a consequence, common ground between true and false worldviews becomes impossible. Accepting Kuyper's concept of antithesis, Van Til sets out to fully explore its philosophical implications.

Cornelius Van Til, the son of a Dutch dairy farmer, immigrated with his family to the United States at the age of ten. Receiving an orthodox Christian education both in Holland and the U.S., Van Til went on to Calvin College and Princeton Theological Seminary (not connected with Princeton University), both bastions of Reformed pedagogy. Proving himself an accomplished student of apologetics, Van Til was chosen by J. Gresham Machen, the conservative Presbyterian theologian, to teach at the newly established Westminster Theological Seminary in 1929. Westminster was, from its beginning, a redoubt for critics of liberal Christianity and a center of orthodox Calvinist scholarship. Van Til remained there until his retirement in 1972.

In the relatively small universe of Reformed scholarship, Van Til soon gained a reputation as a man with strong opinions. His first major publication, *The New Modernism: An Appraisal of the Theology of Barth and Brunner* (1946), was a scathing attack on new trends in Protestant theology. The work positioned him on the militant wing of Calvinist orthodoxy and caused many colleagues to treat him as an outsider. Although Van Til became a productive scholar in the following years, his career was hampered by isolation.[49] Ecclesiastically, he belonged to a small breakaway Presbyterian sect, the Orthodox Presbyterian Church, which took a hard Calvinist line. Academically, he favored an uncompromising brand of scholarship that made him unreceptive to ideas that clashed with his own. When he published articles and books, he did so almost always in non-refereed publications, whose editors offered little critical challenge to his ideas. Both in teaching and publishing formats, Van Til often had trouble communicating, typically using terms without properly defining them or refraining from explaining his ideas through normal give-and-take.[50] To be sure, Van Til's grasp of his subject matter was by all accounts impressive, and he attracted a small group of followers who lauded his work. John Frame, a former colleague at Westminster Theological Seminary and practicing presuppositionalist, is one of those who proclaimed his twentieth century significance.[51] While the adulation of such disciples surely reinforced Van Til's sense of mission, it did little to lessen his isolation from other scholars.

The most consequential difference between Van Til and most of his Reformed colleagues was a divergence in apologetic method, that is, the method of argument used to defend Christianity. Bucking two millennia of Christian tradition, Van Til firmly rejected traditional apologetics, sometimes called "the traditional method" or "evidentialism." The traditional method has always taken for granted the competence of human reason to test truth claims. It assumes the ability of Christians and non-Christians to debate on neutral common ground. Traditional apologists encourage all parties to "argue in a religiously neutral fashion, starting with criteria and facts that are commonly accepted by 'reasonable' men."[52] Under these common-sense assumptions, humans can attain truth through properly observing evidence and using the rules of logic. Van Til, however, calls such assumptions into question. He reiterates Kuyper's point that people carry with them distinct worldviews based on underlying presuppositions that determine how they reason and process reality. Why offer traditional proofs of God or evidence to support the Resurrection of Jesus, he argues, if listeners have presuppositions that distort even the best arguments and predispose them to reach different conclusions?

Van Til maintains that theologians who advocate the traditional method accept the same faulty premises about reasoning as non-believers, that is, they assume they can "begin their thinking without God."[53] To Van Til, they are guilty of the sin of "autonomy" ("self law"). The autonomous mind in its fallen state acts on the basis of its own arbitrary laws and presupposes its own all-knowingness. It can, to be sure, show glimmers of correct understanding from time to time, as seen by its grasp of elements of logic, science, and morality. But, being autonomous, it can only approach these things in reference to itself. It can never put its knowledge into a consistent framework or be sure of its absolute certainty. Nor can it be moved to see the logical necessity of God's sovereignty.

Only a perspective centered on God can present a clear picture of reality and guarantee the truth of knowledge. No fact, according to Van Til, can be seen in isolation from God: "For the Christian, facts are what they are, in the last analysis, by virtue of the place they take in the plan of God." God is "the final point of reference in all interpretation," since only he is capable of giving a full and comprehensive account of reality.[54] As R. J. Rushdoony underscores in his study of Van Til, "this world exists only as a God-created and God interpreted world."[55] The one way for humans to avoid error and to achieve accurate thinking, therefore, is by somehow absorbing God's perceptual framework. One must follow in God's mental footsteps and "think God's thoughts after him." Van Til calls this effort at mental mimicking "analogical thinking." Since human knowledge will never come close to God's knowledge, the most it can aspire to is to become a "finite *replica* of God's knowledge," which occurs when it is fully subject to "God's control and authority."[56] The Christian believer attains correct knowledge by fully accepting God's revelation in Scripture and then using it as a model for reasoning.

Armed with a God-centered worldview, Christians are in a position to abandon the old common-ground defense of Christianity with its ineffective appeals to evidence and logic and its reliance on a 3,000 year-old intellectual tradition. Under Van Til's formula, they can shift the terms of the argument to something far simpler and more direct. They can exploit the enemy's apparent weakness, i.e., his worldview. Taking an aggressive line, they can directly attack its inadequacies and inconsistencies by contrasting it with their own superior worldview. Van Til thus converts Kuyper's concept of antithesis into a well-honed system of critique, intended not simply to defend religion and fend off the enemy, but to reframe the debate.

Van Til's views caused considerable controversy during his lifetime. His main opponents were not humanists or liberal Christians, who were generally unfamiliar with his ideas, but other Reformed scholars who shared his Calvinist beliefs but disagreed with his epistemology. These critics point out that Van Til gets bogged down in circular reasoning, if not downright absurdity.[57] Van Til argues that correct thinking must presuppose (i.e., hold as "an elementary assumption in one's reasoning")[58] God and the truth of the Bible before all else. In effect he is saying that any reasoned attempt to ascertain the truth of God and Scripture cannot be valid since human reason unguided by revelation is flawed. Scripture, rather than the untutored human mind, must be the starting point of any pursuit of truth. Fundamental truths must be assumed *before* one applies one's reason. If asked how God can be proven if he is already assumed to exist, Van Til has a ready answer, which he bases circularly on Scripture itself: no proof for God is required because God is naturally revealed to everyone (Romans 1:18–20).[59] As an apologist for Christianity, Van Til thus wins his argument before he even begins it, since his assumptions are implicit in what he seeks to affirm: i.e. that God and the Bible are true. Such are the advantages of circular reasoning.

Significantly, Van Til concedes the circularity of his argument. But he justifies it by claiming that it is "the only reasoning that is possible to finite man" and that "autonomous" thinking is no less circular, because its own presuppositions foretell its conclusions.[60] On this point, of course, Van Till is on shaky ground, since "autonomous" thinking can, and often does, lead to conclusions that Van Til supports (for example, belief in Christianity), as well as those he doesn't. "Autonomous" reasoning, in other words, is typically linear and open-ended, rather than circular. It is a form of reasoning that Van Til cannot accept, however, because it rests on the mere possibility of success. Any approach to truth must logically *necessitate* the absolute certainty of God and Christianity.

Critics of Van Til have sometimes assumed that presuppositionalism makes discourse between those of opposing worldviews impossible. The doctrine maintains, after all, that believers and non-believers will perceive differently even the simplest of facts. Actually, Van Til takes a more subtle position. On an epistemological level (i.e., with reference to knowledge), he would deny common ground. There is nothing about their knowledge of the world that Christians can convey to non-Christians and be fully understood, and vice versa. Psychologically, however, Van Til sees the possibility of a "point of contact," since all humans are made in God's image and share that intuitive inkling of God already mentioned in our discussion of Calvin, even though the nonbeliever is said to repress it.[61] Unconsciously, non-believers apparently know that their perception of the world is deficient. On the basis of this psychological approach, Van Til advances his own apologetic strategy: to show non-believers the inadequacy of their own worldview in explaining the world, by comparing it with a God-centered framework.

Van Til employs what he calls the "indirect argument," in which he confronts opponents about their allegedly false presuppositions.[62] Diverting discussion from facts to underlying assumptions and worldview, he shrewdly uses traditional (linear) logic to criticize the opponent's worldview, while reserving presuppositional (circular) logic to defend his own. Thus he argues that a non-Christian worldview is inconsistent and unreliable because it presupposes a cosmos that is the product of contingency and chance, with no guarantee from a Christian god that it is true. [63] So far the presuppositionalist is using linear logic to advance his argument.[64] When his own theories are challenged, however, he erects a circular defense. If, for instance, the opponent questions the necessity of God, the presuppositionalist states that logic itself presumes the existence of God the Creator. Since logic is inconceivable without God, one's use of it is tantamount to acknowledging his existence. If the opponent questions the consistency and coherence of Scripture (and the Christian Worldview based on it), the presuppositionalist asserts the inadequacy of human reason to deal with such issues. Because the existence of God and the truth of Scripture are self-evident within a Christian Worldview framework, both questions are viewed as unnecessary or illegitimate.[65] Using traditional logic to criticize opponents while prohibiting its use against themselves, presuppositionalists have thus produced a classic "heads-I-win-tails-you-lose" formula.

This method of argument has become a key forensic tool for today's Christian rightists. It serves them well as a way of challenging the assertions of secularists and justifying their Christian Worldview alternative. An example of the two-pronged style of attack and defense is seen in their campaign against evolution and for intelligent design. Present-day presuppositionalists dismiss the extensive evidence in evolution's behalf as invalid because it is lodged in so-called materialist assumptions. It is part and parcel of a false worldview, they claim, and they use all the traditional forms of logic to attack those assumptions and the scientific ideas that spring from them. By contrast, their defense of their own alternative theory, intelligent design, is essentially circular. Intelligent design does not require decades of scientific research to confirm it because it is self-evident. The hand of a designer is clearly manifest to all, even if many seek to deny it. And if one persists in questioning the reasoning used in the defense of intelligent design, there is a ready biblical backup: Romans 1:18–20. But we are getting ahead of ourselves. The debate over science will be more fully addressed in a later chapter.

It took a while for presuppositionalism to be recognized as a potent ideological tool. Van Til refined it as an apologetic method in the 1940s and '50s, but another theologian was responsible for realizing its true potential. In 1958, that individual wrote a treatise, *By What Standard? An Analysis of the Philosophy of Cornelius Van Til*, extolling presuppositionalism as the basis for a thought system that would shake the status quo. He and a group of followers advanced it as the paradigm for a new biblical age. The author's name was R. John Rushdoony, the father of Christian Reconstructionism.

4

BLUEPRINT: GOD'S LAW

Christian Reconstructionism

One of the favorite refrains of Christian Reconstructionist Gary North is "you can't beat something with nothing."[1] North uses the phrase to chide reluctant Christians unwilling to "go the distance" in fighting the enemy. It is not enough, he maintains, to declare war against secular civilization under the banner of the Christian Worldview. A proper worldview may be a necessary precondition for engaging the enemy, but it does not provide a detailed plan for action. One must have something to replace the old regime, an alternative model that reflects an authentic Christian perspective. To North and other Calvinists of the far right, Christian Reconstructionism provides the only effective answer: a program that applies Christian Worldview concepts to the real world.

R. John Rushdoony, the movement's founder, apparently first used the term "reconstruction" in 1965 to refer to a coming "Christian Renaissance" capable of challenging "humanism and statism."[2] Reconstruction is meant to connote the process of building something from scratch in place of something else that is flawed. In its Christian form, it signifies the establishment of a religio-political order faithful to the dictates of God's will to replace the current godless order. In the eyes of Rushdoony and his followers, a corps of God's elect would undertake the "task of reconstruction," taking the Bible as a blueprint and seeking to apply Old Testament civil codes, often harsh, to contemporary society. In so doing they would establish God's sovereignty over all of society.

Well versed in both Calvinism and Neo-Calvinism, the Christian Reconstructionists considered themselves natural heirs to the Christian

Worldview tradition. Christian Worldview concepts were central to their efforts to forge a distinct brand of theology in the 1970s and '80s. They thus incorporated Calvin's theocentrism, Kuyper's antithesis, and Van Til's presuppositionalist ideas. The uncompromising stance of the Calvinist-Kuyperian outlook, with its hopes of overwhelming secularism and establishing a new age of Christian culture, became part of their identity as a movement.

Meanwhile, the Christian Reconstructionists brought a new, dynamic perspective to Christian Worldview that helped in politicizing it. Prior to 1960, the concept was largely the esoteric concern of orthodox seminarians. During the ferment of the 1960s and 1970s, however, Rushdoony and his allies began to envision broader applications: in particular, they associated Christian Worldview with the possibility of radical change. They brought several new ingredients to worldview thinking that enabled this transformation, three of which stand out as significant: emphasis on a strict covenantal branch of Calvinism, namely, orthodox Anglo-Scottish Presbyterianism; adherence to an optimistic version of millennialism, called postmillennialism; and affinity with American right-wing populism and the economic and political ideas associated with it. We will briefly discuss each of these components.

It is fair to say that a large part of the social agenda of the Christian Reconstructionists is suggested, if not shaped, by their denominational allegiance. Virtually all of the movement's leaders identify with an austere form of Presbyterianism founded on centuries-old confessional statements. Each of them have ties with one of two small branches of Presbyterianism: the Orthodox Presbyterian Church (OPC) and the Presbyterian Church of America (PCA).[3] Both the OPC and PCA are twentieth century breakaways from mainstream Presbyterianism, which they attack for its moderate and liberal tendencies.[4] The two sects derive their principles directly from the Westminster Confession of 1646, the famous creedal statement hammered out during the English Civil War by old-school Presbyterian divines.

Seventeenth century Presbyterianism, a product of Calvinism parallel to the Reformed Church on the Continent, possessed its own distinct coloration and emphasis. Along with such core Calvinist principles as the depravity of man and the unconditional election of God's faithful, it stressed ideas that had special resonance for English and Scottish Puritans. Most notable among them was the idea of a covenant binding God and his people.[5] Such a covenant, found in the Book of Deuteronomy and elsewhere in the Old Testament, specifies an understanding in which God's blessing is offered in return for obedience to his directives. If the people do not comply with God's commands, punishments follow. The focus on covenantal obligations leads naturally to questions about Old Testament law and its application. Such questions, crucial to traditional Presbyterians because of their relevance to Puritan visions of society, occupied months of debate in the Westminster Assembly. It is thus no coincidence that covenantal obligation and biblical law are central concerns for today's Christian Reconstructionists, who in a sense regard themselves as inheritors of the Puritan legacy.

Postmillennialism is a second crucial element embraced by Reconstructionists. Postmillennialism is a form of millennialism that is often contrasted with its more popular sibling, premillennialism. Millennial theories, always an important aspect of Christian theology, are based on prophecies in biblical literature about Christ's Second Coming and the establishment of the millennium, Christ's 1,000 year reign on earth. Different interpretations of Scripture led to the rise of the two predominant schools, each with its own separate views on the timing and conditions of Christ's arrival and the installation of his earthly kingdom. The divergence of opinion is by no means a trivial matter, since a believer's stance on the end of history tends to have a direct bearing on her social and political views, including her attitude on the significance of human action to achieve change.

Of the two kinds of millennialism, premillennialism is the form best known to Americans because of its dramatic rapture scenarios and epic struggles, popularized in Tim LaHaye's Left Behind novels. "Premills," as they are sometimes nicknamed, believe that Christ's coming is close at hand. His arrival is forecast to occur *before* the millennium begins, hence the use of the prefix "pre." The outlook is a pessimistic one, stemming from the assumption that human beings are unable to establish a godly kingdom by their own efforts and must be rescued through divine intervention. As a consequence, the premillennialist tends to attach a low priority to changing the world or engaging in politics. Her mood is one of expectancy and anticipation of unfolding events.

In contrast with premillennialism, postmillennialism calls for a more gradual millennial scenario with full human participation and fewer supernatural props. Postmillennialists believe that Jesus' coming will occur *after* the millennium (hence the prefix "post"). Accordingly, the millennial kingdom must first be achieved on this earth through the work of human beings under the *spiritual* rule of Jesus Christ. The kingdom will be fully consummated only upon Christ's physical return, which is not expected in the foreseeable future. Theologically optimistic, postmillennialists consider it their evangelical mission not simply to spread the Gospel, but to redeem the world, reform institutions, and Christianize civilization. God's kingdom, far from being a hoped-for, externally generated event, is something that needs to be fostered in the present. All of this is in keeping with God's historical plan for his Creation. Significantly, the postmillennial stance toward the world has much in common with the Calvinist commitment to glorifying God's kingdom on earth. Although John Calvin's millennial beliefs were ambivalent,[6] his followers have often leaned toward postmillennialism. Like today's "postmills," they have tended to take an active role in the world. Postmillennial optimism is one of the key motivating elements behind modern Christian Reconstructionism, reassuring its adherents that they are active agents in the unfolding of God's plan.

Contemporary right-wing populism is a third factor behind Christian Reconstructionism's hard-core militancy. Nurtured in southern California, Reconstructionism is in many respects a reflection of Sunbelt conservatism, a populist type of conservatism that favors untrammeled enterprise and disparages Eastern elites, foreign influences, and central government.[7] In their formative years, Reconstructionists showed their colors in such matters by the company they kept. On the political front, they established close ties with the John Birch Society (JBS), the extremist anti-communist organization founded in 1958. R. J. Rushdoony once belonged to the JBS, wrote articles for its publication

American Opinion, and admired its operations and structure, which he compared to the early Christian church.[8] The Reconstructionists have long shared the Birchers' tendency toward xenophobia and penchant for conspiracy theory. Meanwhile, in the economic sphere, Reconstructionists collaborated with conservative foundations like the William Volker Fund, an early supporter of Rushdoony's work, and the Foundation for Economic Education (FEE) based in Irvington-on-Hudson, New York.[9] Staunchly anti-collectivist, Rushdoony and his followers drew inspiration from the free market theories advanced by Ludwig von Mises, Friedrich Hayek, Murray Rothbard, and other like-minded economists. Their glosses on Scripture, not coincidentally, often turn out to be thinly disguised arguments for free market economic policy.

Presbyterian theology, postmillennialism, and ultraconservatism all contributed to the unique approach and agenda of Christian Reconstructionism. Combined with the signature worldview concepts of God-centeredness and cosmic struggle, such elements offered the movement a potent intellectual framework and basis for activism. With these background elements in mind, we can better understand the development of Christian Reconstructionism as a multi-faceted system of thought. First, however, we need to focus on the individuals behind the movement, since personality was to play a special role in its history.

Apostles of a New Paradigm

The proponents of Christian Reconstructionism have long been convinced of their pioneering role. Seeing themselves as the carriers of a new theology that will change how people see the world, they claim to offer a paradigm for knowledge that will redefine truth and a program based upon that paradigm that will inaugurate a new Christian age. Their striking zeal and determination, reinforced by theological certainty, have inspired gargantuan publishing efforts and years of sacrifice for the cause. Because of such efforts, their ideas have shown a startling resiliency in the face of multiple challenges, including ostracism, internal discord, and eventual organizational decline.

Given its visionary doctrines, Christian Reconstructionism could not have asked for a better agent to present its program to the world than Rousas John Rushdoony. Rushdoony fits the image of a prophet. His gaunt physique, long beard, and piercing eyes convey the impression of a stern patriarch called upon by God to perform a special mission. Rushdoony was driven throughout his life by a profound hostility to secular civilization and a fierce commitment to the literal pronouncements of Scripture. His proposed solutions to world problems were authentically radical, and his rhetoric harsh and polemical. With no permanent ties to any academic or research institutions, Rushdoony followed his own path, starting out as an isolated voice in the wilderness and ending up as the revered leader of an elite band of Christian ultra-conservatives committed to changing the course of civilization.

Rushdoony was born in 1916 in New York City, the son of Armenian refugees recently arrived from the turmoil in their native Turkey. Descended from a long line of clerics, Rushdoony had the role of missionary stamped on his genes. Just as consequential was his consciousness of belonging to a once oppressed minority. In his upbringing, he apparently heard many times the retelling of Armenian massacres at the hands of the Turks.[10] Rushdoony thus had deep reasons for seeing the world as inhabited by implacable forces that needed to be confronted and defeated at all costs.

While the Rushdoonys historically were members of the Apostolic Armenian Church, R. J. Rushdoony's father broke family tradition by receiving ordination in the mainstream Presbyterian Church. After a few years in the United States, the elder Rushdoony settled down in Kingsburg, California and founded his own Armenian-speaking parish.[11] His son Rousas, fully imbued with conservative Christian training in his youth, naturally gravitated to the ministry after attending the University of California at Berkeley. Becoming ordained in the Presbyterian Church like his father, he went on to serve as a missionary for eight years with American Indians in Nevada and as a pastor of his own congregation in Southern California in the 1950s. Eventually, Rushdoony's austere faith drew him to a strict, Calvinistic form of Presbyterianism. He joined the small Orthodox Presbyterian Church

(OPC) in the late 1950s, where he remained in good standing for about 15 years.[12] During this period, Rushdoony applied himself to the study of theology, finding time to write articles for religious journals.

Given his uncompromising approach, Rushdoony was understandably receptive to the doctrines of Neo-Calvinism being propagated by Abraham Kuyper and his followers. He was particularly impressed by the then obscure theologian, Cornelius Van Til. When he first came upon a book by Van Til, Rushdoony saw its pivotal importance and reviewed it enthusiastically. The intellectual encounter was transformative, leading eventually to his first book publication, *By What Standard? An Analysis of the Philosophy of Cornelius Van Til* (1958). Rushdoony showed enthusiasm both for Van Til's concept of a Bible-centered epistemology and his views on the dangers of human autonomy. Armed with this framework, he assumed the role of critic in earnest, producing books at the rate of about one per year over the next 20 years.

In his writing and research, Rushdoony soon ventured beyond the confines of theology and philosophy. Unrestricted by the specialized norms of academe, he covered such areas as education, history, psychology, law, politics, economics, and science. Although the breadth of his writings leaves him vulnerable to the charge of shallowness, one cannot simply dismiss him as a dilettante, for Rushdoony showed considerable skill in the way he applied his orthodox religious framework to different areas of experience. In the first decade of his writing career, he employed that framework in the work of demolition, critiquing multiple segments of American secular culture. His proposed radical solutions were to follow later.

In the summer of 1965, Rushdoony established the organization that was to embody the Reconstructionist cause for many years, the Chalcedon Foundation. At that time, he issued the first of his monthly newsletters, later called the *Chalcedon Report*, which continue to the present day. The word Chalcedon refers to the Council of Chalcedon, a conference of bishops held in 451 A.D. that attempted to shore up Christianity's fundamental doctrines. Rushdoony claims that the Council stripped human government of what he refers to as its "messianic" pretensions, its ambition to offer a worldly form of salvation. He calls the Council a milestone in the establishment of the "Christian foundation of Western culture," heralding the victory of Christ over Caesar.[13] In his first monthly newsletter, Rushdoony sets up a simple choice between two claimants to the "throne" of universal government: the "state" and the "Holy Trinity."[14] Later newsletters would call attention to the encroachments of statism and the onset of social anarchy in the absence of religious authority.

In 1973 Rushdoony finally offered his corrective for a fallen society: the outline of a Christian system of law and government, presented in the form of a 900 page tome. *The Institutes of Biblical Law*, whose title mirrors Calvin's *The Institutes of the Christian Religion*, marks the real "coming out" of the Reconstructionist movement. For all of the importance Reconstructionists attach to it, the *Institutes* has no pretensions to being great literature, consisting of little more than a collection of footnoted sermons delivered between 1968 and 1972.[15] Nonetheless, it is remarkably broad in scope. Organized around the Ten Commandments and the case laws associated with them, the book serves as a guide to contemporary legal, moral, and social issues viewed in the light of literal Old Testament standards. Since the Commandments are largely couched in negative terms ("thou shalt not" as opposed to "thou shalt"), the book inevitably focuses on the intricacies of crime and punishment. It is here that it has generated the most controversy.

Rushdoony did not stop writing after the publication of *The Institutes*. With the bountiful support of certain financial angels of the far right,[16] he continued to publish books and issue his *Chalcedon Report* for a couple more decades. But now his emphasis was less on scholarship than on appealing to a larger audience. Evangelical opinion-makers had begun to tune into his works by this time, and he could probably begin numbering his loyal readers in the thousands.[17] In writings that tended to be shorter and less rigorous than his earlier works, he conveyed to any who would listen that Christian Reconstructionism was the wave of the future.

Rushdoony was particularly successful in his middle years in attracting, training, and employing a cohort of future leaders at Chalcedon. Gary North, Greg Bahnsen, James Jordan, and David Chilton were some of the acolytes who passed through the organization and absorbed the founder's vision and purpose. To be sure, Rushdoony did not succeed ultimately in keeping the movement united or disciplined. His authoritarian temperament eventually drove most of his young tutees out of the fold and into separate splinter groups during the late 1970s and early 1980s. But this mini diaspora also revitalized the movement by encouraging new thinking. The two most renowned of Rushdoony's disciples to break away and establish their own brands of Christian Reconstructionism were Greg Bahnsen and Gary North.

Greg Bahnsen, the most academic of the Reconstructionists, was born in 1948 and grew up in the suburbs of Los Angeles.[18] Raised as a member of the Orthodox Presbyterian Church (OPC), he remained in that denomination for the rest of his life either as congregant or minister. Falling under the influence of Van Til and Rushdoony when still in high school, Bahnsen began writing for Rushdoony's Chalcedon Foundation while attending Westmont College in Santa Barbara. He rounded out his education by securing an advanced degree at Westminster Theological Seminary (WTS) in 1973, where he studied directly under Cornelius Van Til, and a PhD in philosophy at the University of Southern California in 1978.

Bahnsen's academic credentials seemed to make him an ideal candidate for a teaching career in one of the leading conservative seminaries. Events turned out differently, however. Early on, Bahnsen's unconventional theology began to raise red flags among Reformed Christian traditionalists. His master's thesis at WTS, "The Theonomic Responsibility of the Civil Magistrate," which defended the applicability of Old Testament laws to modern societies, caused uneasiness among the faculty. "Theonomy" (literally "God's law") was a central element of the new Christian Reconstructionist movement, and Bahnsen did not hide his sympathies with it. After working briefly with Rushdoony at the Chalcedon Foundation, Bahnsen went to teach apologetics at Reformed Theological Seminary (RTS) in Jackson, Mississippi, where he developed a small student following.[19] However, the publication in 1978 of *Theonomy in Christian Ethics*, an expanded version of his master's thesis, made him persona non grata in the academic community. RTS failed to renew his contract in 1979, and WTS showed no interest in recruiting him as a replacement for the newly retired Van Til. The rejection of Bahnsen, one of its intellectual stars, was a harsh blow to the early Reconstructionist movement because it dashed any hopes for establishment recognition. The perceived injury continued to fester, setting the stage for a bruising ideological struggle in the following decade between traditional Reformed seminarians and unaffiliated Reconstructionists over claims of orthodoxy.[20]

Faced with a dead end in academia, Bahnsen moved back to California, where he established an OPC church in 1980, and took a teaching position at Newport Christian High School. His diminished status, however, did not halt his advocacy for theonomy and Christian Reconstruction. If anything, it probably increased his commitment to the cause by freeing him from institutional restraints. During the 1980s, when controversy raged in right-wing Christian circles over questions about the application of biblical law, Bahnsen forcefully defended theonomic orthodoxy.[21] His crowning effort as an apologist, however, was in behalf of the arch apologist himself, Cornelius Van Til. Bahnsen edited and annotated a tome containing a broad selection of Van Til's works,[22] knowing that Van Til's presuppositionalism and Reconstructionism would stand or fall together. Soon after completing the manuscript in 1995, he died suddenly from a blood platelet problem.

While Bahnsen served as the principal academic apologist for theonomy, Gary North became the movement's intellectual gadfly on a broad range of issues. Moreover, as Rushdoony's influence faded during the 1980s, North took on the role of chief strategist for the movement, guiding it through controversy and directing much of its publishing program. Born in 1942 and raised in a non-religious family, North converted to evangelical Christianity at the age 17.[23] He won a state scholarship to Pomona College and later transferred to the University of California, Riverside. Throughout his college years, North showed strong conservative leanings, taking special interest in both free market economics and biblical studies. One of his intellectual goals was to explore the ostensible connection between them. Encouraging him in this endeavor was R. J. Rushdoony, whom North first met at a summer seminar in 1962. From their first encounter until the end of the 1970s, Rushdoony played a key supportive role in North's career, providing him with encouragement, funds, and eventually a full-paying job. Reflecting their close personal relationship, North eventually married Rushdoony's daughter.

After his graduation in 1963, North pursued his biblical and economic interests. With Rushdoony's assistance he attended the Westminster Theological Seminary in 1964, where he studied briefly with Cornelius Van Til. In the years that followed, North continued to do "sporadic work on biblical economics," as he describes it.[24] Having immersed himself in free market theorists like von Mises and Hayek, he soon took to writing articles for *The Freeman* and other conservative economic publications. These were later collected in one of his early books, *An Introduction to Christian Economics* (1973). Meanwhile, he returned to the University of California, Riverside, where he obtained his history Ph.D. in 1972 with specialties in economic history and Puritan economic thought. The following year, North followed Rushdoony's call to serve on the staff of the Chalcedon Foundation and later to edit Chalcedon's *Journal of Reconstruction.*[25]

As a published writer and then editor, North had high ambitions for the budding Reconstructionist movement. Having witnessed firsthand the upheaval in the universities, North believed that modern thought and culture were in a state of severe crisis. Predictably, he came to regard presuppositionalism as the best corrective approach to knowledge and thinking.[26] North was fond of invoking Thomas Kuhn's work, *The Structure of Scientific Revolutions* (1962), which views stages of intellectual history in terms of paradigms that govern the direction of human thought.[27] North believed that the current modernist paradigm was ripe for replacement. Projecting optimism about a new Christian age of thought, he edited a collection of essays in Van Til's honor in 1976 (*Foundations of Christian Scholarship: Essays in the Van Til Perspective*) focusing on different fields of knowledge from a Van Tillian point of view.

As the 1970s played out, however, it became increasingly obvious that such optimism was, at best, premature. The problem was not so much opposition to the new ideas from secular forces or religious moderates as it was resistance from within the conservative Christian community itself. Reformed Christian theologians at institutions like the Westminster Theological Seminary increasingly viewed Christian Reconstructionism as a threat to traditional Christianity. And evangelical activists, initially attracted by the movement's militant spirit, reacted ambivalently to its bold biblical agenda. The seeds of division were definitely visible, even as the Religious Right was gaining steam.

An even more immediate problem for Reconstructionists, however, was division within their own ranks, the result of ideological and personal factors. Around 1980, the first major rift in the movement occurred: a falling out between Rushdoony and North that was to have significant implications for the future of the movement. The immediate cause of the split was seemingly trivial: Rushdoony found one of the articles submitted by North for his *Chalcedon Report* to have been doctrinally faulty, "heretical," as he termed it. It was an article on the symbolism of the Passover entitled "The Marriage Supper of the Lamb." North withdrew the article and was content to let the matter drop, but Rushdoony took a hard line: it was either recant in writing or face discipline. The disagreement spiraled out of control, North was fired, and a permanent chasm separated the two men.[28] North left southern California and relocated to Tyler, Texas, where he established his own research center. While still acknowledging Rushdoony's key role in the movement, he no longer felt constrained to conceal their differences. And once he was independent, North was able to give attention to his own priorities.

The theological aspect of the split did not fully come out in the open until years afterward. Interestingly, it showed the younger man taking the side of orthodoxy and the older man playing the role of heretic. According to North, the dispute over the article was peripheral to their more fundamental disagreement over the authority of the Church. It was well known in the Chalcedon community that Rushdoony had severed his connections with the Orthodox Presbyterian Church in the early 1970s after a period of becoming gradually estranged from it. North traces the beginning of Rushdoony's change of attitude to a messy divorce in 1956, which put him, as a minister, in an awkward position with church authorities.[29] As Rushdoony cooled toward the OPC, he gradually moved away from orthodox Presbyterianism and adopted a loose form of non-denominationalism, condemning the authoritarian tendencies of hierarchical church government.[30] This directly affected his theology, which came to question the authority of the Church in creedal, sacramental, and judicial matters.[31] Around the time of his break with the OPC, Rushdoony instituted his own Sunday Bible meetings at Chalcedon. His Bible study group gradually mutated into a "patriarchal home church," in North's words, and by 1991 had begun administering the sacraments.[32] In reaction, North finally went public with his criticism, claiming that Rushdoony had replaced the church's authority with that of the family head, i.e. himself. To North, the dire result was Christian "patriarchalism" and the "cult of the family."[33]

North's differences with Rushdoony were not limited to the matter of church authority. He accused Rushdoony at times of improperly applying Old Testament law[34] and too readily accepting the legitimacy of the U.S. political system and Constitution.[35] But the two differed most significantly in the areas of temperament and strategy. Rushdoony preferred the role of isolated prophet, issuing books and newsletters on general matters while separating himself from day-to-day controversies. Gary North viewed such a posture as far too timid, calling it the "Dwight Eisenhower" strategy.[36] Instead, he chose a high profile approach that involved publicly confronting opponents, especially on issues of ideological purity. After his break with Rushdoony, he became the active face of the movement.

In the early 1980s, North set up the Institute for Christian Economics (ICE) in Tyler as his publication arm. Fortunately for the movement, he had both the writing and organizational skills necessary for an active publishing campaign and, like Rushdoony, the external financial backing to keep it going.[37] The steady stream of publications coming out of Tyler in the following decade, titles written by himself or fellow writers, is testimony to the productivity of his efforts. The writings tended to fall into one of three categories: texts that offered a blueprint for a reconstructed society and justified it in biblical terms; books discussing movement strategy; and polemical works directed at Reformed Christian and premillennial opponents who opposed the Reconstructionist approach. The publication offensive put Reconstructionism on the map as a Christian ideological alternative and made it a force to be reckoned with.

The 1990s saw a gradual diminishment of Reconstructionist activity. Greg Bahnsen's death in 1995 was a blow to the movement's morale and marked the end of its period of high productivity. Individuals, however, carried on in their own fashion. R. John Rushdoony's unconventional practices continued to isolate him from many of his fellow Reconstructionists, although he issued his *Chalcedon Report* from his outpost in Vallecito, California, on the edge of the Sierra Nevada Mountains, until his death in 2001. A band of Rushdoony stalwarts continue to keep the periodical going. Gary North's publishing activities peaked around 1990 and slowly declined to the end of the decade, by which time he had become involved in his financial investment newsletter, *Remnant Review*. His dire forecasts about the Y2K crisis, which failed to materialize in 2000 as he predicted, diminished his credibility. Still, North continued to engage sporadically in political controversy, as shown by his book, *The War on Mel Gibson* (2004), which attacked the liberal media. Currently, probably the most active member of the movement is Gary DeMar, the present head of American Vision, a Reconstructionist think tank based in Atlanta. DeMar is the author of a number of books defending Reconstructionism, several home schooling texts, and occasional critiques of premillennialism.

As a distinctive movement, Reconstructionism no longer creates the shock waves in the evangelical community that it once did. Its strident claims are made less frequently and, when heard, carry less weight. But its diminished role and reduced profile can also be taken as evidence that it has accomplished a good part of its purpose: namely, to change the parameters of discussion and bequeath its biblical presuppositions to other Christian activists. Its argument for societal transformation is now accepted, although with significant qualification, by a majority of religious rightists. It is hence time to examine more closely the contours of the Reconstructionist position. It is based on two central features: first, a blistering critique of modern secular society and the thinking that underlies it; and second, an espousal of an alternative Christian order that provides an answer to all the defects of the former. Without further ado, we move on to these two topics.

The Enemy: Human Autonomy

By any definition, autonomy refers to self-governance, the condition of being guided by one's own laws. In common parlance, it is a term with positive connotations. It can refer, for example, to the mental maturity attained when a child develops into a self-sufficient adult. Or it can describe the political status of a region that assumes the chores of self-government. Autonomy is a quality necessary to normal personal and political development, one generally associated with responsibility, independence, and flourishing. But in the lingo of Reconstructionism and Christian Worldview, autonomy takes on a dark meaning: it symbolizes the waywardness of fallen mankind. When God's commands must be followed faithfully, autonomy equates to rebellion against him. The idea of autonomy as rebellion is implicit in the standard verses of Romans 1:18–32, which expose the rift between God and idolaters. Calvin calls it by such names as pride and disobedience. Kuyper, Van Til, Rushdoony, and later Christian worldviewers condemn it by name, identifying it with modern apostasy. But the Reconstructionists carry the critique of autonomy to an unprecedented level, denouncing its impact on every aspect of culture and charting its historical progression from Adam and Eve to the United Nations. With scholarly single-mindedness they calibrate its influence, associating it with humanistic ambition, "messianic" utopianism, and state control. The story of mankind becomes an ongoing moral drama in which the forces of autonomy, aligned with Satan, are pitted against the forces of God.

Much of this drama is seen occurring on the institutional level. The sin of autonomy finds its most typical expression in the secular state, which claims legitimacy from ungodly sources (often the people). It is guilty, like the erring individual, of being a law unto itself, setting itself up as the governing authority of last resort. For worldviewers who view God's authority as paramount, this amounts to poaching on God's territory. Like Kuyper before them, Reconstructionists regularly cite the Tower of Babel (Genesis 11:1–9) as the consummate symbol of the autonomous state.[38] For Rushdoony, the project at Babel is a human attempt to establish a "one-world-order," suppress differences among people, and make mankind its "own Messiah, savior, and god."[39] Babel is the first of several examples of the overreaching state in biblical literature. It is mirrored later on in the Egyptian and Babylonian monarchies and the Roman Empire.[40]

R. J. Rushdoony sometimes refers to the Babel model as a "unitary" state because of its apparent claims to omnipotence and disavowal of transcendent authority. In contrast to the "unitary" state concept with its exclusivist claims, Rushdoony offers his religiously correct alternative: the "two-power" idea, associated with Augustinian doctrine and the Council of Chalcedon of 451 A.D. The two powers, representing the divine and human orders, were meant to be separate but not equal, according to Rushdoony. Human institutions were to be distinct from God's realm while, at the same time, falling clearly under God's purview. The Chalcedon formula, however, was more an ideal than a reality in Christian history. In later centuries, the medieval Catholic Church abandoned the two-power idea by merging the two realms, at least according to Rushdoony's view of papal history. Pope Innocent III (1161–1216) adopted the concept of the Church as "the divine-human bond of heaven and earth, *the* Kingdom of God on earth," with jurisdiction over all peoples and institutions.[41] The Church was thus apparently mimicking the Roman imperial idea of a unitary human order on earth. Only with the onset of the Protestant Reformation was the unitary concept challenged once again. Rushdoony sees Calvin, who relied heavily upon Augustinian doctrine, as a key agent in reviving the distinction between earthly and divine orders and returning the earthly order to its subservient position.[42]

After the Reformation, however, human autonomy took on a new and ominous form, according to Reconstructionist writers. Developments in religion, science, and philosophy gave impetus to independent thinking and, in the process, changed the way humans looked upon God and government. In the field of religion, heretical weeds began to sprout in the garden of Protestant Christendom and produce runaway varieties. Calvinist doctrine met its most significant challenge in Arminianism, the seventeenth century doctrine advanced by Jacob Arminius (1560–1609) and later identified with Methodism and popular evangelicalism. Arminianism stressed human free will and the possibility of salvation for all comers. Endowing humans with implicit control over their own fate through their freedom to accept or refuse the Gospel message, it undermined God's power of predestination. It dashed the notion of a divinely determined plan, a key ingredient of a God-centered theology.[43]

Science and philosophy, however, are the prime examples of the new autonomy. Gary North views physicist Isaac Newton (1642–1727) as a key figure in this trend, one who laid the "philosophical and cultural foundations of modern atheism."[44] Newton represented the new tendency to employ reason to understand the physical world. Newton's use of mathematics to explain gravity and other concepts made the mechanics of the universe comprehensible to human minds. By portraying God as the architect of universal physical laws, Newtonianism dealt a blow to the notion of God as a force capable of overruling the material laws of cause and effect when it pleased him. Out of the Newtonian concept arose the Enlightenment idea of the universe as a mechanism set in motion by a cosmic clockmaker. In contrast to God's ever watchful role, it offered an abstract framework congenial with deism or even pantheism.[45] Natural law became the idiom of the day, creating a conceptual means to establish universal moral standards. Reconstructionists dramatize these tendencies by giving them a conspiratorial twist. Behind Newton's espousal of universal principles, they see the commitment to a humanistic religion, with all the qualities of an ardently held faith. Citing Newton's side experiments in alchemy, North suggests the scientist was searching for a "leap of being" and the "deification of man." Referring to events that occurred generations after his death, North and Rushdoony attempt to tie Newton to revolution and the subversion of Christian civilization.[46]

The philosopher Immanuel Kant (1724–1804), who is more closely associated with the idea of autonomy than any other major thinker, is an obvious target for Reconstructionist historians. Following the lead of

Van Til, Rushdoony attacks Kant for trying to solve the question of knowledge "apart from God,"[47] meaning without reference to God and the Bible. He complains that Kant showed little interest in metaphysical issues relating to ultimate truth and the nature of God, focusing instead on the more practical need to shore up human knowledge against the claims of skeptics. Kant believed that knowledge of the sensory world was possible through the synthetic power of the human mind. While he did not deny God's existence–he was a believing Christian–Kant consigned God to a noumenal (beyond the senses) realm that could not be apprehended with certainty. In so doing, he furthered the trend toward a less defined and less personal concept of divinity. Rushdoony, not surprisingly, sees this as a direct affront to the Almighty. With characteristic hyperbole, he views Kant's reliance on the activity of the human intellect as equivalent to the "solution" worked out by Satan and Eve: "man seeks to solve 'the problem of God' by becoming God in his own eyes."[48]

Rushdoony is equally dismissive of Kant on moral matters. He scornfully connects Kant's argument for moral autonomy with the "triumph of natural law philosophy." Kant appeals to a moral law that can form the basis of a universal ethics and is evident to all humans without the aid of Scripture. To a writer like Rushdoony, this approach is akin to pantheism, relying on the assumption of a normative order in the universe and a human mind that can discover it through reason. Such an approach is thus anti-Christian and anti-God. Rushdoony, following Calvin and Kuyper, prefers to see the universe as "fallen and perverted" rather than normative, and human reason as corrupt rather than benign. The only thing that can produce moral order is an external corrective: God's word as conveyed in Scripture. To Rushdoony, the Kantian argument for individual autonomy in the realm of morality can lead only to a debilitating form of relativism.[49]

The Reconstructionists knew they had to cast Kant, the greatest philosopher of the Enlightenment, as the archenemy of religion. This was not as easy or plausible as it might seem, however. Far from displacing God, Kant makes him the final guarantor of universal law and a morally ordered universe.[50] What he does reject is the arbitrary

God of Calvinist imagination, the predestinating autocrat who displays his wrath and keeps humanity on a short leash. Kant supports human autonomy within God's ordered universe because he sees it as a key to responsible action. His commitment to freedom is deeply felt, a reflection of his animus toward submission to unquestioned authority.[51] Indeed, he sees slavish adherence to the doctrines of particular sects as a threat to civil order and contrary to the aims of Christianity itself. He lived in a Europe, it should be remembered, which bore the scars of two centuries of religious conflict. The warfare between Catholics and Protestants, with its millions of victims, amply demonstrated that the contending creeds of Christianity could not guarantee a stable moral order.[52] Kant's concept of human autonomy was an attempt to universalize morality and put it on a firm basis in the interests of mankind. His "categorical imperative" can be viewed as a universalized version of the Golden Rule.[53]

Autonomy assumes special significance for Reconstructionists in the realm of politics. The state in their eyes is autonomy's major manifestation. Founded on the despised Enlightenment principles of reason, humanity, science, and democracy, the modern state is typified in their eyes by the excesses of the French Revolution.[54] By serving as a substitute for God, it takes on the likeness of a human religion. Rushdoony uses the pejorative label of "messianism" to describe the state's high-minded goals. It assumes a "messianic" character by attempting to improve the lot of humanity and focusing on earthly salvation in lieu of the eternal kind. Serving as "the priestly mediator of the good life," the state commits the ultimate blasphemy against God.[55]

Popular democracy, which emerges in its modern form in the wake of the Enlightenment, becomes a favorite target of Rushdoony's wrath. He associates it, like the state, with the French Revolution. Its rise in both the French and American contexts is a function of the growth of state power. As Rushdoony puts it, "the democratization of society goes hand in hand with the divinization of the state. Power and right are withdrawn from God and given to the people." Indeed, he commonly portrays democracy as the voice of the people substituting for the voice of God ("vox populi, vox dei").[56] Rushdoony's discussions of democracy are so vitriolic that they seem almost intentionally hyperbolic. In one essay he calls it a leveling force, a destroyer of moral distinctions, and a breeding ground for sexual perverts, pornographers, hedonists, drug abusers, and anarchists. Elsewhere he considers democracy a precursor to tyranny, an instrument in the hands of the rabble. And again, it is "totalitarian" because it replaces God's revealed order with the new "divine right" of the people.[57]

Rushdoony turns to American history for lessons on the threat of expanding state power and popular democracy. Rushdoony approves of the U.S. Constitution in its original form because he thinks it was designed to perpetuate a traditional Christian order. In his view, the United States was created as a republic controlled by an elite with "simple faith and strong virtues."[58] As such, it was never intended to be a democracy guided by the broad will of the people. Instead it embodied an organic form of localism that checked majority rule and the leveling influence of the state. He calls this localism "Christian feudalism," by which he apparently means a system of "local power and protection" where the prevailing values were those of Reformation Christianity.[59] The American Revolution, meanwhile, was not a true revolution, but rather a "conservative counter-revolution" that enabled the machinery of localism to continue almost without alteration.[60] Rushdoony admits that the decentralized ideal of American republicanism was not to endure for long. As property qualifications for voting were gradually reduced in the early 1800s and power moved from the localities to the center, the virtuous U.S. republic began to show signs of decline. The devolution of power into the hands of so-called irresponsible elements, most notably the un-propertied masses, marked the end of the sanctity of property, resulting in "the steady confiscation of wealth, property, and income through taxation."[61]

Rushdoony condemns not only democratization, but social reform of any kind, which he views as subversive of God's providential order. A major target is the Unitarian Church, one of the key progressive forces in nineteenth century America. Reconstructionists despise Unitarianism for its disavowal of the Calvinist tenet of human depravity and its failure to stress God's righteous justice. It errs by emphasizing an ethics based on the Golden Rule and the practice of Christian compassion. Rushdoony denounces it as "the religion of humanity" looking to "the perfection of man in paradise on earth."[62] He cites its support for public education as a key example of its drive for institutional perfection. In Reconstructionist eyes, public education usurps the family's role in the edification and religious instruction of youth. Horace Mann, a Unitarian proponent of public education, is portrayed as a subversive figure who flouts Calvinist traditions and abets the encroaching power of the state.[63] Public schools take on a "messianic" function by serving as the secular instruments of society's salvation.[64]

Reviewing America's sectional conflict, Rushdoony blames the Unitarians for their role in the abolitionist movement and their support for the Union cause. He casts his sympathies with the South in the Civil War because of its stout defense of localism and its adherence to a Calvinist, God-fearing form of Christianity. The war on slavery he rejects as being anti-Christian because "the revolutionary re-ordering of society would be far worse than anything it sought to supplant." And he quotes a Southern preacher who advocates relying on "the delicate mechanism of Providence" to work out the imperfections of human society.[65] Because suffering is a necessary ingredient in a world shaped by God's rewards and punishments, Providence's "delicate mechanism" is apparently far preferable to any serious reforms to alleviate human misery. The model Protestant republic is meant to eschew human intervention as much as possible so that God can freely work his will on the world.

For Rushdoony, the idea of a divine order probably receives its most serious nineteenth century challenge, however, not from reformers, but from science. The older Newtonian paradigm of a clockwork universe, which eased the Calvinist God into semi-retirement by substituting Nature's order for God's personal supervision, is now replaced by a more radical Darwinian paradigm. Rushdoony, with typical hyperbole, portrays Darwin's view of Nature as that of a "blind, unconscious energy" devoid of all law or regularity and infused by chance.[66] He takes the theory of evolution as an example of autonomous science stripping the world of its last vestiges of providential meaning. In political and social terms, it leaves humans the lone custodians of human society and gives impetus to human legislation and statist centralization. Gary North develops this theme further in an essay on the growth of "humanistic sovereignty," maintaining that while Darwinism begins by emphasizing man's humble origins in the natural world, it ends by enthroning him as a unique and controlling life form. As usual, North puts a conspiratorial spin on the thesis. State planners and messianic reformers, once rid of any notion of God, step into the gap by becoming his predestinating replacements.[67]

In the twentieth century, a new breed of bureaucrats, planners, educators, internationalists, and do-gooders become the contemporary face of human autonomy. These secular "priests," conditioned to the dominant role of the state, work in tandem with it. They inculcate secular values through the public school system, administer welfare to the masses, and use the confiscatory power of taxation to achieve their secular goals.[68]

The overreaching nation state, however, is just one aspect of the political trend undermining God's sovereignty. International organizations, most notably the United Nations, offer a further example of the "religion of humanity" in action. The U.N. represents the doctrine of "salvation by law" applied worldwide. Rushdoony denounces the U.N.'s opening Preamble, which declares the need "to save succeeding generations from the scourge of war." Such "saving" clearly is intended to occur through human international law rather than Christian regeneration. It is to take place in an environment of religious neutrality without reference to the Christian God.[69] As such it is illegitimate in the eyes of Rushdoony, who sees religion and God's will as anything but neutral. The United Nations is simply an autonomous entity serving as a substitute for the Christian God.

Rushdoony's approach amounts to a direct attack on universal standards of morality. Thus he readily condemns world-renowned ethical leaders who do not share his anti-humanist assumptions. Albert Schweitzer, the Christian theologian whose medical work in West Africa made him a symbol of humanitarian service, is portrayed not as a practitioner of love but as the "autonomous man" who "seeks to be his own god" by going beyond biblical mandates. Rushdoony regards Schweitzer's identification with the poor and less fortunate (the non-elect in many Calvinists' eyes) as misguided and "promiscuous," leading to the subversion of "ethical standards and distinctions."[70] Mohandas Gandhi, the proponent of peaceful civil disobedience in the cause of social justice, receives similar treatment. In the American context, Rushdoony views moderate and liberal Christians practicing the social gospel as deluded sentimentalists working out a form of self-hatred. Motivated by guilt, they practice a "law of hate, masquerading as a law of love." As he sees it, the helping hand is something to be offered only to those who have first proven themselves deserving. The maxim "love they neighbor" is meant to be strictly limited, mandating love at a distance with a calculated respect for others' persons, property, and "God-given immunities."[71] Empathy is not one of its attributes.

Christian Reconstructionists essentially make human autonomy the catchall equivalent of ungodliness and idolatry. They use the term to demean any human achievement, deed, or act of compassion that is done without the direct oversight of the biblical God. The anti-autonomy theme carries an important educational message. It reminds followers that the best of ideals are nothing compared to fidelity to God's word and covenant. It provides a ready framework for viewing the actions of non-Christians as a perversion of God's order. And it prepares the way for a powerful response. Since neutrality is impossible in Reconstructionist thinking, there is only one acceptable alternative to the self-law of autonomy: God's law.

The Antidote: Biblical Law

Reconstructionists use the word "theonomy" to refer to law that is divinely decreed. Sometimes rendered as "God's law"(from the Greek words for "God" and "law"), the term specifies law as revealed by God through Scripture.[72] To most Christians, God's law is generally identifiable with the Ten Commandments delivered to Moses at Mount Sinai.

They tend to confine themselves to the moral laws embodied in the Commandments as interpreted and amplified by Jesus and the later Apostles. But to ardent biblical literalists, the Ten Commandments are only a preface to a much larger "treaty or covenant" made by God with the Hebrew nation that included the codes outlined in Exodus, Leviticus, and Deuteronomy.[73] This large corpus of laws provided rules for Hebrew daily life and had moral, ceremonial, and civil applications. Central among them are an array of civil case laws that deal with everything from the calculation of tithes to the treatment of husbands who slander newly wedded wives. Reconstructionists treat virtually all of these Hebrew codes, except for the strictly ceremonial ones, as binding for all Christian nations. Since the Old Testament laws are supposed to reflect God's perfection and unchanging holiness, they are seen as valid for all time.[74]

The Old Testament codes are most notable for their stress on crime and punishment. In careful detail, they specify a long list of moral and criminal offenses and the penalty for each type of offense. By modern standards the punishments are draconian, but Reconstructionists justify their severity as necessary for rooting out evil.[75] No mercy is shown for the serious offender, since, as Rushdoony interprets it, "sin does not exist apart from the man." The maxim about loving the sinner and hating the sin Rushdoony takes to be sentimental nonsense.[76] "Wicked persons" are to be removed as the surgeon removes "a hopelessly diseased organ to save the body."[77] Capital punishment is dictated for offenses of varying gravity. The crime of murder requires the death penalty for the perpetrator, but so do a multitude of other infractions including adultery, sodomy and bestiality, homosexuality, rape, incest, incorrigibility in children, Sabbath breaking, kidnapping, apostasy, witchcraft, sorcery, false pretension to prophesy, and blasphemy.[78] Today, many of these offenses (Sabbath breaking, apostasy, false pretension to prophesy, blasphemy) are actions protected by the First Amendment to the U.S. Constitution, while others (homosexuality, witchcraft, sorcery) are regarded as noncriminal acts in all countries of the world outside of a handful of radical, modern-day theocracies.

Reconstructionists bravely try to rationalize this distinctly arbitrary system of penology. Rushdoony insists that the fundamental goal of biblical law is not the exaction of punishment but the "restitution of God's order." When that order is defiled or upset by sin, it can only be restored through God's justice.[79] God's justice is, in good part, reflected in the famous *lex talionis* of the Old Testament ("eye for an eye, tooth for a tooth"), which mandates a penalty in direct proportion to the offense of the wrongdoer. By being proportional, the principle of talion purports to restore judicial balance. The taking of a life for a life, underscored by the line "Whoso sheddeth man's blood, by man shall his blood be shed" of Genesis 9:6, appeals to theonomists for its symmetrical expression of "just recompense."[80] For similar reasons, theonomists give restitution a central role for lesser offenses such as theft, making redress to the victim a substitute for a prison sentence. But some types of penalties cannot easily be justified in terms of balance or restitution, especially those involving victimless "crimes" like irreligious acts or lifestyle offenses. What sort of justice would allow these offenses to receive the same punishment as murder? Theonomists respond simply that because such crimes, and ultimately all crimes, are crimes against God and his law-order, the appropriate punishment is entirely in God's hands. As the ultimate offended party, God has the authority to decide what penalty is adequate to achieving restoration: it is "what the crime warrants in God's eyes."[81] The result, obviously, is a penal system tied to God's will and impenetrable to human reason.

Reconstructionists make the controversial claim that theonomy is supported by Jesus' teaching in the New Testament, or at least not contradicted by it. In so doing they brush aside two millennia of Christian tradition and interpretation. Declaring the old Hebrew case laws to be valid in the Christian era, they treat the two Testaments as one seamless fabric. Their view is based largely on their reading of one passage from the Book of Matthew (Matthew 5:17–20) in which Jesus tells his followers that he has not come to destroy "the law and the prophets" but to fulfill them. As it turns out, Greg Bahnsen contorts the meaning of key words to produce the desired interpretation. Specifically, he misconstrues "fulfill" (the Greek "pleroo") to mean "confirm," as if Jesus were ratifying a traditional corpus of laws.[82] But linguistic problems are the least of Bahnsen's difficulties. He seems to be tone-deaf to the context of the passage in question, in which Jesus outlines a freer interpretation of the law and a softening of the "eye for an eye" formula.[83] Generally, Jesus says little about the old judicial laws, or when mentioning them, typically shows a preference for broader moral principles. Most Christian commentators see a discontinuity between Old and New Testaments on such matters, portraying Jesus as one who gives special weight to the spirit of the law.[84]

The concept of theonomy, in fact, has found almost no support even from Reformed Christian theologians. Calvin himself forcefully rejected the application of Old Testament laws to Christian societies in the *Institutes of the Christian Religion*, his magnum opus.[85] Moreover, the Westminster Confession of 1646, a document expressing British Calvinist opinion of the time, also declines to support the application of Mosaic laws to modern Christian societies.[86] The document explicitly states that the old case laws have "expired" (chapter XIX.4). Ardent Reconstructionists, deeply vexed by such lack of support for their theories, do their best to explain away the discrepancies,[87] but have found few takers for their views.

Indeed, the theonomist position on the current utility of Old Testament laws has never gained much support outside of the Reconstructionist movement. Christian Worldview advocates of the Religious Right from Schaeffer to Dobson have mostly steered clear of the controversial issue. Still, it would be incorrect to see theonomy as irrelevant to Christian Worldview thinking. Its tendency to blend religion and law is very much in harmony with Christian Worldview premises. Since moral sins and civil crimes are both seen as offenses against God, there is no inconsistency in lumping the two categories together. The Reconstructionists are simply confirming the classic view expressed in Romans 1, which brackets the worst of criminals with sinners and idolaters, and makes them all subject to God's wrath. Whether or not the specific penalties in Deuteronomy are endorsed, the religious view of law is common to both theonomy and Christian Worldview.

Theonomy also expresses an attitude deeply embedded in Christian Worldview: the endorsement of a highly punitive form of divine justice. Reconstructionists are quite explicit about godly vengeance. While Rushdoony repudiates vengeance on the human level, he does not hesitate to stress it on the divine.[88] He highlights divine will and the role of animus and jealousy in his portrait of God's character. And he expresses no apologies for it: "The fact that jealousy is associated repeatedly with the law, and invoked by God in the giving of laws, is of cardinal importance . . . . The law of God is not a blind, impersonal, and mechanically operative force," he declares.[89] In line with this interpretation, those who transgress the law present a direct personal affront to God's authority and must reap the results. God's human deputies, who are responsible for carrying out the penalties in Deuteronomy and Leviticus, become the avengers of God's wrath. Some on the Religious Right, especially activists in the anti-abortion movement, have taken these ideas to extremes, with tragic consequences.

Reconstructionists make the restoration of God's law-order their fundamental historical mission. However, while God's law-order is spelled out explicitly in biblical texts, questions still arise about the shape and administration of such a system in contemporary terms. What would society look like, and how would political and economic institutions function? Christian Reconstructionists, leaving nothing to chance, are happy to provide us with detailed answers to such questions.

Reconstructing Society

Using the Bible as their road map, selectively as always, Rushdoony and his followers are bent on "reconstructing" the social order from the ground up. Their plan is a comprehensive one, encompassing every sector of society. Their purpose is to bring about a righteous order beginning with the individual and the institutions of daily life and proceeding to the nation as a whole. When speaking of "government," they speak of it as applying not simply to centralized civil government, but to all the disparate units of society: self, family, church, business, etc.[90] These units, similar to the "spheres" of society spoken of by Neo-Calvinists, constitute distinct "realms of authority" with defined responsibilities for the maintenance of moral order. Rather than being accountable to a central civil authority, they are accountable directly to God. Each Christian individual, family, church, business, and nation maintains a covenantal relationship with God, in which they accept his explicit guidelines and know that their compliance will be rewarded with divine blessings, and non-compliance with disfavor.

Reconstructionists look to selected passages in Scripture for the duties of each of the governing units. For the individual, it is to fear God (Ecclesiastes 12:13) and follow God's commands. For the family, it is to teach obedience to one's children, instill the fear of God, and provide moral and general education (Deuteronomy 6:4–7; Proverbs 4). For the church, it is to shepherd its members and be attentive to their welfare (Acts 6:1–6; Acts 20:28). For the state, it is to preserve law and order and attend to matters of crime and punishment (Romans 13:1–4).[91] Excessive meddling by the state is perceived as a human intrusion in the working of the other units and a threat to God's order. Ever mindful of the example of Babel, Reconstructionists strictly limit the state's role and seek to empower countervailing smaller units.

Reconstructionists are generally comfortable using the word "theocracy" to describe their concept of godly rule. Rushdoony characterizes theocracy as a "a government over every institution by God and His Law."[92] Not surprisingly, he and his fellow Reconstructionists look to ancient Israel as a general model for it. The Hebrew kingdom had many features that appealed to their traditionalistic, anti-statist mentality: it was rule-based, decentralized, and non-bureaucratic. The one element that fully united the kingdom was God himself: "Even though there was not a political centralism in Israel, there was a covenantal centralism: the word of God,"[93] observes Reconstructionist Gary DeMar. God's word, as conveyed in Scripture, was the basis for how the nation was ordered and ruled.

The ideal regime of the Reconstructionists, accordingly, features an emasculated state apparatus outside the areas pertaining to law enforcement and war, in combination with a well-ordered private sector and a vigorous religious establishment. Under this arrangement, churches and other religious organizations take over the state's normal role in administering social policy, leaving the central government to handle justice-related and military responsibilities. New forms of revenue collection would reflect this new allotment of functions. Thus the central government would relinquish most of its powers of taxation, including the power to "redistribute wealth" through "discriminatory" distinctions between taxpayers. Rushdoony proposes a simple national poll tax set at an equal amount for all citizens (Exodus 30:11–16), requiring the same contribution from the common worker as from the CEO. With no trace of irony he states that a poll tax would "avoid the oppression of the rich."[94] Other Reconstructionists, realizing the poll tax to be somewhat insufficient, accept the possibility of income taxation at the county level for up to ten percent of an individual's annual income. Upper levels of civil government would obtain revenues by taxing lower levels of government. According to Gary North, "This would decentralize power with a vengeance."[95] Meanwhile, Reconstructionists look to the revival of the church tithe to cover expenses for the expanded activities of religious institutions. The tithe is the one-tenth of income that Christians were once expected to pay their church annually. The modern neglect of the tithe is portrayed as an abdication of biblical responsibility, an act of theft equivalent to "robbing God."[96] In the Reconstructionist view, the decline of tithing in the churches enabled the "messianic" state to take over most social services. Their tithing policy would return the church to its proper prominence in the political order.

Reconstructionists take a strong interest in the economic configuration of their hypothetical Christian regime. Looking to Scripture as a model for economic activity, they focus on the "dominion task" assigned to all humans by God, the task specified in the command to "be fruitful, multiply, . . . and have dominion" (Genesis 1:26–28). The best way for the godly to fulfill this obligation, as they see it, is through the productive use of property, especially land, and the active investment of wealth. The failure to put land and riches into productive activity is indicative of sloth and a missed opportunity to glorify God. To be sure, Reconstructionists frown on accumulation and hoarding for its own sake, as this serves man's ends rather than God's. While stressing ownership, they consider property rights less than absolute since God is the actual owner of his Creation and human owners merely stewards.[97] However, by insisting on its sacrosanct nature and its immunity from taxation by government, they confer upon property a virtually untouchable status in civil terms.

Unlike Neo-Calvinists such as Kuyper and Dooyeweerd, who view Christianity as "neither socialistic or capitalistic,"[98] Reconstructionists believe that neutrality on economic systems is unacceptable because it makes the Bible irrelevant on a matter of key importance. For them, Scripture condones laissez-faire capitalism. As Gary North sees it, a marketplace left to itself is biblical because it allows individuals to demonstrate their stewardship and work out their salvation on God's terms without external interference. A pure capitalism facilitates a form of divine justice, rewarding those who are faithful to biblical mandates and penalizing those who are unfaithful to them (Deuteronomy 8 and 28).[99] The reward-punishment concept is an expression of the covenantal contract that exists between God and his creatures. The tie between economics and religion here finds an echo in Max Weber's well-known thesis connecting the Protestant ethic and the spirit of capitalism,[100] whereby individuals work hard to accumulate capital and wealth believing that prosperity is a sign of being among the elect.

Reconstructionists believe that "humanistic" intervention, however limited, damages the ability of the market to serve God's purposes. Thus they look askance at government regulations because they require firms to answer to human regulators for their conduct rather than to God. Social Security and government safety nets are ruled out because they relieve individuals of having to bear full responsibility for their lives. Because government aid comes out of general tax revenues, an indulgent government stands guilty of the unforgivable offense of "stealing" from some to help others. Reconstructionists do concede that the state should play a limited role in economic affairs, mainly as guardian of the integrity of the market system. Thus it is needed to guarantee fair play by punishing economic crimes such as fraud and by ensuring the reliability of "weights" and "balances," i.e., the dependability of exchange in the marketplace (Leviticus 19:35–36). But its mandate in the commercial sphere goes little further.[101]

A minimalist role for government pertains also in the area of finance. Reconstructionists challenge the state's authority to control currency or even print money. It is their belief that the creation of money is motivated by the human desire for power and can only lead to the adulteration of the money supply (Isaiah 1:22: "Your silver has become dross, your wine mixed with water"). The inflation that allegedly results is an evil because it represents a fraud against the people, an "invisible tax" equivalent to theft.[102] The Reconstructionists consider various drastic alternatives. They view with some favor the adoption of a strict gold standard, with gold defined as the medium of exchange. "Hard money" has the merit of preventing government from creating money and limiting its ability "to grow beyond biblical boundaries."[103] Even more preferable, because it eliminates direct state interference entirely, is a system where the private sector determines the currency. A biblically based solution would "have the state policing private issuers of gold and warehouse receipts to gold" and then collecting "its taxes in a specified form of private currency."[104] As for money lending, Reconstructionists oppose the universal modern practice of fractional reserve banking, which enables loans to be created on the basis of relatively small amounts of deposits. Reconstructionists like Gary North maintain that the time-honored practice contradicts biblical injunctions against "multiple indebtedness," as suggested in maxims about lending money in Exodus 22:25–27. It is not only implicitly fraudulent, North argues, but results in the possibility of bank runs and increased inflation. It poses a threat to God's "civil law-order."[105]

Much of the Reconstructionist program dealing with commerce and finance is hardly original, having been inspired directly by the writings of right-wing economic theorists. Economists will recognize in them the arguments of libertarians, anarcho-capitalists, and Austrian School economists, all of whom endorse an extreme version of laissez-faire capitalism. North and his fellow writers are essentially channeling such theories, embellishing them at times, and giving them a Christian basis and justification.

Most economists who identify as Christians reject the Reconstructionist model as an example of zealous biblical literalism applied selectively. The model is vulnerable to criticism not just in economic terms, but in biblical ones. For example, it puts far more weight on the ancient Hebrew prescriptions of the Old Testament than on Jesus' later sayings on wealth, poverty, and justice. Jesus condemns a rigid approach and says nothing that would exclude government-based actions to deal with poverty and systemic injustice.[106] Even in the old Mosaic codes, there is plenty to contradict the Reconstructionist obsession with untrammeled free markets. Laws to address the needs of the poor include the law on gleanings, which requires that landowners allow the "poor and the stranger" to gather crops at the corners of fields and the leftovers after reaping (Leviticus 19:9–10). Measures aimed at enhancing the economic security of the Hebrew population include the Jubilee Law (Leviticus 25), requiring that land be returned to its original owners every fifty years. The law was intended to prevent the undue concentration of wealth and protect families from the "relentless economic forces in society."[107] Whether the Jubilee provisions are taken literally or figuratively, they obviously provide theoretical justification for something North strongly opposes: legislative restrictions on the free market in behalf of the distressed.[108] Overall, the biblical record hardly supports North's model of a free market of buyers and sellers. In fact, in the entire Old Testament, there is no mention of any law dealing with the sale of land, and not a single instance of an Israelite willingly selling land beyond his family circle.[109] The risk-averse tribal economy of the ancient Hebrews seems a bizarre model on which to base a radically unregulated capitalist system.

One inevitably asks how citizens' rights and freedoms would fare under a "reconstructed" republic. While Rushdoony uses the phrase "radical libertarianism" to characterize his brand of theocracy, his "libertarianism" is more about God's liberty than the people's. To the extent that freedom applies to the individual, it is conceived in terms of freedom *from* secular government rather than freedom *to* act freely in one's interests. In Rushdoony's republic, God and his law are offered as a form of deliverance from the tyranny of the state. The desired result is the "self-government of covenant man."[110] That is, citizens are seen as "working members" of a new realm created to serve God's purposes in accordance with the biblical covenant. But for those who do not see themselves as covenant-bound, Rushdoony's "liberty" would appear to offer little room for deviation. Gary DeMar, a Rushdoony follower, states the matter candidly: "There can be no autonomy among the citizenry. Anarchy–power invested in the individual to do what he or she feels is right–is not tolerated by God."[111] The citizen is plainly forbidden from following his or her moral compass if it conflicts with an orthodox interpretation of biblical norms.

The hypothetical biblical republic, in addition, establishes religious qualifications for political participation. Office holders are restricted to those who "understand that they derive their authority from God." Such leaders are voted into office by what Demar calls "a godly citizenry,"[112] suggesting an electorate limited to the faithful. Gary North is even more explicit. He believes that "the long-term goal of Christians in politics should be to gain exclusive control over the franchise."[113] He declares that anyone refusing to recognize God's covenant should be denied political rights because "he has no lawful right to enforce God's civil laws on others."[114] Not stopping there, North believes that such citizens should be deprived of citizenship in the same way that "strangers" were deprived of it in ancient Israel.[115]

However fanciful the Reconstructionist plan for a Christian kingdom might appear, a small group of zealots seems convinced it can be implemented after a long struggle. Advocates like North think that matters can eventually be brought to a head through consciousness-raising, cultural warfare, and confrontation with the "humanist" establishment, which he sometimes refers to as the "humanist theocracy."[116] People will flock to the Christian cause and help to usher in a Christian republic in place of the present system. North and other Reconstructionists deny that they aspire to revolution in the classic sense. They are not revolutionaries because, as postmillennialists, they have a long-term view and lots of patience. They are not the hatchers of plots, but merely the vehicle for God's purposes: "The Lord will exalt us when He is ready, and when He knows that we are ready."[117] The Christian kingdom is apparently brought to fruition in stages through the force of persuasion: "Christian Reconstructionism begins with personal conversion to Christ and self-government under God's law; then it spreads to others through revival; and only later does it bring comprehensive changes in civil law."[118] The process could take a long time. Still, Reconstructionists do not conceal their preference for a quicker turnaround. North envisions near-term scenarios that involve the fall of humanist civilization under its own weight. Comparing today's "society of Satan" with the "collapsing Roman Empire," he sees an opportunity for Christians to take advantage of the inevitable chaos to follow. "This is why we need a remnant," he states. "We need men and women who know, in advance, that a crisis is coming."[119]

The Legacy of a Movement

Given its controversial nature, it is somewhat remarkable that Christian Reconstructionism has received so little public exposure over the years. Although R. J. Rushdoony was writing about biblical law as early as the 1970s, he was virtually unheard of in the mainstream media until as late as 1987, when Bill Moyers made his PBS documentary *God and Politics: On Earth as It Is in Heaven.* Moyers devoted one third of his TV special to Christian Reconstructionism, including an interview with R. J. Rushdoony himself. Even after that, few investigative reporters were interested enough or had the necessary background to cover the doctrinal aspects of the movement. Two notable exceptions were sociologist Sara Diamond, who stressed the movement's role as a catalyst for dominionism, and journalist Frederick Clarkson, one of the first to examine Reconstructionist ideology closely and take it seriously.[120] General coverage picked up in the 1990s and afterward, but still remained in journalistic byways rather than in the main thoroughfares. Even within the evangelical community, media coverage of Christian Reconstructionism was initially limited.[121] The reason, however, was not so much ignorance of its existence as caution, distaste, or fear of public embarrassment.

What seems beyond dispute is that, while the media either slept or looked away, Christian Reconstructionism was having a major impact on the Religious Right. For two decades starting in the 1970s, Reconstructionism filled an intellectual vacuum in conservative evangelical circles. Its scores of publications came to monopolize the political and economic sections of Christian bookstores, and Christian activists eagerly sampled the new doctrines. Robert Billings, the first executive director of the Moral Majority, admitted that if it weren't for the writings of R. J. Rushdoony, "none of us would be here."[122] While a certain aura of taboo hung over Reconstructionism because of its radicalism, many Christian activists turned to it for inspiration. In the words of another Christian leader, "Though we hide their books under the bed, we read them just the same."[123] While most Religious Right leaders chose not to support Reconstructionism publicly, some like Jerry Falwell and D. James Kennedy openly endorsed books written by its advocates. Others like Pat Robertson invited avowed Reconstructionists such as R. J. Rushdoony to appear on their TV programs. By the late 1980s, the Christian Right had incorporated much of Reconstructionism's biblical vision. According to Jay Grimstead, a major strategist of the movement, "There are a lot of us floating around in Christian leadership . . . who don't go all the way with the theonomy thing, but who want to rebuild America based on the Bible."[124]

Over time, much of the language, argumentation, and angry tone of Reconstructionism, if not all of its doctrinal fine points, became identifiable features of the Religious Right. The movement's leadership adopted a basically Rushdoonian critique of contemporary America and conveyed it to the troops on the ground. The average evangelical's indoctrination was probably unconscious, as Gary North has suggested: "the ideas of the Reconstructionists have penetrated into Protestant circles that for the most part are unaware of the original source of the theological ideas that are beginning to transform them."[125] The impact on Pentecostal and charismatic Christians was especially marked. These groups were particularly susceptible to theological influence because of the doctrinally "amorphous" nature of their religion. The fusion of doctrine and emotion that resulted from such interaction was potentially explosive. In the words of Reconstructionist preacher Joseph Morecraft, "God is blending Presbyterian theology with charismatic zeal into a force that cannot be stopped!"[126]

Today some advocates for the Religious Right downplay the continuing influence of Reconstructionism. Conservative journalist Anthony Williams, for example, describes Christian Reconstructionism as a "small, insignificant sect" with little political relevance. He calls claims of its influence on the Religious Right "dominionist fantasies."[127] Some Christian rightist leaders, like James Dobson and Charles Colson, studiously ignore Reconstructionism as though it never existed. Even individuals with past ties to Reconstructionism often attempt to distance themselves from it. For example, Herb Titus, John Whitehead, and Howard Ahmanson, former students and associates of R. John Rushdoony, insist that they are no longer strict followers.

Disagreements over the legacy of Christian Reconstructionism seem to arise from different ways of measuring its influence on the Christian Right. If one measures it by the clout of its self-declared followers, then its impact seems fairly marginal. The few bona fide Christian Reconstructionists still on the scene, notably Gary DeMar at American Vision, Inc. in Atlanta and a few holdouts at the Chalcedon Foundation in Vallecito, consider themselves a separate movement and seem to exert little direct influence on the Religious Right. While Christian rightists coordinate activities with outspoken Reconstructionists from time to time,[128] they part company with them on their more controversial positions, especially the imposition of Old Testament legal codes. They can thus disassociate themselves from Christian Reconstructionism by washing their hands of its most notorious policy prescriptions.

If, on the other hand, one measures Reconstructionist influence by its tangible impact on the Religious Right's agenda and outlook, its influence is obvious. The ambitious goals of today's religious rightists dovetail in many key respects with those of Christian Reconstructionism. We have seen how the Reconstructionists expanded Christian Worldview beyond its theological and epistemological framework. As a result of this expanded vision, Christian Worldview took on broad scientific, historical, legal, political, and economic dimensions. In the areas of history and the sciences, for example, the Reconstructionists attempted to undermine accepted methods of treating evidence by actively applying the presuppositional approach to knowledge. Their approach fostered the development of Christian revisionist history and helped to legitimize intelligent design theory as an alternative to evolution. In the law, while they failed to gain lasting support for the Old Testament codes, they furthered the perception of Scripture as a model for civil law and helped to elevate the legal authority of the Ten Commandments in popular venues, if not yet in official ones. In political affairs, they helped to demonize the modern secular state by portraying it as a false usurper. Their assertion of God's sovereign claims facilitated the rise of dominionism, the notion that Christians are best suited to carry out God's commands in the political sphere. Finally, in the realm of economics, Reconstructionists were instrumental in popularizing "biblical economics," which argues for an extreme form of free market capitalism.

The full ramifications of Reconstructionist influence will be touched upon in later chapters when we examine Christian Worldview in today's polarized environment. But first, we need to follow the most recent stage in the formation of the Christian Worldview: namely its shaping under the guidance of Francis Schaeffer and those after him, who were able to transform it into a popular ideology that could motivate conservative Christians and challenge the prevailing culture.

5

MISSION: RECLAIMING AMERICA

Schaeffer: A Call to Action

Calvin, Kuyper, and Rushdoony were the formulators of grand ideas. Uncompromising and systematic, they drew lines in the sand and spawned distinct theological schools. Francis Schaeffer, by contrast, was a popularizer. While Schaeffer lacked the acuity of his renowned predecessors, he knew how to communicate and persuade. He could read the minds of everyday Christians, speak to their guts, and give voice to their concerns. Schaeffer fully understood both the dynamic potential of Kuyper's doctrines and the critical power of Christian Reconstructionism. He saw these two expressions of the worldview impulse as potent tools in confronting what he saw as the existential threat of secularism. But as a practicing evangelizer, Schaeffer was inclined to filter and modify such ideas in order to reach his audience. He made thorny concepts palatable by glossing over the sharp edges of Calvinist doctrine. Not overly concerned about doctrinal consistency, he introduced his own improvements when he deemed them appropriate. His central aim was to present the Christian Worldview as a justifiable creed of protest, a biblical rallying point against the secular status quo.

Schaeffer's orthodox training for the ministry brought him into early contact with Christian Worldview thinking. Having studied under Cornelius Van Til at Westminster Theological Seminary in the 1930s, he became well versed in Calvinist and Neo-Calvinist theology, along with the new epistemology of presuppositionalism. He explicitly used a presuppositionalist framework when he first put his thoughts into book form in 1968. In *Escape from Reason* and *The God Who Is There*, he took the Bible, inerrant and unchanging, as the framework for answering all of life's questions. Only by starting with the reality of God and his word, he maintained, could one arrive at an authentic worldview.

In deference to his diverse evangelical audience, however, Schaeffer applied presuppositionalism less consistently than either Van Til or the Reconstructionists. Schaeffer, rather than treating his biblical presuppositions as self-evident in all instances, sometimes employs traditional argumentation to support them, using plain evidence to substantiate their truth.[1] He admits that presuppositions must on occasion be consciously chosen on their merits: "Most people catch their presuppositions from their family and surrounding society the way a child catches measles," he states. "But people with more understanding realize that their presuppositions should be chosen after a careful consideration of what worldview is true."[2] This is the same as saying that presuppositions can be arrived at through "autonomous" choice. On that basis, one neutral commentator calls him a "rational" presuppositionalist as opposed to an "authoritarian" one.[3] Some observers on the right have critiqued him harshly for his lack of orthodoxy on the issue.[4]

Schaeffer also borrows selectively from Christian Reconstructionism. He was familiar with at least some of R. J. Rushdoony's writings and reviewed one of his books on tape.[5] Like Rushdoony, Schaeffer strongly endorses Reformation views of law and liberty.[6] His *A Christian Manifesto* (1981) lifts whole sections verbatim from Reconstructionist works dealing with seventeenth century Christian views on government and civil resistance.[7] On broader questions, Schaeffer accepts much of the Reconstructionist framework: for example, the denunciation of autonomy and the secular state, the critique of secular law, and the commitment to war against humanism. Moreover, he assumes the preeminence of God's authority in human governance: "The civil government, as all of life," he declares, "stands under the Law of God." When human authorities ignore God's law, they are "not to be obeyed."[8] But, as in the case of presuppositionalism, Schaeffer hedges somewhat. In one notable passage where he considers the use of force in defense of God's law, he seems to realize the inflammatory nature of his words and walks back his rhetoric. He pointedly rejects "any kind of a theocracy" and supports the protections of the First Amendment: "There is no New Testament basis for a linking of church and state until Christ the king returns," he states.[9] But because these caveats conflict with his forcefully argued stand on the primacy of divine law in the political realm, they come across as less than convincing. At the very least, they make him vulnerable to criticism for wanting to have it both ways and leave his work burdened with ambiguity.[10]

Schaeffer is prone not just to inconsistency, but to a certain naïveté in scholarly matters. Like his Neo-Calvinist predecessors, he sees history playing out on the unidimensional level of worldview, with little role for socio-economic and other factors. He thus tends to analyze trends in simplistic, either-or terms that are unconvincing under close scrutiny. The Reformation, which he automatically identifies with Calvinism, is a glorious age, while the Renaissance, which he associates with humanistic excess, is quite the opposite. He views the advent of modernism as simply the triumph of one worldview struggling for dominance over another worldview, having little to do with urbanization, democratization, and other trends.[11] Schaeffer frequently leaps to conclusions on the basis of scanty evidence. In tracing the foundations of American constitutionalism, for instance, he places unusual emphasis on the obscure Scottish Presbyterian thinker, Samuel Rutherford (1600–1661), who espoused the idea that the ruler was subject to God's law. Schaeffer claims that Rutherford was a formative influence on the American Revolution, although he produces no evidence to bolster the assertion.[12] Historians, including Christian ones, have concluded that Schaeffer's writings are of little use to the serious student.[13]

However vague on the facts, Schaeffer was highly effective in moving readers. Ronald A. Wells compares Schaeffer's combative style to that of the jeremiad delivered from Calvinist pulpits in centuries past, with denunciations of moral corruption and appeals for a return to the faith.[14] Schaeffer envisions civilization on the edge of an abyss, teetering towards an uncontrolled freedom that can only lead to "chaos or to slavery under the state."[15] In conducting his verbal assault against secular government, Schaeffer calls for a form of activism heretofore unprecedented in evangelical circles. Making parallels with the American

Revolution, he suggests that direct confrontation might be appropriate in resisting the abuses of the state. He speaks not simply of political and legal action, but civil disobedience. As already discussed, the issue that provides ready tinder for organized resistance is abortion, the cause célèbre featured in Schaeffer's books *Whatever Happened to the Human Race?* (1979) and *A Christian Manifesto.* The legalization of abortion with the approval of the federal courts is part of a narrative of betrayal that would soon energize a cohort of Christian soldiers from Jerry Falwell to Randall Terry.

Although Schaeffer's overall message was a potent motivator, its contradictions became apparent as time went on. Indeed, his followers after his death soon divided themselves, depending on which aspects of his thought they stressed, into two general groups: the zealous and the zealous with reservations. The zealous included the leading crusaders of the Religious Right, figures like Jerry Falwell, Pat Robertson, Tim and Beverly LaHaye, James Dobson, D. James Kennedy, Randall Terry, and others. These leaders stressed confrontation with the established order and advocated its replacement by a Christian-based order. Schaeffer's more cautious side, on the other hand, was reflected in the second group of followers.[16] These disciples, including evangelical intellectuals like Chuck Colson and Nancy Pearcey, advocated a more social-cultural form of Christian engagement, less political than the first type but still aggressively anti-secular. Both groups, and the tendencies they represented, will receive attention in the next two sections.

The Dominionist Urge

When Jerry Falwell founded the Moral Majority in 1979 it was, at least on paper, open to all comers regardless of their religious leanings. While the movement could hardly hide its evangelical roots, it was portrayed as a broad political alliance of "moral" Americans in opposition to liberal values and policies. This stance was stressed in Falwell's book, *Listen America!*, which lamented America's moral decay and laid out the broad outline of a solution. Holding the Bible up as a source of inspiration for America's healing, it asked "concerned moral Americans" to join "bible-believing Christians" in bringing about renewal.[17]

In the wake of Reagan's victory in 1980, however, a new mood began to take hold. Freshly conscious of their power in the political sphere, Christian activists began to articulate their goals in overtly Christian terms. As already discussed, Francis Schaeffer evoked the Protestant Reformation and defined the issues in orthodox Christian terms in *A Christian Manifesto* (1981). But those who followed in his footsteps demonstrated the lurch toward Christian militancy even more strikingly. One of these was John W. Whitehead, a Schaeffer acolyte who declared in a book published the next year (*The Second American Revolution*) that law must be centered in the Bible: "Law in the true sense is bibliocentric," he states, "concerned with justice in terms of the Creator's revelation."[18] In the conclusion to the book, he calls for a second American Revolution against humanistic culture, a revolution that would empower Christians and be founded upon "the Bible in its totality."[19] At about the same time, televangelist Pat Robertson came out with *The Secret Kingdom*, which seemed to endorse a Christian-run political order: "God's intention," the book states in one section, "was that his world be governed and subdued by those who were themselves under God's sovereignty." [20] Meanwhile, another Christian activist, Jay Grimstead, was launching a new organization, the Coalition on Revival, aimed at uniting the Christian Right's factions behind a specifically Christian approach to government and society. On the basis of what we know about them, Whitehead, Robertson, and Grimstead were not Christian Reconstructionists, either by definition or intent. But by seeming to condone a specifically Christian solution to the problems of America, they were not far removed from the Reconstructionist camp. In common parlance they were what are often called "dominionists."

Dominionism is generally defined as a theology mandating that Christians take control over the whole of society and shape it according to Christian principles.[21] The idea is a natural offshoot of Christian Reconstructionism, although not synonymous with it.[22] The term dominion comes from the familiar passage in Genesis (1:26–28), sometimes called the Dominion Mandate (or Cultural Mandate), which commands humans to "subdue" the earth and have "dominion" over every living thing. The Genesis verses actually refer to God's plan for *all* of humanity and speak to humans generally, not to Christians or Jews. Reconstructionists argue, however, that any dominion by humans over the earth is illegitimate unless it occurs under the aegis of God. "Man," Rushdoony states, "was created to exercise dominion under God and as God's appointed vicegerent over the earth." He deems any other form of human dominion "perverted" and a "temptation of Satan."[23] Rushdoony goes on to claim that the dominion command is reaffirmed in the New Testament. He correlates the mandate in Genesis with Jesus' call to his followers to go out and "teach all nations"(Matthew 28:18–20), often referred to as the Great Commission.[24] Jesus' Great Commission has traditionally been understood to mean spreading the Gospel rather than anything as crass as subduing or taking command. The relating of the two passages can thus be considered one of Rushdoony's bolder strokes, enabling him to fuse political militancy with evangelism and to press for a specifically Christian form of dominion. Gary North endorses this interpretation, stating that Jesus' Commission to teach the nations "is basic to the dominion assignment" and requires putting nations "under the rule of God."[25] As he states elsewhere, "How can we disciple the earth if we are not involved in running it?"[26]

Christian Reconstructionists, of course, do not stop at the mere notion of Christian rule. Dominion for them involves rule according to the precise specifications of biblical law, a notion that most contemporary Christian rightists, preferring a less overt form of dominion, would consider unnecessarily controversial. In consideration of these different interpretations of dominionism, writers Chip Berlet and Matthew Lyons distinguish between two different types: "hard dominionism" to describe the Reconstructionist imposition of biblical law, and "soft dominionism" to denote "more limited systems of Christian control."[27] The division draws a line between those insisting on strict fidelity to the biblical model and those, more attuned to public opinion, willing to settle for a more general framework.

Whether hard or soft, the idea of dominion became widely disseminated in Religious Right circles within a few years. Notions about building God's kingdom became common currency among rightist evangelicals as their movement gained momentum. Dominionism in one form or another became closely associated with Christian Worldview. While all sectors of the Religious Right seemed drawn to the new thinking, Pentecostals and charismatic Christians played an especially prominent role in its spread. As mentioned earlier, the emotionalism inherent in their type of religion and the very vagueness of its theology made it susceptible to mutation in unexpected directions. New leaders soon emerged who were able to harness the old religion to the cause of political and social activism. Their purported access to spiritual powers seemed, if anything, to strengthen their resolve to take on enemies in the earthly realm.

Pat Robertson, a charismatic in the prophetic mode, is representative of the shift toward dominionism by "enthusiastic" Christians.[28] Robertson, long renowned in charismatic circles for his spiritual gifts, used his reputed clairvoyance for years to make predictions and interpret God's judgments.[29] Although at first he showed little interest in getting involved in politics, after Reagan's election the sheer momentum of the Christian movement pulled him in a political direction. In 1981 he formed a grassroots national organization called the Freedom Council with the aim of fighting for "the rights of believers."[30] Before long he was making political pronouncements and identifying with rightist positions. By 1984 he was stating openly that only Christians and Jews were qualified to govern the nation and that "God's people would soon hold sway in Washington."[31]

Another key Pentecostal leader, Earl Paulk, emerged in the 1980s to proclaim the theology of Kingdom Now, commonly linked with dominion theology. The pastor of a Pentecostal church in suburban Atlanta, Paulk was undoubtedly aware of prevailing dominionist currents within Reformed and evangelical Christianity. However, he drew his primary inspiration from a strain of Pentecostalism called Latter Rain, which stressed spiritual revival in the present and repudiated the premillennial belief in Jesus' imminent return. The Latter Rain sect was a particularly dynamic form of Pentecostalism. It allowed room for fresh ideas by placing special authority in inspired "apostles and prophets" empowered to receive God's unfolding insights.[32] Paulk readily stepped in to assume the role of prophet and created a movement in line with his own priorities. Most notable of these was establishing God's kingdom on earth in the present chaotic era. Giving a socio-political twist to Latter Rain's revivalist teachings, his Kingdom Now movement called for confronting oppressive worldviews and "demonstrating" via revivalism the kingdom in all spheres of life.[33] Paulk's version of dominionism, though resisted by more established Pentecostal churches, had an electrifying effect on congregations where it took hold.

Given the increased involvement of diverse leaders like Robertson, Paulk, and Falwell in the Religious Right, questions naturally arose about the shape of the movement's agenda. While there seemed to be growing consensus on the need for an overall Christian solution to current evils, there was ambiguity about what a future Christian order would look like. What should be the movement's stance on the nature of government, the role of law, the place of the free market, and similar issues? Given the movement's centrifugal tendencies, many leaders saw the need to settle on basic principles and establish ideological discipline. Their aim was to give new substance and solidity to the Christian Worldview so much talked about by Francis Schaeffer. One of these leaders, Jay Grimstead, a northern California Pentecostal with dominionist views, formed an organization called the Coalition on Revival (COR) in 1982 with such a purpose in mind. Grimstead organized several private conferences involving hundreds of Christian rightists to hammer out a series of "worldview" positions. In the process, he was able to bring to the table all segments of the Religious Right. They included, for example, fundamentalists Tim and Beverly LaHaye, Don Wildmon, and Josh McDowell; charismatics Randall Terry and Dennis Peacocke; and Reformed Christians D. James Kennedy and Frank and Edith Schaeffer (the surviving son and wife of Francis). Significantly, several representatives of Christian Reconstructionism, generally considered an outlier by religious rightists, were also included, notably R. John Rushdoony, Gary North, David Chilton, and Gary DeMar.[34]

In 1986 COR unveiled a set of seventeen "worldview documents" encapsulating the ideological viewpoint of the Religious Right coalition.

The documents provide a revealing snapshot of Christian Worldview thinking at that time, reflecting the dominant influence of Neo-Calvinist and Reconstructionist ideas. Addressing topics such as government, law, economics, science, and the arts, they offer principles on how to "apply the truth of the Bible to all spheres of life and ministry."[35] Seeking to avoid opening past wounds, the COR documents shun all reference to two outstanding issues of disagreement among rightist evangelicals: eschatology (end-of the-world theology) and biblical law. Otherwise, their outlook is comprehensive and far-reaching. The documents advance the idea of an identifiably Christian political and legal system centered on the sovereignty of the Christian God and the authority of Scripture; they affirm God's rule over the various "spheres" of society, in the Kuyperian sense; they promote an interpretation of Scripture that justifies uncurbed capitalism and a minimal public sector; and they articulate a theistic approach to the understanding of science and truth. The positions were to be taken as "fundamental and non-negotiable truths and mandates," and coalition participants were expected to sign a "Solemn Covenant" signifying agreement with them, to be honored without exception until the signer died or was raptured.[36]

While COR was key to instilling ideological unity in the Christian Right at a critical point in time, its institutional influence began to wane in the early 1990s following some negative publicity. Journalist Frederick Clarkson reported at the time on the bizarre activities of a political group created under COR's auspices, the National Coordinating Council (NCC).[37] The NCC was advocating a number of extreme measures, such as the abolition of public schools and across-the board elimination of federal institutions like the IRS and Federal Reserve. It made no secret of its aim to Christianize whole sectors of society and to install Christian rightists as sheriffs with the aim of setting up county militias.[38] To make matters worse for COR's image, facts were leaking about its connections with Christian Reconstructionism. In reaction to these disclosures, a number of leaders, including Tim LaHaye and Don Wildmon, openly disengaged from the organization.[39]

COR's notoriety, however, hardly spelled the decline of dominionist influence on the movement. Dominionism had become too well entrenched for it to suffer anything more than a temporary setback. During the 1980s and early 90s, in fact, other religious rightists were gravitating toward variations of the dominionist approach. Two prominent examples that will receive closer attention later on should be mentioned. One is a group sometimes referred to as the Regent constitutionalists, associated with Pat Robertson's Regent University Law School. This school of thinking, developed by evangelical legal advocates Herb Titus, John Whitehead, John Eidsmoe, and others, argues for "returning" America's constitutional system to its supposed Christian foundations. They make the case for the law's early Christian foundations through a handful of selected biographical and textual references that they magnify to the utmost. Most notably, they claim Christianity to be a source of the English common law by emphasizing the Christian background of jurists like William Blackstone (1723–1780) and their reference to the "laws of nature," a phrase with religious overtones in some contexts. Blackstone's influence in colonial and post-colonial America and the one-line evocation of "the Laws of Nature and of Nature's God" in the Declaration of Independence are, almost by themselves, enough to show that American law is Christian-based. Upon such thin reeds rest the Regent constitutionalists' God-centered interpretation of the American legal system.[40]

History revisionists touting the United States as a "Christian nation" make up another group with dominionist tendencies. Like the Regent constitutionalists, Christian revisionists promote a Christian view of the American founding, but they go further in espousing a specific American Christian identity and agenda. Appealing to patriotic impulses and rejecting standard historical approaches, they argue for Christianity's special status in the public sphere and an end to church-state separation. Their main advocates are amateur Christian history buffs like Texan GOP operative David Barton and itinerant pastor Mark Beliles.

It is clear that within about a decade the Religious Right had reached a general consensus on the major features of its program. Various factions, to be sure, would continue to stress their own favorite points and differ over issues like the scope of the Dominion Mandate. But the broad tenets of their ideology had become fixed. As time went on, Christian rightist leaders increasingly turned their attention to inculcating and promoting this ideology amongst their own followers. Not surprisingly, instruction in Christian Worldview became essential to their efforts. With emphasis on forms of ideological instruction, we briefly survey the movement's recent developments.

The Battle for Hearts and Minds

In 1990 James Dobson and Gary Bauer published *Children at Risk: The Battle for the Hearts and Minds of Our Kids*, a book expressing a major concern facing the Religious Right: how to keep young Christians, confronted with societal influences in the schools and media, within the orthodox Christian fold. The authors called the struggle to retain the loyalty of young people the "Second Great Civil War."[41] They saw it as a war for the control of children's minds fought between faithful Christian parents, on the one hand, and teachers and government bureaucrats with different priorities, on the other. The problem for the Religious Right was, of course, more acute than simply ensuring Christian faith. It involved ensuring fidelity to a set of orthodox doctrines, to a particular worldview that could instill in the upcoming generation a sense of urgency over the current state of affairs and a desire to fight the enemies of Christianity to the last rampart.

After a decade of activism, it was evident that the movement had failed to convey adequately its worldview to its own captive audience, or even to establish a means of doing so. While Schaeffer had succeeded in popularizing the concept of Christian Worldview and while dominionists had worked to codify its doctrines, movement leaders were not yet prepared to offer a worldview curriculum suitable for classrooms and Bible study groups. The work of constructing a pedagogical method lay ahead of them. Fortunately for them, philosophically oriented Christian Worldview teaching methods had been tried for over a decade in more academic settings. Several evangelical intellectuals, inspired by the works of Abraham Kuyper and by the early philosophical writings of Francis Schaeffer, had produced books introducing the concept of

Christian Worldview and demonstrating its alleged superiority over other worldviews. James W. Sire's *The Universe Next Door*, first published in 1976, was one of the more popular efforts in this apologetic genre.

The first major Christian rightist to offer the basics of Christian Worldview in a teaching format was a man with a long history in evangelicalism, David Noebel. Noebel's Summit Ministries, located at the foot of Pike's Peak in Colorado, had functioned as a training center for Christian leaders since 1961. Noebel was long known for infusing his religion with the canons of social conservatism and anti-communism. Early in his career, for instance, he authored a pamphlet entitled "Communism, Hypnotism, and the Beatles" that portrayed rock music as a Soviet plot to indoctrinate American youth. In the 1970s and '80s, he played a key role in the highly public crusade against homosexuality associated with celebrity Anita Bryant. But Noebel's principal contribution to the orthodox Christian cause was his grand apologia for Christian Worldview, published as a 900 plus page tome entitled *Understanding the Times: The Religious Worldviews of Our Day and the Search for Truth* (1991). This volume, which has served for years as a textbook in numerous conservative Christian institutions and home-school settings, presents arguments for Christian Worldview within a comparative framework. It attempts to demonstrate Christian Worldview's superiority over other worldviews in answering "life's searching questions," and takes the reader on a journey through philosophy, ethics, psychology, law, politics, history, and other branches of knowledge. Its chapters are amply garnished with quotations from R. J. Rushdoony, Francis Schaeffer, Charles Colson, and other worldview advocates.

Noebel's book marks the beginning of a trend of selling Christian Worldview to the evangelical masses. It signals the emergence of a new type of Christian rightist literary form: primers, guides, and exegeses on Christian Worldview. In recent years several formulations of Christian Worldview have emerged, reflecting different shades of opinion on the Religious Right. Three are especially worthy of mention: the first, an orthodox approach popular with doctrinaire Calvinists like D. James Kennedy; a second somewhat more cultural approach linked with Charles Colson, Nancy Pearcey, and other Francis Schaeffer loyalists;

and a third revivalist approach embraced by many Pentecostals and charismatics. We touch briefly on each of the three types.

The orthodox formulation of Christian Worldview is best demonstrated in the writings Dr. D. James Kennedy, a minister of the ultra-conservative Presbyterian Church in America (PCA) and founder of Coral Ridge Ministries in Fort Lauderdale, Florida. An outspoken televangelist and inspirational speaker until his death in 2007, Kennedy preached to millions of listeners on the need to "reclaim America" for Christ. His worldview incorporates elements from both Neo-Calvinism and Christian Reconstructionism. Borrowing from Abraham Kuyper, he sees life properly divided into "spheres"(i.e., family, church, school, nation, humanity, the world) that need to be brought under direct submission to God. While Kennedy avoids the Reconstructionists' insistence on biblical law, he pushes the dominionist precept that every Christian "should be working to Christianize" all spheres of life, including the state.[42] Like Rushdoony, he merges the Old Testament idea of asserting dominion with the New Testament mandate to spread the Gospel, making them a combined mandate for all Christians.[43] Meanwhile, Kennedy bolsters his dominionist position with Christian revisionist history,[44] offering arguments for "America's godly heritage" similar to those advanced by revisionist historian David Barton. The narrative of a great Christian nation, once peopled by God-fearing patriots and defenders of liberty only to be betrayed in our own time by secular humanists, plays readily into the "reclaim America" version of events.

Kennedy's Christian Worldview approach, with its emphasis on bringing the nation under a Christian umbrella, has gained traction in the world of politics, where subtlety has little weight and grievances go a long way. Politicians such as Palin, Bachmann, DeMint, Gingrich, and Huckabee are typical purveyors of the "Christian nation" trope, having all essentially declared war on secular America. For them, freedom of religion is synonymous with freedom for Christianity, separation of church and state is proof of a secular conspiracy, and minority religions like Islam pose an existential threat to the nation.

Chuck Colson and other acolytes of Francis Schaeffer offer a second, less politically oriented, version of Christian Worldview. Colson came to Christian evangelism from the world of politics, having worked as a political operative in the Nixon administration and spent seven months behind bars for job-related felonies. His experiences served as a cautionary reminder of the dangers of zealous political involvement. Subsequently, Colson was swept up in the fervor of the evangelical movement and drawn to the Schaefferite cause. Avoiding Washington political intrigue, he founded his Prison Fellowship Ministries to evangelize the underclass and promote the idea of a new Christian culture. Like other cautious Schaefferites, Colson began to worry about the drift toward Reconstructionist ideas within the Religious Right and believed the movement needed to be purged of its overtly theocratic associations.[45] A steadfast admirer of Abraham Kuyper, he fully accepted the notion of antithesis and the war against secularism but believed that Christian goals could be achieved largely through cultural, as opposed to political, struggle. Accordingly, he has stressed the Christianization of education, business, the media, the arts, along with church and family. His popular book *How Now Shall We Live?* (1999), written in collaboration with evangelical intellectual Nancy Pearcey, focuses mostly on society, preaching the virtues of a biblically oriented social order submissive to God's authority.

Nancy Pearcey, who has developed a distinct profile of her own, likewise promotes a more cultural application of worldview ideology. A former student of Francis Schaeffer's at l'Abri and a devotee of Neo-Calvinism, Pearcey has gained prominence as a leading female intellectual in the evangelical movement. She has been a strong advocate of creationism and, most recently, intelligent design (ID).[46] Addressing the issue of worldview in her book, *Total Truth: Liberating Christianity from its Cultural Captivity* (2004), Pearcey attacks the intellectual face of modernism, lecturing on the negative impact of today's philosophy, psychology and science. She sees Darwinism as a prime target because, in her view, it represents the heart of the enemy's materialist worldview. Pronouncing the modernist worldview bankrupt, Pearcey offers the Neo-Calvinist alternative: a heart-felt commitment to

God and Scripture, which becomes the basis for an authentic view of the world. She bemoans the fact that most Christians today assume that religious truth is simply a matter of individual belief. To the contrary, she contends, people must be made to realize that orthodox Christianity is "objectively" true, ready to challenge science and secular knowledge on questions of factuality. Only if the gospel is restored "to the status of public truth" will Christianity be liberated and allowed to fulfill its destined role in redeeming culture.[47]

For all their efforts to downplay politics and dominionism, it is important to remember that Colson and Pearcey fully endorse the Christianization of America as a nation and society. In *How Now Shall We Live?* they emphasize not just "spiritual restoration" but "the restoration of all God's creation" in every corner of life. Like their more orthodox allies in the movement, they deny a "dividing line between things sacred and secular." They explain what this means in practice: "We are to bring 'all things' under the lordship of Christ in the home and the school, in the workshop and the corporate boardroom, on the movie screen and the concert stage, in the city council and the legislative chamber."[48] When they touch upon politics, they echo some of Francis Schaeffer's awkward inconsistencies. Most notably, they seem to shun theocracy and yet accept government "ordained" by God and a higher law that trumps human law.[49] Finally, Colson and Pearcey make no distinction between the transformation of the social order and conventional evangelism. They support the Reconstructionist notion, mentioned earlier, that equates the Dominion Mandate of Genesis ("subdue the earth") with Jesus' call to "teach all nations."[50] Their rejection of dominionism[51] should thus be taken at something less than face value.

The Colson-Pearcey version of Christian Worldview has served as an influential educational model in Religious Right circles. Devoid of triumphalist rhetoric and possessing a philosophical veneer, the approach has drawn support from leaders as different as Rick Warren, a self-styled moderate, and James Dobson, a combative traditionalist. For many years, Warren represented a traditional sort of evangelism, oriented toward spiritual concerns. But more recently Colson has been able to bring Warren around to a more activist, "world-redeeming" point of view. In 2006, he and Warren jointly collaborated on a worldview study curriculum called *Wide Angle: Framing your Worldview*, aimed at more mainstream Christian audiences.[52] Meanwhile, James Dobson, long concerned with reaching America's Christian youth, has adopted a similar curriculum but with a more systematic and hard-edged approach. In 2005, his Focus on the Family began the Truth Project, a training seminar covering the 12 major disciplines, including philosophy, science, history, anthropology, and politics. Aimed especially at college students, the course stresses rightist talking points on intelligent design, stem cell research, global warming, postmodernism, and other current issues. It prudently soft-pedals doctrinaire Calvinism, featuring a team of lecturers with diverse religious backgrounds. It stands as one of the slicker presentations of worldview ideology.

A third version of Christian Worldview, dominionist in tone but with revivalist features, is associated with the Pentecostal, charismatic wing of the Religious Right. The fastest growing representative of this constituency today is the New Apostolic Reformation (NAR), a movement that has taken off both domestically and internationally under the leadership of C. Peter Wagner. The NAR shares many of the features of Latter Rain and the Kingdom Now movement of Earl Paulk, discussed earlier. Like them, it places special authority in spiritual leaders with credibility in the Pentecostal community who receive God's unfolding plan and put it into practice on earth. Referred to as "prophets and apostles,"[53] these leaders accept earthly dominion as a key element of God's plan. Like other dominionists, they see God calling on Christians to transform the world both socially and spiritually.

Until recently the NAR did not give much attention to the worldview concept. Because of its emphasis on emotion and spirit, the movement seemed rather indifferent to the idea of an intellectualized theology. This attitude has changed. Cindy Jacobs, an NAR prophet who now accepts the need for a Christian Worldview, offers some explanation for the new emphasis. She states that revivals and crusades by themselves can only go so far in facilitating real change. While they may be powerful for a time, they usually sputter out or get short-circuited by "anti-God philosophies."[54] To attain genuine reformation requires instilling an unshakeable attitude in the minds of believers: "Our minds need to be discipled before we can disciple a nation," she says in bold print in her book, *The Reformation Manifesto* (2008).[55] Jacobs asks her readers to pray for the Lord to "come as a divine surgeon" into their thinking in order that God's "will be done on earth as it is in heaven."[56] The thoughts that God implants surgically come in the form of a "heavenly perspective," that is, a "God-centered, biblical worldview."[57]

Jacobs' version of Christian Worldview, firmly endorsed by apostle Peter Wagner,[58] borrows much from the Calvinist/Reconstructionist template. Indeed, Wagner openly describes NAR theology as directly descended from Calvin, Kuyper, and Rushdoony.[59] In common with these thinkers, it portrays the rise of humanism as part of a strategy to undermine Christianity. It views all true law as coming from God, stresses the importance of God's covenant, and fully supports the notion of Christians taking dominion over the human realm.[60] In addition, because of the Pentecostal stress on supernatural forces, the NAR also extends its campaign for dominion into the spiritual area. Dominionism entails not simply Christianizing the world, but also overcoming unseen, satanic forces that ostensibly control the minds of unbelievers and debase civilized life. The NAR is thus known for its public vilification of "false religions," such as Islam, and its massive prayer rallies directed against demonic "strongholds." Its intent in these displays is to prepare the way for the new kingdom through transforming consciousness and invoking God's powers. It essentially spiritualizes Christian Worldview, imprints it in the minds of believers, and acts it out in collective rituals.

The three versions of worldview just discussed reflect somewhat different approaches to Christianizing society and culture. Nonetheless, there is much more that unites Kennedy, Colson, and Wagner than divides them. All adhere to a core model of worldview that embraces antithesis, truth, and the Christianization of society. The model can be boiled down to a settled formula that is easily conveyed to followers, a kind of catechism supplying answers to a list of FAQ's about the world. Its positions on everything from autonomy to worldview conflict are steadfast and predictable. It has a special terminology, a ready means of categorization, and a caste of villains and heroes. It has a list of favored quotations and passages–Romans 1 topping the list–to underscore its philosophy. And it contains one organizing principle that underlies all the others: God's sovereignty over every aspect of human existence.

Our coverage of current worldview thinking in this chapter is by no means exhaustive. Christian Worldview is still evolving and warrants our continuing attention. But it is time to address Christian Worldview in a broader context, particularly as it relates to current public discourse. Whether one likes it or not, many of the issues in our culture and politics are being framed in Christian Worldview terms. The Religious Right has shown an ability to articulate its worldview perspective with greater skill than any other force on the political landscape. Using that perspective, the movement has helped to frame debate on abortion, secularism, evolution, family values, responsibility, religious freedom, the public square, government, church and state separation, and constitutional principles. The danger for all Americans is that its message is pitched to exploit some of the darker aspects of human nature, to appeal to its fears, prejudices, and resentments. All too often it repudiates the democratic values of today's open, pluralist society. The next three chapters deal with the main elements of Christian Worldview and their effect on public debate. Those elements are antithesis, truth, and the concept of the earthly kingdom. The chapter on Christian jihad discusses the confrontational posture of Christian Worldview and its dynamic and motivational role in the Religious Right; the chapter on total truth focuses on the conflict between presuppositional and evidence-based thinking, most notably as it plays out in the areas of science and history; and the chapter on the coming kingdom discusses worldview strategies involving government, economy, law, and constitutionalism.

PART III:
Christian Worldview in Action

6

CHRISTIAN JIHAD

Targeting the Enemy

"Those who believe, fight in the cause of Allah, and those who disbelieve, fight in the cause of Satan. So fight you against the friends of Satan." This passage from the Qur'an (4.76) portrays a world divided between the followers of the Almighty and his enemies. It suggests the necessity, if not the inevitability, of struggle between irreconcilable forces. For Islamic commentators, the passage explains what drives those who wage Islamic holy war, or jihad. The words show that the jihadist's motives are pure, unsullied by personal interest or desire for conquest.[1] For many outsiders, particularly distrustful Christians, they are proof of something quite different: evil intentions and a tendency to violence. The satanic enemy stigmatized by such a passage, they point out, often takes the shape of Christianity and Christian civilization. But all interpreters would agree that the passage stresses conflict, based on the incompatibility of opposing beliefs, and that its purpose is to fortify and arouse the faithful.

The idea of incompatibility expressed in terms of spiritual warfare, however, is an idea that is hardly unique to Islam. It is common to many religions, including Christianity, and rooted in their holy books. The Bible, for example, is well known for portraying a God who conducts wars against satanic forces and at times condones the annihilation of peoples of other faiths. Zealots across all religious traditions are drawn to such themes and give them unwarranted emphasis. The Religious Right is no exception when it comes to stressing the more militant elements of its religious tradition. Ironically, if one replaces the word

"Allah" with "God" in the passage from the Qur'an above, it harmonizes very nicely with today's Christian Worldview thinking.

Holy warfare against the enemy has always been a key element of Christian Worldview. It is implicit in the classic passage from Romans 1, which differentiates God worshippers from idolators, and is enshrined in Abraham Kuyper's concept of "antithesis." It takes on ominous features in the writings of Rushdoony, Schaeffer, and others who speak of secular tyranny and the need for Christian Reformation. And it remains a central principle of today's Religious Right, which sees itself persecuted by, and perpetually at war with, humanist forces.

"Culture war," a term that came into wide usage after the publication of James Hunter's book, *Culture Wars: The Struggle to Define America,* in 1991, quickly became a battle cry of the Christian Right. Pat Buchanan's evocation of cultural warfare at the 1992 Republican National Convention energized social conservatives by spotlighting the high stakes involved: "There is a religious war going on in our country for the soul of America," he stated. "It is a cultural war, as critical to the kind of nation we will one day be as was the Cold War itself."[2] His words are an indication, if any were needed, that religious rightists view culture war as more than a conflict over values. It is for them a struggle for civilization with cosmic significance, one in which the fate of the world seems to hang in the balance. The enemy is larger even than international Communism: it is the modern world itself.

The Religious Right's continuing emphasis on struggle has served as a key means of advancing its agenda. The movement frames issues in terms of good and evil to generate outrage and exclude the possibility of compromise. It wages public campaigns around tactical "wedge" issues, involving sensitive points of controversy, to gain popular allegiance. And it focuses its ire on enemies who are easily stereotyped. The enemies on its short list include secularists, homosexuals, feminists, Muslims, liberals, environmentalists, and "activist" judges, all targets whose actions are magnified and vilified. Thus during the George W. Bush era, religious rightists were able to transform a disagreement over the feeding tube of a brain-damaged hospital patient, Terry Schiavo, into an example of "judicial tyranny" and court-approved murder, after the courts attempted to resolve it. They have framed the movement to legalize gay marriage as an attempt by gays and lesbians to destroy traditional marriage. And they have construed a trend towards religious inclusiveness during the holiday season as sure proof of a "War on Christmas." Such exercises have not only impeded dialogue, but have fostered a narrative showing that society is captive to dark forces from which it needs to be liberated.

Demonization and conspiracism, commonly identified with such tendencies, are no strangers to the American scene. They are typical of a mindset that surfaces from time to time during periods of national discord. Chip Berlet and Matthew Lyons define demonization as a process of labeling "a person or group . . . as totally malevolent, sinful, and evil." This usually occurs in the context of dehumanizing people regarded as "inferior or threatening." Conspiracism is a tendency to assign "tiny cabals of evildoers a superhuman power to control events." It sees conflict as a "transcendent struggle" in the apocalyptic mode and "makes leaps of logic in analyzing evidence."[3] Demonization and conspiracism are often closely interrelated. In America's past, for instance, one sees the two behaviors blended in attempts to brand Jews as disreputable individuals and, simultaneously, powerful manipulators. Identifying enemies as conspirators becomes a way of enhancing their demonic qualities by personalizing their evil and overstating their power. Seen as creatively destructive, such groups become a perverse mirror image of the forces identified with goodness and light.

Richard Hofstadter's classic study of political paranoia places these behaviors, especially conspiracism, in historical context. Hofstadter suggests that a paranoid style of thinking emerges in history when "whole systems of values" seem to be under threat.[4] In the face of an imagined foe endowed with almost supernatural powers, the paranoid mind suffers acute frustration and a feeling of powerlessness. In extreme cases, it perceives the enemy as part of a grand conspiracy or "motive force" in human history and views the outcome of this conspiracy in apocalyptic terms.[5] Hofstadter wrote in the period of the early 1960s, when conspiracism was a striking feature of populist right-wing organizations. The most famous example at the time was the John Birch

Society (JBS), which stigmatized whole sections of the populace and regularly evoked the Communist menace.

Not coincidentally, conspiracism is a key element of Christian rightist thought and rhetoric. Congenial to the polarized framework of Christian Worldview, it has clear roots in Reconstructionist attitudes. Reconstructionists make no secret of their conspiracist leanings. R. John Rushdoony, who was both Reconstructionist and writer for JBS publications, warmly subscribes to the concept of "history as conspiracy."[6] For him, history is not the product of "blind, impersonal forces." To the contrary, because it is guided by God and expressive of his Creation, it must be perceived in terms of "Christian personalism."[7] History becomes "a personal conflict between the forces of God and anti-God, Christ and antichrist, with the ultimate victory assured to God and His Christ."[8] In this conflict, the vile schemes of the enemy come into play. Rushdoony finds support for his conspiratorial framework in biblical texts such as Psalm 2, which records the beginning of a heathen revolt against the Hebrew kingdom. In these verses, God laughs at the folly of those who rebel against him. He sets up his loyal king or messiah, and endows him with the power to break the heathen with a "rod of iron." The people must either side with God against the conspirators or face destruction.[9]

In light of their penchant for narratives of intrigue, it is not surprising that Reconstructionists recycle many of the familiar conspiracies of history, although within their own distinctly Christian framework. Thus the Freemasons and Illuminati, fomenters of plots and revolutions, are featured as the implacable enemies of Christianity seeking to advance their own rival religion.[10] The big central banks, viewed as anti-Christian by virtue of their desire to be "as God" and their manipulation of an unbiblical debt economy, are shown to be in covert alliance with financial organizations like the Federal Reserve. And the United Nations is seen as the enemy of orthodox Christianity, having as its end the salvation of man and the establishment of a "humanistic" world order.[11]

These well-known conspiracies, however, are mere sideshows compared to what looms in the eyes of the biblically informed. As Gary North opines, "there are conspiracies, and then there are *Conspiracies.*"[12]

The truly big one is the Conspiracy that Satan manages as a holding company for all the others. Firmly planted on American soil and allowed to grow over time, it has come to threaten the biblical foundations of Western civilization.[13] It is, in a word, the Establishment. Over the last century, the Conspiracy has succeeded in annexing American society's major institutions: "church, State, the media, big business organizations, the prestige universities, and the banking establishment." In the process, it has gradually gained respectability ("capturing the robes," Gary North calls it) and exerted control over the "climate of opinion."[14] Like all the great intrigues in history, it has achieved enough credibility to deny that it is a conspiracy at all. In the words of Rushdoony, "The successful and continuing conspiracies of history are never admitted to be conspiracies. Their known activities are extolled as virtues and patriotic works, never as illicit activities. Legitimacy is the reward of success."[15] Meanwhile, the Conspiracy carries out its strategy against God through cultural propaganda and misinformation, flattering the people and tempting them toward infidelity in the same way the serpent appealed to Eve with his famous words: "Ye shall be as Gods."[16]

The Reconstructionists skillfully frame the Establishment Conspiracy in worldview terms. They foster the image of a dominant humanist ideology, a rival religion to Christianity, with a throng of false worshippers who have prospered in the modern secular age and occupy positions of power. This modern worldview has a distinct "theology" whose aim is to mold the world according to humanist ideals, as outlined in our earlier discussion of Reconstructionism. R. J. Rushdoony typically refers to it as "the religion of humanity," using a term coined by the 19th century French positivist, Auguste Comte.[17]

The conspiratorial rhetoric of the Reconstructionists sets the tone for later religious rightists, who are eager to portray their secular opponents in menacing forms. Some Christian authors, notably Pat Robertson, adhere to conventional conspiracy theory for their framework. A premillennialist, Robertson uses a familiar cast of freemasons, trilateralists, and international bankers to bolster his prophesy of impending one-world government and the coming Antichrist, as forecast in the Book of Revelations.[18] Most Christian rightists, however, emphasize conspiracy in its worldview sense. Francis Schaeffer is the first Religious Right leader to focus on humanism as a worldview threat, a "religion" substituting itself for Christianity and Christian values.[19] While he stops short of speaking of a humanist "conspiracy,"[20] his references to the "manipulative" efforts of government, the intelligentsia, and the media to propagate humanist ideas imply as much.[21] The most influential conspiratorial treatment of humanism appeared in 1980: Tim LaHaye's widely read book, *The Battle for the Mind*, which borrowed much from Schaeffer's ideas.[22] By associating humanism with collusion and deception, LaHaye helps to make it (and its stand-in, "secular humanism") a sinister term in the right-wing lexicon.

The humanist movement, both secular and otherwise, is not in itself a fabrication on the part of LaHaye and others. A small number of American intellectuals, many of them Unitarian ministers, articulated a humanist philosophy in a statement of principles in 1933 called the Humanist Manifesto. A second revised Humanist Manifesto II, more secular in tone, was signed by a different convention in 1973. The fact that both manifestoes emphasized principles outside the fold of doctrinaire religion made humanism an inviting target for Christian fundamentalists like LaHaye,[23] even though the humanist movement was hardly known to most Americans. Its relative obscurity may actually have enhanced its usefulness to conspiracy hunters, since it evoked the image of a small clique of outsiders.

LaHaye finds humanism to be particularly loathsome because he believes it hides its true colors behind a cloak of high-sounding ideals. To LaHaye, humanists insinuate their values into the public mind by using a vocabulary that means one thing to easily duped Christians and something else to humanists.[24] He exposes the philosophy's true "destructive" nature by revealing its five basic components: namely, atheism, evolution, amorality, human autonomy, and one-world socialism.[25] Like other Christian commentators, he claims that it is a religion with a "well-defined theology" masquerading as a neutral viewpoint in the schools and media, while the Christian viewpoint is excluded from the same forums. LaHaye views the humanist vanguard as an arrogant elite numbering about 275,000 people, a small enough group to remain unobserved but powerful enough to assert "mind control" over the American people. It works behind the scenes to thwart the will of the Christian majority, exercising power over the "four vehicles of mind control"–education, the media, humanist organizations, and government.[26] In 1980 LaHaye predicted that without a Christian awakening, humanists would achieve their "goal of a complete world takeover by the year 2000"[27] (although treating the subject 20 years later, he prudently omits a timetable for enemy takeover).[28]

Humanism is just one of many faces of the modern secular worldview. Christian worldviewers also visualize it in its scientific form, identifying it with a matter-oriented approach to life. The main target in this rendering is Darwinism, which has long been deeply troubling for Christian worldviewers. Kuyper himself believed that Darwin's theory was antithetical to Christianity because of its lack of a spiritual component, although he did not reject outright the findings of evolutionary science when considered within a theistic framework.[29] His worldview successors went much further, attacking Darwinism as a sinister worldview and tabulating its baleful influence. R. J. Rushdoony held that it robbed nature of its "deified" status and identified it with statism, positivism, and other man-centered isms.[30] Francis Schaeffer associated it with a "material-energy, chance concept of reality" that laid the basis for situational ethics and a system of arbitrary law.[31] Contemporary theorist Nancy Pearcey maintains that "scientific materialism," which she ties to Darwinism, leaves people with a fragmented view of life and fails to provide them with the certainty that Christian Worldview provides.[32] She sees its effects evidenced in relativism, postmodernism, social engineering, birth control, and *Roe v. Wade.*[33]

Other Christian Worldview commentators bring Darwinism closer to home, showing it surfacing in America's public schools and corrupting the youth. According to one right-leaning Christian educationalist, public school classrooms are little more than psychology laboratories "where the child is taught that he is an animal linked by evolution to the monkeys."[34] Atheism and immorality are the inevitable consequences. When GOP leader Tom Delay famously linked the student killings at Columbine High School in 1999 to the teaching of evolution in the schools,[35] he was voicing accepted dogma in Christian worldview circles. Televangelist D. James Kennedy leaps to even broader conclusions about Darwin's impact. He calls evolution "the Big Lie" that "has deceived hundreds of millions of people and has probably brought about more deaths than any other view in the history of the world." The *Origin of Species* becomes a foundation for the acts of Hitler, Stalin, and Pol Pot.[36]

Some Christian rightists, meanwhile, prefer to portray the enemy worldview in supernatural terms. They focus on a popular strand of thought known as New Age philosophy, a combination of Eastern religion and self-transformational psychology that has received much media attention in recent years. The New Age movement is an appealing target because, unlike humanism or Darwinism, it can be easily identified as a religion. Since it defines itself in spiritual terms, its presumed anti-Christian tendencies can readily be exposed. Reconstructionist writers view New Age tendencies as expressive of a search for meaning by those committed to a godless worldview.[37] Pat Robertson characterizes such beliefs as "tailor-made for a secular elite looking for a philosophy."[38] The sinister underside to this popular quest for spirituality is that New Age ideas deny the biblical God's authority and reject Jesus Christ's atonement. The worldview they represent commits the ultimate blasphemy of deifying man. "Cosmic humanism," as some worldviewers term it, conveys the idea that "every individual is God and God is every individual." It enables humans to become attuned to divine powers by reaching "unity of consciousness."[39]

Christian rightists tend to treat New Age thought as if it were a unified creed. They reduce its many elements to a one-world religion with an "agreed-upon body of doctrine" and an "active core" of proselytizers.[40] Presenting it in this form, they are able to claim that the movement has a well-defined, sinister purpose. In the mid and late 1980s, a cottage industry of fundamentalist publications sprang up warning of a New Age plot to destroy Christianity.[41] These books describe a movement that spreads more like an "organism" than an "organization" and disseminates its heretical message in movies, books, and television programs.[42] Prophets of the right do not hesitate to portray New Age philosophy in the dark language of premillennialism and end-of-times tribulation. They describe it as a tool of Satan "to catapult his Antichrist to power" and to unite all religions into one World Religion. It will destroy, they say, all vestiges of Christianity and form the basis of a new tyranny.[43]

The Pentecostal wing of the Christian Right takes obsession with the occult to yet another level. As mentioned earlier, the New Apostolic Reformation (NAR) movement focuses on defeating sinister forces by mobilizing its followers to participate in "spiritual warfare." Its modus operandi is revealed most vividly by its activities in certain Third World nations, where minority religions and animistic traditions are easy targets. Typically, it identifies the presence of evil religions in local communities, endorses the destruction of books and objects associated with such religions, and conducts rallies against "idolatry," appealing to the power of the Holy Spirit.[44] While the NAR has found less opportunity to express overt bigotry in the United States, its demonization of so-called enemy religions is a subtext for many of its programs and activities. It regularly promotes mass events, sometimes perversely advertised as "reconciliation ceremonies," that include a heavy amount of sectarian vitriol. Islam, Catholicism, and other religions are often targeted.[45]

The confrontational rhetoric, wedge-issue campaigns, and organized intolerance of today's Christian Right represent a major extension of the idea of "antithesis" developed by Abraham Kuyper over a century ago. Kuyper fully realized the concept's power as a mobilizing tool when building his anti-modernist movement, but he was realistic enough to downplay it when he was acting on a wider stage and needed to advance national goals. Current worldview activists simply do not share Kuyper's sense of limits. Their obsession with antithesis, and their use of demonization and conspiracism to amplify it, has placed them in a dark world of their own making. This, it hardly needs to be stated, has affected the way they interact with others and exert influence in our political life. Finding common ground becomes unthinkable.

This confrontational posture has always been an attribute of the Christian Right. One can take the position, as we do in this book, that such a posture is born of the movement's uncompromising ideology and that culture war is the inevitable product of it. But, to be fair, let us consider for a moment the Christian Right's position as seen through its own eyes and by its own standards. Is there some basis to its rigid, dualistic view of the world? What are we to make of its view that it is simply reacting to a counter-ideology, a secular worldview that is equally determined to assert its exclusive view of truth? By this way of thinking, current conflict is the product of discord between two similar but irreconcilable moral outlooks fighting for supremacy. Some years ago, an academic writer proposed a "culture war" framework along these lines to explain what he viewed as unavoidable cleavages in American society. His view has since become accepted media opinion. What is noteworthy is that the author of the framework is a sociologist with an ostensible claim to scientific neutrality. His arguments are thus worthy of close inspection.

Framing Culture War

A year before Pat Buchanan delivered his famous speech on culture war, a sociologist from the University of Virginia, James Davison Hunter, published a work that would help make "culture war" a household term. His book, *Culture Wars: The Struggle to Define America*(1991), offered a catchy way of envisioning cultural conflict in America. It seemed to confirm academically the Religious Right's theory of worldview struggle, while appearing to remain neutral toward the combatants themselves. Using military terms like "warfare" and "the front," the book portrays a new kind of ideological conflict in America between forces committed to diametrically opposed "truths." It asserts that the two dominant worldviews are generally inelastic, mutually exclusive, and allergic to compromise. Hostility is seen as unavoidable and worsening.

Although written a generation ago, Hunter's book continues to influence thinking about religion and politics in contemporary America. The idea of antagonistic worldviews in perpetual struggle has come to be assimilated not just in right wing circles, but also by much of the media and public at large. Culture war has become the favorite term for portraying the rhetorical divide in American life, even though the idea of ideological conflict is generally alien to most Americans. A number of years ago, journalist Frederick Clarkson openly challenged the culture war framework set forth by Hunter by exposing the author's bias in his treatment of the subject.[46] We reopen the discussion here in an attempt to further elucidate the issue, addressing an underlying weakness in Hunter's theoretical approach.

Hunter's dramatic picture of a face-off between worldviews with their own truth claims raises several questions. Key among them is the question of whether the author's "orthodox" and "progressivist" worldviews are truly comparable, or whether he is postulating a kind of false equivalency between them. Is "culture war" an appropriate term for a conflict that shows, as this one seems to, certain asymmetrical aspects? Is the conflict best understood as one between clashing versions of "truth," or can the tensions be explained in some other way? Before we deal with these questions, however, it is worth examining how the author presents his argument for culture war.

From the beginning of his book, Hunter sets out to stress polarity and confrontation. He starts by presenting the views of maximalists on the two sides of the cultural divide, those who are the front-line gladiators in America's debate over social issues. To Hunter, they represent the essence of today's public culture: two sides locked in combat, fighting for unshakeable principles and making exclusive claims to moral legitimacy. He defines cultural conflict as hostility based on "different systems of moral understanding," at the core of which are compelling views of moral authority and "moral truth." Since such views "have a character of ultimacy to them," they are naturally conducive to conflict. Followers embrace their moral systems passionately–so passionately, in fact, that they are moved to seek domination over competing ones: "The end to which these hostilities tend is the domination of one cultural and moral ethos over all others." A seemingly inevitable struggle for dominance between "systems of moral understanding" is thus basic to Hunter's argument.[47]

Although cultural divisions have been present throughout American history, they did not assume their contemporary form until about the

1960s, according to Hunter. In the past they typically manifested themselves as sectarian conflicts between religious groups: e.g., between Protestants and Catholics, Christians and Jews, conventional Christians and unconventional ones (Mormons, Jehovah's Witnesses, and the like). Rooted largely in theological and ecclesiastical disagreements, these conflicts could take ugly forms, but because the participants held in common a Judeo-Christian tradition informed by "biblical symbols and imagery," they at least shared, in Hunter's view, some underlying assumptions about the ordering of society.[48] During the second half of the twentieth century, however, a more elemental kind of cultural conflict resulting from a period of social change, emerged to take the place of the old sectarian divisions. The new type of conflict was founded on "differing worldviews" representing what Hunter calls the "impulse toward orthodoxy" and the "impulse toward progressivism."[49]

The new sources of disagreement are more fundamental than the old ones, according to Hunter. What now separates the two sides is not theological disputes, but divergent "assumptions about how to order our lives." This divergence is reflected in disagreement on an array of issues from abortion and gay rights to stem cells and public education. Lined up on one side are religious conservatives who base their worldview on an "external, definable, and transcendent" authority, e.g., Scripture in the case of Protestant evangelicals, or Church teachings in the case of conservative Catholics. This authority creates absolute moral standards and makes it impossible to revise those standards on the basis of reason or experience. On the other side are progressives who draw their authority from "the spirit of the modern age, a spirit of rationalism and subjectivism."[50] The progressive worldview is guided by the Enlightenment search for universal ethical principles that have "the human good" as their highest goal.[51] Although the two sides generally identify with conservatism and liberalism respectively, Hunter insists that their controversies are basically *cultural* rather than political in nature. They involve "matters of ultimate moral truth" above and beyond current political issues.[52] As such, they are not amenable to compromise.

Hunter's concept of conflict has two prominent features: a tendency to see conflict dualistically and a tendency to construe it in religious terms. Regarding the first point, Hunter perceives two main forces, the orthodox and the progressive, with little concern for whatever opinion falls between them. He portrays the two opposing forces as feeding off their mutual antagonism, embracing tactics and goals that seem to echo each other. This condition he calls "symmetry in antipathy," a situation where each side inflates the power of the other and employs inflammatory rhetoric.[53] He further illustrates this mirror quality by contrasting the two sides' conflicting positions in a range of areas, e.g., history, family, law, politics, and the arts, as one might compare photographs with their negatives. Secondly, by portraying worldview struggle as a struggle over ultimate truth, Hunter essentially elevates it to a religious level. Hunter calls the two sides in the culture war "faiths," applying the term not just to the Religious Right, but to the secular camp. In other words, godless humanists qualify as religionists every bit as much as the worshippers of Christianity. Hunter justifies his religious terminology by offering a very broad definition of religion: "at the heart of religion," he states, "are its claims to truth about the world."[54] Based on this spacious definition, the current "culture war" is a "struggle for power" between aggressive, irreconcilable "faiths," each of them intent on enforcing its own vision of truth and reality.[55]

Hunter's picture of conflicting faiths locked in battle seems almost a flashback to Reformation-style religious conflict, where opposing branches of Christianity sought to impose their exclusive views of truth on the populace at large. In the same spirit, Hunter's dualism and religious framing also echo the Christian Worldview perspectives outlined by Abraham Kuyper, R. John Rushdoony, and Francis Schaeffer. These theologians, it will be remembered, see reality in terms of a dualistic collision of worldviews, each with its own exclusive perception of moral truth and the world. Like Hunter, they cast the struggle in ultimate terms where each side is striving to assert its own "religious" view. The theologians of Christian Worldview naturally identify the two forces with truth and error, God and Satan, Christian faith and modern apostasy. Hunter, who is obliged as a professional sociologist to adhere to standards of neutrality, naturally declines to use such terminology.

Based on his advocacy outside the classroom, however, Hunter, seems to have non-neutral assumptions on worldview matters, as Frederick Clarkson has well observed.[56] Hunter played an important role in the famous 1986 Alabama Textbook Case as a consultant for Pat Robertson's National Legal Foundation (NLF). The case was brought by Christian conservatives against the Mobile Board of Education to protest what they claimed was "secular humanism" in public school textbooks. As a witness for the Christian plaintiffs, Hunter strongly supported their argument that secular humanism was "the functional equivalent of religion."[57] Based on the omission of certain historical references to religion, he opined that "secular humanism of a sort is a dominant ideology of public school textbooks, at least the ones reviewed."[58] Hunter's arguments incorporate the Christian Worldview's critique of secularism, both its claim that all strongly held belief systems are, by their very nature, religious, and its denial of the possibility of neutrality. While these arguments initially persuaded a district court judge to rule in favor of the plaintiffs, his opinion was unanimously reversed by the federal circuit court, which found no evidence that the textbooks, through errors of omission, were advancing a "religion of secular humanism" or inhibiting theistic religion.[59]

Hunter's concept of "culture war," proposed several years later, essentially reflects the losing position he supported in the Alabama Textbook Case. Both in his testimony and his book, he makes it appear that the contending sides are fighting over ultimate truth claims. To be sure, one can agree with Hunter that "orthodox" and "progressive" forces are at loggerheads on many issues and assemble opposing facts to support their positions. But a close inspection indicates that the parties actually hold different types of objectives and argue for different types of things. For the orthodox camp, truth is something absolute, contained in inerrant texts or teachings. It is propositional, containing such moral axioms as "life begins at conception," "wives must obey their husbands," and "homosexuality is a perversion of nature." Winning the culture war means advancing these orthodox certainties at all costs. On the progressive side, by contrast, truth is far more elusive. Not dictated through revelation, it is what one aspires to by a variety of means, including experience, reason, and received wisdom. As such, it is not simply a catalogue of certainties and moral propositions. Indeed, if one looks at the progressive coalition, which includes moderate Protestants and Catholics, secularists, minority religionists, political liberals, and various independents, one struggles to find a propositional moral "truth" that is common to all, beyond perhaps a universal maxim like the Golden Rule. As Hunter himself concedes at one point, among progressives "truth tends to be viewed as a process, as a reality that is ever unfolding," rather than a list of "unchangeable" assertions. It is an intangible that is guided by the "spirit of the modern age."[60] But Hunter refuses to consider the next logical step, which is to recognize that progressives might not be defending a view of "truth" at all. They are clearly defending something, but Hunter strains our credulity by asking us to imagine them manning the barricades to defend a "truth" vaguely identified with the spirit of modernity.

What progressives are defending is, in fact, something quite different than a version of truth. They are concerned not with verities, as Christian rightists are, but with rights and freedoms. The most important of these is the freedom to arrive at truth by one's preferred means and to act accordingly. The primary goals are freedom to choose, self-expression, flourishing, and a climate of open-mindedness toward diverse opinions and life-styles. Human autonomy is valued rather than denigrated. Even when progressives take a strong stand on an issue like abortion, they act not in behalf of a truth claim, but in behalf of a liberty claim, a right to privacy and free choice.[61]

Naturally, when the argument between opponents becomes one of rights versus truth, rather than a version of truth versus an opposite version of it, the calculus changes significantly.[62] Disagreement may be intense, but the dualistic culture-war framework no longer applies since that framework assumes belief systems to be rigid and cast in the same mold. In actuality, the two sides are talking past each other because they have very different points of focus. They are concerned with different kinds of things. It just so happens that one type of concern is well-suited to the American democratic context, while the other is quite alien to it. Defending rights is a key element of the American ethos. The historical expansion of rights to workers, blacks, women, gay people, and others is central to our identity as a people and nation. Asserting exclusive claims to truth and attempting to impose them on society at large, on the other hand, is outside of that ethos. Because it challenges the assumptions of an open, popular democracy, such a posture threatens its stability and very existence.

Hunter's orthodox Christians would, of course, not take kindly to this analysis. If progressives are understood to be fighting for a type of freedom rather than an ultimate truth, they cannot readily be portrayed as worshippers of a "religion" that competes with and threatens Christianity. If Christianity is not under direct attack, antithesis becomes problematic, if not irrelevant. And without antithesis, struggle is not mandatory and the logic behind a Christian Worldview in defense of truth, and in opposition to the enemies of truth, is called into question. Furthermore, if liberty rather than truth is a matter at issue, the Religious Right's fraught position on questions of freedom and choice necessarily comes into focus. Its hostility to human autonomy and its rejection of a level playing field for all beliefs becomes glaringly evident. In essence, when truth is not preeminent, Christian worldviewers are forced to give up what they see as their one major advantage in their battle with the enemy. Their worldview becomes hugely vulnerable.

The focus on truth is clearly essential to the Religious Right's posture vis-à-vis the world. By spotlighting truth, Christian worldviewers are able not only to elevate the significance of their struggle, but to affirm the unique legitimacy of their viewpoint. Readers will recall from an earlier chapter how Cornelius Van Til, the father of presuppositionalism, played a critical role in building Christian truth on a seemingly impregnable biblical foundation. It will be our aim in the next chapter to show how this doctrinaire approach to truth has helped to advance the Christian Right's ambitious claims.

7

TOTAL TRUTH

Theistic Facts

The idea of truth has always occupied a central place in the Christian tradition.[1] Representing Christianity's highest ideals, it has commonly been associated with divine attributes. In some cases truth has been identified with the person of Jesus Christ himself ("I am the way, the truth, and the life"–John 14: 6). In others it has been linked with the Gospel message or the news of Jesus' redemptive role and resurrection, providing devout followers with a framework of meaning and giving their religion an aura of authority. In recent centuries, biblical Christians have taken to identifying truth with the text of the Bible, holding it to be an infallible product of God's wisdom. In all of these instances, the invoking of truth also serves a closely related purpose: to distinguish Christianity from other religions and to allow it to assert its unique claims.

As might be expected, those trained to argue in Christian Worldview terms endorse the key role of truth in their thinking. Like other Christians, they believe in a truth that has divine attributes and makes unique claims. But worldviewers take their claims a giant step further than traditional believers. They broadly expand the definition of truth and its worldly applications. The reason for this is obvious. As promoters of a Christian ideology with hopes of reestablishing its preeminence in the public sphere, they see themselves in competition with secular opponents who have made contributions to knowledge in all areas outside of theology. To challenge them on their turf, worldviewers see the need to expand their own knowledge assertions and throw cold water on the secular alternatives.

Truth in their hands, therefore, is no longer confined to what one would consider religious truth. Relying on the old framework of Romans 1,[2] they essentially have God, who is assumed to be the world's Creator and Definer, stand in as the referee of all truth, religious and secular alike. The Christian who has acquired knowledge of the Creator and his purposes (in large part through reading Scripture)[3] is thus said to have a decisive advantage over the non-believer since the Christian's access to God's viewpoint allows him to see reality with clarity and absolute certainty. Truth becomes everything that "is" by reason of the fact that God has made it so. It can be understood as comprising all of reality from apples to zebras, as perceived through the Creator's spectacles. Viewpoints based on different worldview assumptions become not only erroneous, but by implication an affront to the biblical God because of their denial of his role in creating the world and his ownership of it.

Cornelius Van Til helped to give this broad interpretation of truth currency through his theory of presuppositionalism, already discussed, in which a commitment to God and a biblical framework became the foundation for true knowledge. Van Til believed that a Christian Worldview provided a new, correct way of seeing reality. To justify this position in evangelical terms, he cites Paul's Epistle to the Colossians 3:10: "[Ye] have put on the new *man*, which is renewed in knowledge after the image of him that created him." For Van Til, Jesus came into the world not just to save humanity or lead it to righteousness, but to put it on the path to epistemological health.[4]

R. John Rushdoony, who wrote the first book-length commentary on Van Til, affirms the latter's emphasis on truth in its worldview sense. Following Van Til, he sees Jesus as one who made possible the knowledge of truth about the world. "The true interpretation of reality is possible only in terms of the triune God, of whom Jesus is the declaration or exegesis," he states.[5] Since all of reality is "God-created" and "God-interpreted," "no fact is a fact apart from God."[6] Facts must be regarded as "theistic facts."[7] Rushdoony castigates the autonomous non-believer for seeing facts as independent entities, "brute facts" as he calls them, which have no apparent meaning beyond what human reason assigns to them.[8] He uses the metaphor of the emperor who has no clothes to ridicule those who take on the role of neutral observer and do away with the biblical God standing behind reality. Non-believers may understand some bits and pieces of truth, he concedes, but since they wear "the colored spectacles of the covenant-breaker"[9] and do not allow themselves to see things through God's eyes with the aid of Scripture, they cannot arrive at a consistent view of the whole. They are condemned, in his eyes, to a chaotic, even nihilistic, worldview.[10]

Francis Schaeffer was also firmly committed to the idea of a God-based truth, considering it necessary for meaning and certainty. Like his Christian Worldview predecessors, Schaeffer takes the assertion that God is objectively true as his starting point.[11] If God is objectively true, then Scripture must be so as well, since it represents God's direct revelation.[12] By presenting reality as God sees it, the Bible serves as a template for true knowledge about the world.[13] "True truth," as Schaeffer sometimes refers to the truth God stands behind,[14] leads not just to certainty, but to intellectual coherency. It offers the believer a "unified field of knowledge" in which all things are related to each other by their common reference to a creator God.

Schaeffer acolyte Nancy Pearcey uses an Orwellian label, with no qualms, for this unified conception of truth: "total truth." Truth so named is unitary and indivisible as well as comprehensive. It eliminates distinctions between types of truth, especially between spiritual truth, on the one hand, and tangible fact, on the other. For her, putting angels and rocking chairs into the categories of "subjective" and "objective," respectively, is to accept the erroneous idea of a divided knowledge. She and Schaeffer call this traditional division a "two-story" method of knowing because it relegates belief to the "upper story" of unverifiable ideas while associating what is known through the senses with the "lower story" of objective knowledge. It epitomizes, they contend, the inconsistent and fragmented modernist worldview.[15] They prefer to see truth in terms of a one-story system with God at the core and the Bible as framework, where all truth both spiritual and material is divinely certified. The one-story rationality they embrace is not one that begins from human reason. It is a "theological rationality" that radiates from the testimony of Scripture.[16]

Contemporary worldviewers like Pearcey see themselves in a long-term struggle over how truth is perceived. They understand, of course, the challenges of instilling a God-centered approach to knowledge in a modern, secular society. To surmount them, they believe that evangelicals must jolt themselves out of "their metaphysical timidity" and mount a vigorous intellectual offensive in culture-war fashion. "If Christians hope to engage effectively in the *culture* war, we must be willing to engage the underlying *cognitive* war," Pearcey states.[17] Her desire to inaugurate a biblical way of perceiving reality resembles in some respects the Reconstructionist ambition to establish a "new paradigm" for the ages that would replace humanistic knowledge with knowledge based on biblical presuppositions.

One has to be impressed by the salesmanship of today's worldview activists. They make no bones about their desire to consign science and evidence-based methods of investigation to the dustbin of history. And yet they have few reservations about co-opting the language of science and philosophy, and bending it to their own purposes. Thus they readily appropriate concepts used and validated by inquirers over the centuries, concepts like reality, coherence, logic, fact, thought, knowledge, objectivity, and rationality. The result is an entirely new framework that transmutes words and serves up combinations like "theistic rationality," "objective God," "thinking God's thoughts," and "total truth." Only through constant repetition are these unlikely abstractions able to pass in the world of reasoned discourse.

The cognitive war against reason and proven methods of inquiry, however, is much more than linguistic gimmickry. It involves a whole different way of treating facts. In this regard, Christian worldviewers have been eager to put their theories into practice. To understand their methods, we consider two areas where they have applied them: science and history. For Nancy Pearcey, modern science is the main target for radical reassessment because of its reliance on testable, physical evidence. Darwinism, a prime example of this approach, embodies the scientific paradigm that she is convinced must be discarded. Once it is replaced, she believes it will then be possible to restore a "robust concept of creation" to our knowledge of the world and an idea of God's active role in it.[18] Francis Schaeffer, for his part, tends to focus on history as a means of fostering a biblical perspective. He lectures on the alleged Reformation roots of Western civilization, with God as the reference point for all human activity. Human history, seen through a divine lens, becomes a way of properly understanding the world. In the following sections, we will examine these approaches to religiously correct knowledge.

Theistic Realism vs. Science

Phillip Johnson, a stalwart defender of the Christian Worldview and a leading critic of contemporary science, sees himself on a truth mission. His purpose is to expose the errors of the current scientific worldview, as he calls it, and provide an alternative. He offers a solution in the form of a parable: A vehicle is driven through a canyon with no easy exit. At some point the driver is forced to halt because of a large log obstructing the road. Since the log is too big to move, his only hope of clearing it away is to break it into smaller units. Observing cracks along the log's bark, the driver inserts a metal wedge into the largest one and, by pounding on it, expands the opening and eventually splits the log. By so doing, he is able to remove the log and proceed on his way.

In Johnson's parable, the log stands for what he sees as the biggest obstacle to the pursuit of truth in contemporary culture: the philosophy of naturalism, which apparently lies at the root of modern science. Naturalism is understood by Johnson to be a doctrine that assumes the real world to consist exclusively of matter and energy resulting from purely physical processes. The crack in the log is naturalism's apparent inconsistency: while it claims to be factually objective, it exhibits a close-minded dogmatism in Johnson's eyes. The wedge in the parable stands for the effort to bring "long-neglected questions to the surface" and introduce them "into public debate."[19] Key among such questions is the role of God in the creation and formation of the world. In the minds of biblical Christians, science has avoided these issues by focusing exclusively on natural phenomena.

Christian worldviewers like Johnson seek to challenge these ostensible limitations by declaring that truth about the world is not confined to what is empirically verifiable. Echoing the views of Schaeffer and Pearcey, they declare that modern science erroneously overlooks the truths revealed by God, most notably the truth of Creation. They call themselves "theistic realists," holding that God is "objectively real" and that his word cannot be safely ignored.[20] They believe, of course, that God directly reveals himself in Scripture. But even in the absence of Scripture, they believe that the average person can apprehend God through the simple reliance on one's mental faculties, since God makes his role in the design of things obvious to all.[21]

The most prominent example of this approach is the concept of "intelligent design"(ID). Because it offers a simple and understandable concept of divine intervention, intelligent design theory has emerged as a favorite Christian response to Darwinian evolution. Postulating a supernatural designer, generally unspecified, to explain life on earth and the differentiation of species, ID theory challenges the empirical foundations of modern science on a major front. For Johnson, it represents the "wedge" that splits the log of naturalism.

The Christian rightist effort to undermine science, sometimes called the Wedge or Wedge movement, originated in the early 1990s out of Phillip Johnson's fervent public efforts to discredit Darwinism. Significantly, Johnson was not himself a scientist, having progressed no further than high school in his scientific training. But he was a motivated student in other areas, succeeding as a legal scholar, earning a position on the Berkeley Law School faculty, and publishing a textbook on criminal law. Sometime in the middle of his career, Johnson faced a mid-life crisis following a divorce. At the age of 38, the Berkeley professor gave himself "to Christ," which, in his own words, led him to question why other intellectuals like himself were "so dominated by naturalistic and agnostic thinking."[22] A sabbatical in England and a chance encounter with evolutionary theory in 1987 cemented his resolve to combat the "materialist" foundations of modern culture. Darwinism became the focal point of his campaign. His book *Darwin on Trial* (1991) was the first in a series of works to assert the need for a new kind of science that allowed for divine explanations of physical processes. Conferences soon followed, and the Wedge movement was launched.

The movement's full agenda, however, did not receive widespread attention until at least the late 1990s, when a document issued by the Center for the Renewal of Science and Culture (CRSC), the leading organization promoting ID, appeared on an internet site.[23] The Wedge Document, as it is referred to, presents a sweeping attack on what it calls "scientific materialism" and a detailed plan for defeating it and replacing it with an alternative science consistent with the Christian Worldview approach. It outlines a strategy to be implemented over defined periods, proposing three phases of activity: research and publication, publicity and opinion-making, and cultural confrontation and renewal. Research in behalf of ID is featured in the first of the three phases. Significantly, however, publicity and cultural confrontation receive the lion's share of attention in implementing the strategy.

The far-reaching scope of the strategy becomes obvious from the document's preface. The attack on evolution is to be merely the opening offensive of a much larger "cultural" campaign. The CRSC "seeks nothing less than the overthrow of materialism and its cultural legacies," which are evident in every mode of culture from "politics and economics to literature and art," but most notably science. It blames materialist science for portraying humans as "animals or machines," fueling "moral relativism," eroding "personal responsibility," and producing failed approaches to "criminal justice, product liability, and welfare." At the same time, using rhetoric reminiscent of Christian Reconstructionism, it blasts "materialist reformers" for spawning a "virulent strain of utopianism" and advocating "government programs that falsely promised to create heaven on earth."[24] As a way out of the cultural morass just described, the CRSC unveils its multifaceted program to overthrow the materialist paradigm and return to "bedrock principles." A key priority in achieving its aim is reopening "the case for a broadly theistic understanding of nature."

Intelligent design theory is accepted as the most obvious means to introduce this "theistic" approach. Still, ID advocates have been ambivalent about conveying an openly religious message. In some settings, they admit the religious thrust behind ID theory. Phillip Johnson is typical when he openly argues that intelligent design is a species of "theistic realism." His colleague Nancy Pearcey likewise champions ID alongside Christian Worldview. The Wedge document itself argues for a "science consonant with Christian and theistic convictions" and considers Christians to be the movement's "natural constituency."[25] On the other hand, advocates are wary of overplaying the religious basis of ID in public debate, aware of the constitutional problem of introducing religion into tax-supported venues, such as public school classrooms. In courtroom settings, they firmly deny ID's religious inspiration. The inconsistency remains a sticking point, as ID supporters seek establishment legitimacy for their theory while simultaneously trying to mobilize conservative Christians behind it.

Where they have the most difficulty, however, is in establishing ID's scientific credentials. ID's claims to qualifying as real science are damaged by two factors: its association with the older, Genesis-inspired theory of origins called "creationism," and the insubstantial record of scientific research by its practitioners. Old-style creationism, long embraced by Christian fundamentalists, has always insisted on God's personal role in the creation of the universe as outlined in the Book of Genesis. ID theory is silent on the Genesis account, while articulating a concept of design and an active designer that is at least consistent with it. The ID approach has thus attracted many former creationists interested in appealing to a wider audience. In doing so, however, it has buttressed the impression that it is simply a cover for the older theory.[26]

Meanwhile, in the area of research, ID supporters have failed to produce experiments in the laboratory able to convince even the most persuadable of scientists. In the years since ID has emerged as a concept, few if any peer-reviewed articles have been published on the subject.[27] The claim that natural things are the product of intelligent design is an argument based on simple analogy rather than scientific method. It states that the universe, a flower, the human eye, etc. are creations analogous to products endowed with order in the human world and hence, by inference, requiring the work of an intelligent creator. Unfortunately, such assertions cannot be tested by empirical scientific experiment. They have possible meaning for poets and theologians but little value for the working scientist.

Still, the primary aim of ID advocates has never been to persuade the scientific community, which overwhelmingly dismisses the concept as useless. Their purpose has always been to persuade a jury of average citizens that it is a convincing alternative to evolution. ID spokespersons have loudly claimed that Darwinism is "on trial," and their public campaign has been waged in the manner of a courtroom battle.

It is well to remember, however, that the legal approach to sifting evidence and determining fact is significantly different from the scientific method, as philosopher Robert Pennock has pointed out. Scientists in the empirical sciences strive for truth by making hypotheses and testing them with evidence. The process is often laborious, leading ultimately to the kind of truth written in "lowercase" letters. Truth is tentative rather than "all or nothing," since results are always subject to revision in the light of new evidence. Scientific evidence must therefore be seen as coming in "varying degrees of strength." It is strongest when supported in a cumulative sense, as when it is confirmed by thousands of independent findings and by an edifice of scientific applications, as in the case of evolutionary theory.[28]

Advocates for ID, not surprisingly, are uncomfortable in this world of judicious empiricism, preferring an environment where true is True and false is False. They welcome a setting where debate is conducted on a stage and the skills of the lawyer are at a premium. Trial lawyers, unlike scientists, make their case for a client in an adversarial environment. They attempt to present a one-sided view of things often by raising enough doubts about the opposing view to permit them to claim victory for their side. The framework favors only two alternatives, with no range of possibilities between them.[29] The process becomes a form of head-on combat of the sort relished by Christian worldviewers.

In the court of public opinion, the ID movement could not have picked a better warrior for its cause than legal expert Phillip Johnson. Although Johnson may be an amateur on science and scientific method, he is proficient in the methods of courtroom debate. As a skilled attorney, Johnson seeks both to discredit the scientific community and present a caricature of evolutionary theory. He argues that the theory of evolution is a dogma held by a zealous scientific elite. The evolutionist is the "blind" ideologue asserting his hegemony in the science classroom and insisting on the exclusion of any theories that suggest supernatural explanations. The ID proponent, in contrast, is made to appear like the reasonable "skeptic" fighting for open-mindedness and the right to free speech.[30] In his substantive arguments, Johnson knows that he need not prove his theory correct to win his case. If he can raise sufficient doubts about the prevailing theory in the mind of the "jury of public opinion," he advances his favored alternative by default.[31] Negative argument rather than counter hypothesis becomes the favored mode of engagement. Thus the bulk of his book, *Darwin on Trial*, is devoted to picking holes in evolutionary theory by narrowing the definition of proof, pointing to whatever gaps still exist in the fossil record, separating micro from macro evolution in the mind of the non-specialist, and conducting evidential skirmishes around the edges.

But Johnson's real argument against evolution is ideological. He wishes essentially to brand evolutionary theory as the poster child of atheistic materialism, an alternative religion parading under the banner of objective science. Calling mainstream science a worldview, he dubs it "scientific naturalism." He maintains that scientific naturalism is a dogmatic philosophy based on presuppositions that either implicitly deny God's existence or, at the very least, exclude any meaningful role for God in the lives of "natural creatures like ourselves." Scientific naturalism, in his words, rules out a God who can "do anything that makes a difference."[32] To buttress his claims, he regularly quotes from a number of known atheists and philosophical materialists like Richard Dawkins and William Provine who disparage religion and present a generally mechanistic picture of the cosmos.[33] Johnson implies that these individuals speak for the scientific community as a whole.

In his attempt to attach a worldview label to science, however, Johnson uses semantics to sow confusion. Johnson's "scientific naturalism" is actually a conflation of two different viewpoints: *metaphysical* naturalism and *methodological* naturalism.[34] The first of these, metaphysical naturalism, does indeed assume physical matter, generally in combination with energy, to be the basis for all reality and existence. The viewpoint has a long history and characterizes the thinking of philosophers like Lucretius, Holbach, Feuerbach, and modern-day scientists like Richard Dawkins and Steven Pinker. However, to fuse this view with *methodological* naturalism and to present it as the "dogmatic" position of modern science is misleading demagoguery. Methodological naturalism is simply a method of approaching and understanding the facts of nature by weighing empirical evidence. Far from making a broad philosophical statement, it takes no position on ultimate questions of God and existence, about which scientists hold different opinions depending on their religious or philosophical beliefs. Methodological naturalism is committed simply to the use of empirical evidence to support its conclusions. These conclusions can hardly be called dogmatic since, by the rules of inductive experiment, they can be modified at any time by new evidence.

To be sure, the empirical evidence admitted by the scientific method precludes evidentiary claims of miracles and supernatural intervention. But this limitation, rather than demonstrating anti-theistic bias, is necessary to the conduct of science as a discipline. Without it, science would be unable to exist. Scientists require the presence of order and predictability in the natural world for them to have any confidence in their observations and experiments. As Robert Pennock has pointed out, "without the constraint of lawful regularity, inductive evidential inference cannot get off the ground."[35] This constraint hardly makes science the dogmatic religion that Johnson claims it to be.[36]

Johnson's efforts to construe science as a materialistic religion, however, are just one part of his polemic against "scientific naturalism." He opens a second front by questioning science's claims to objectivity. Johnson turns for support to the controversial philosopher of science, Thomas Kuhn, who over the years has been invoked by thinkers of both the left and right to question the reliability of human knowledge. Kuhn's influential book, *The Structure of Scientific Revolutions* (1962) casts science's trustworthiness in some doubt, challenging the idea that science represents the gradual advancement of knowledge on the basis of a constant set of assumptions. Instead Kuhn offers a model in which science proceeds by revolutionary bursts and involves value-laden assumptions about how the world works. Science, he maintains, is guided at any given time by core sets of premises, called paradigms. Paradigms provide a framework for scientific research and determine the sorts of questions that scientists ask. When a paradigm no longer answers the challenges of the day, i.e., when new problems seem to resist solution and anomalies arise, a crisis is created forcing a breakthrough to a new paradigm that enables science to progress. The Copernican Revolution represents the most famous of such breakthroughs, when the paradigm of heliocentrism (a sun-centered viewpoint) replaced geocentrism (an earth-centered viewpoint). Nineteenth century Darwinian theory, which substituted natural selection for the biblical theory of creation, is a second example.

Now, after a century and a half, Johnson wishes to show that the Darwinian paradigm has outlived its usefulness. It is the product of a discredited framework, in his opinion, that is unable to answer fully the kinds of questions raised by ID theorists and others. Furthermore, it is no longer born out by new, supernatural ways of viewing reality.[37] Like many other commentators, Johnson uses Kuhn to advance a relativistic view of human scientific knowledge. But here he seriously oversimplifies Kuhn's thesis. While Kuhn believed that the choice of a paradigm was influenced by one's norms and values, he did not go so far as to reject the ability of science to discover objective knowledge. Nor did he question the importance of empirical evidence for ascertaining facts. Johnson's use of Kuhn to discredit scientific methodology in this sense is quite illegitimate.[38]

Johnson not only embraces the views of iconoclasts like Kuhn, but he often uses the language of postmodernism and deconstruction to discredit the possibility of objective human knowledge. He associates the work of mainstream science with mythmaking and manipulation rather than facts and truth. Thus he pictures Darwinism as a "creation story," and sees science as having "a virtual monopoly on the production of knowledge."[39] Openly indebted to postmodernism, he actually considered titling his first anti-evolution book *Darwin Deconstructed* before later deciding on *Darwin on Trial*.[40] Johnson, ironically, is far more critical of the scientific enterprise than the old-style creationists, who sought legitimacy for their theories under the rubric of science even while adhering to Scripture. He differs from them in his embrace of the worldview critique of human reason and autonomy. In unison with today's Christian worldviewers, Johnson comes across as a thorough relativist on the subject of human knowledge.

Significantly, Johnson rarely provides a positive argument for intelligent design or for a new and improved science that might support it. Indeed, Johnson's books fail to deal forthrightly with what is surely the most conspicuous weakness in his own position: the lack of a consistent methodology for ascertaining fact. Johnson realizes that elaborating on a scientific method of his own would mean having to commit himself on the sticky problem of evidence. He understands that working scientists, and even attorneys for that matter, regard "supernatural evidence" as an absurdity since there is no consistent methodology for ascertaining it. "Miraculous explanations" are frowned upon not just in science labs but in courtrooms. Thus rather than subjecting himself to embarrassing questions, he astutely avoids the issue of evidence, especially when addressing sophisticated audiences. When asked by Robert Pennock at a public lecture if empirical evidence could be derived from Scripture, Johnson declined to answer positively. But not wanting to paint himself into a corner or offend his religious followers, he also did not explicitly reject the possibility.[41]

The furthest Johnson goes in offering a methodological alternative to mainstream science is to support "theistic realism" in his later books. The theistic realist is one who is convinced that "God is objectively real, not merely a concept or fantasy" and proceeds on the basis of this assumption.[42] The conception borrows from Van Til's presuppositionalism and Francis Schaeffer's similar unified field of knowledge founded on the reality of a biblical God. Johnson admits that theistic realists need to give a fuller picture of their "theory of knowledge," but instead of providing such a picture, he reverts to his bedrock assumptions, his worldview starting point. He quotes two passages from Scripture and simply asserts them to be true. [43] The first passage, from the opening three verses of the Gospel of John, refers to the "beginning" of things: "In the beginning was the Word, and the Word was with God, and the Word was God. . . . All things came into being through him." The second passage is the famous polemic from Romans 1, encountered in our earlier chapters. It asserts that God's power and divine nature is "evident" to all. Those refusing to recognize the obvious are idolaters "without excuse" who form corrupt images in their minds of natural things. These resisters represent, of course, today's practitioners of science.

Johnson's "theistic realism," in a word, is a set of assumptions he finds in Scripture that separate the cognitively correct from the cognitively incorrect. Those who are not among the former he deems to be misled (and damned). Johnson dodges the issue of methodology by returning to one of the favorite themes of Christian Worldview: the view that the presuppositions underlying one's worldview determine the truth of one's outlook. For him, the replacement of false presuppositions with correct ones remains the key to the attainment of truth about the world, just as it did for Kuyper, Van Til, and Schaeffer.

To his frustration, Johnson realizes that the acceptance of a new faith-based paradigm is not so easy for those conditioned to a "naturalistic" culture. Referring to encounters with scientists who are not as truth-minded as himself, he states: "it is pointless to try to engage a scientific naturalist in a discussion about whether the neo-Darwinist theory of evolution is *true.* The reply is likely to be that neo-Darwinism is the best scientific explanation we have, and that *means* it is our closest approximation to the truth."[44] Johnson thinks that to pursue a question to some point short of absolute certainty is to make peace with the insidious disease of relativism. He fails to understand that the cautious approach to truth is a key strength of the scientific viewpoint.

While Johnson had reason to expect resistance to his truth mission from the mainstream scientific community, he was unprepared for the strong opposition he found in certain unlikely corners of it, notably among Christian scientists. He reports that in his visits to universities, Christian professors, no less than non-religious ones, needled him on questions of evidence and method.[45] Discussions were often "acrimonious," he concedes. One can surmise a double-edged reason why Christian researchers would be among his harshest critics. Johnson's attacks raise questions about their role not only as scientists, but also as Christians. On the one hand, Johnson throws into question their activity as researchers, requiring them constantly to look over their shoulders for theological validation. On the other hand, he narrows the definition of faith by dictating the correct way to conceive of God's role and character. Johnson's deity is the controlling, interventionist God of Calvin. He declines to consider the vast range of theistic possibilities beyond that, including a God who might oversee a universe in which chance and freedom are necessary components. His rhetorical framework is a model of simplicity, allowing for only two defendable religious possibilities: an overbearing God or no God at all.[46]

In spite of resistance among academic scientists, there is evidence that the Wedge movement, boosted by worldview supporters like Johnson and Pearcey, has increased public skepticism in the United States about evolution. Although ID's status as a science has recently been rejected in the federal and state courts, most recently in the Dover, Pennsylvania textbook case of 2005 (*Kitzmiller et al. v. Dover Areas School District*),[47] its defenders continue to lobby successfully in statehouses around the country for recognition of educational alternatives to evolution. Undeterred by legal roadblocks, ID advocates regularly change their tactics to present their case in new and imaginative ways. Thus if the teaching of intelligent design is banned in the public schools, they react by promoting closely related alternatives in the school curriculum: the teaching of "evidence against," the "strengths and weaknesses of," or the "critical analysis of" evolution, or simply a "full range of scientific views."[48] These tactics have had measurable success, particularly in conservative sectors of the country. The pivotal state of Texas, which many textbook publishers look to as a bellwether, is one place where traditionalists have made major assaults on the classic science curriculum.

Beyond the teaching controversy, the Wedge movement has had a big impact on the way scientific issues are treated in today's political debates. A few decades ago, science and scientists were viewed with respect across the political spectrum. Scientific matters usually transcended partisanship, and legislation on issues like air and water standards, wilderness designation, tobacco smoking, food labeling, and research funding had friends on both sides of the aisle. Those idyllic days are gone. Right wing political forces now tend to view the science community with hostility, as if the warfare between science and theology of ages past were once again a reality. The Religious Right's role in this new state of affairs is unmistakable, as religious conservatives with no love for science hold virtual veto power over Republican candidates for national office in many states. The result is a kind of Republican groupthink on scientific issues, at least at the federal level, where anti-scientific forces use ideological talking points and the either-or format of Christian Worldview to advance arguments. They now present a virtual united front on key issues like stem cell research, environmental regulation, and global warming. On a recent congressional bill restricting the EPA's authority to alleviate greenhouse gases, for example, not a single Republican cast a dissenting vote.[49]

Science, of course, is not the only area of knowledge that has come under assault from Christian Worldview advocates. History too has become a prime target. Like science, it has been hit with demands to redraw its boundaries and admit a new sort of truth into its vestibules. Supporters of empirical and fact-based approaches to history must now defend themselves against the claims of Christian providentialists. As with science, the fight over history has become a high-stakes game, overflowing into classrooms, court opinions, and legislation. We assess this second battlefield in the next section.

Providential History vs. History

The early summer of 1787 was a difficult moment for America's founders. The Constitutional Convention held in Philadelphia to thrash out ideas for a new constitution seemed at a stalemate. Delegates from twelve of the American colonies had been cooped up in secret chambers for over two months, apparently stymied by disagreement between delegates of the small and large colonies over the issue of representation. Proposals had been made by each side and quickly rejected by the other. During this impasse, Benjamin Franklin rose from his seat to observe that little thought had been given to God's influence over the affairs of men. Accordingly, he proposed that henceforth prayer be introduced at the beginning of meetings to seek the assistance of God in all of their future deliberations. After discussing the motion, the combined body agreed to have clergymen lead prayer in future meetings. Its resolution was implemented at least in part, and the happy effects were soon evident: the political logjam began to break. Roger Sherman introduced the famous Connecticut Compromise proposing a bicameral legislature with a senate and house. The delegates' prayers seem to have been answered at a crucial moment, marking a turning point in the formation of the American Republic.[50]

This, or something similar to it, is what school children in thousands of Christian academies and home settings find recorded in their history texts. They learn that the Almighty is a defining presence at key moments of human history, ready to guide events to a felicitous conclusion when needed. The version of events related by mainstream historians, on the other hand, provides a more nuanced picture. Benjamin Franklin did, by all accounts, rise on June 28, 1787 to suggest that prayer be instituted at the commencement of future meetings. But far from acquiescing to his suggestion, the delegates declined to vote on the motion after discussing it. Franklin wrote in his own notes that, except for three or four people, nobody thought prayers were necessary. Nor is there any evidence that prayers were ever introduced in the Convention proceedings thereafter. Rancor between delegates continued for weeks following Franklin's suggestion before a preliminary compromise on representation was reached on July 16. Necessary agreement on all issues seems to have been achieved not through supplication or miracle but through laborious human effort and perseverance.[51]

The two versions of events rely on some of the same contemporary evidence about the Convention proceedings, especially James Madison's detailed transcriptions. But the inspirational version borrows from a questionable Christian source, blends it into the narrative, and cuts out facts from Madison and others that don't conform to it. The Christian source is a thick tome by the Congregational minister Benjamin F. Morris entitled *The Christian Life and Character of the Civil Institutions of the United States*, a mainstay of many an old church library. Published in 1864, the book contains hundreds of documents, some of dubious accuracy, interspersed with editorial commentary, all aimed at demonstrating the wholesome Christian character of America's civic foundations. The inspired version of the Franklin prayer story is presented full-blown in its pages without a source reference. Morris appears, however, to have borrowed the story from an earlier Christian work, E. C. Miguire's *The Religious Opinions and Character of Washington* (1834), which in turn acquired it from an obscure letter to the *National Intelligencer* of August 26, 1826. The letter, by a certain William Steele to his son, narrates the Christianized version of events by his friend, the then dead Jonathan Dayton, a former member of the Constitutional Convention from New Jersey. Unfortunately, the inspired version is one man's (Steele's) memory of another man's (Dayton's) memory of what occurred some 25 years in the past, a version contradicted by all other contemporary sources and events.[52]

However tenuous the faith-based evidence, it nonetheless fits nicely into a preconception of what most Christian worldviewers believe history consists of. History, according to early Puritan historians and most of today's Christian rightist advocates, is "providential," i.e. marked by God's guidance and oversight. By this view, God is "Sovereign over His creation . . . and is at work in significant, and seemingly insignificant, events to accomplish his purposes for mankind."[53] Human figures throughout history are used for God's purposes, much as Moses and David were used in biblical Israel. God assumes a guardian role over his developing creation and is not reluctant to intervene as he sees fit. The Christian Worldview readily incorporates these ideas of providential history, which are consistent with the Calvinistic view of God's watchful authority over his creation. Abraham Kuyper, the father of Christian Worldview, explicitly embraces them. Kuyper refers to "the great work of the Holy Spirit in history," in which God providentially enters the hearts of individuals to make things happen. The doctrine of Calvinism, for instance, far from being invented by men, is a "fundamental interpretation" granted by God to mankind, "of which Calvin was only the first to become clearly conscious."[54]

God's providential guardianship makes him not simply a mover of human beings; it makes him a judge of their behavior. God is known as much for his ability to reward and punish as he is for his role in planting seeds of consciousness. The biblical narrative of Israel shows God bestowing favor on that nation as long as it maintains fidelity to him, but retracting it when it loses its way. In the modern context, Kuyper mentions God's discretionary power to dispense liberty to peoples that are deserving of it while withholding it from those who have proven themselves unworthy.[55] Christian Reconstructionist historians like R. J. Rushdoony and Gary North are also strong believers in judgmental acts of divine intervention. As proponents of Mosaic law, they focus on his blessings and cursings in accordance with the terms of the Hebrew covenant. For them, history takes on meaning under the umbrella of God's constant surveillance.

Today's Christian history apologists vary in the degree to which they stress the providential, but almost all hold providential assumptions.[56] Mark A. Beliles and Stephen K. McDowell, evangelical authors of the popular textbook, *America's Providential History*, are major proponents of the providential approach, emphasizing America's role as the chosen nation of God. They take note of America's blessed geography, speak of God's aid on the battlefield and at political turning points, and warn of the dangers of losing his favor. David Barton, while best known for attempting to document America's Christian past in human documents, also believes that God picks sides and acts accordingly. As he puts it,

"Nations, like individuals, *will* be recompensed for the actions and stands they take under the watchful eye of God."[57]

Christian providentialists oppose mainstream history for much the same reason that ID advocates oppose mainstream science. They view it as materialistic, un-purposeful, and devoid of meaning. R. J. Rushdoony, an important precursor of today's revisionist Christian historians, disdains any history that fails to acknowledge God's "predestined purpose." History whose meaning is created by man he derisively calls "humanistic history," which he equates to a "frail and shaking ladder, resting on no foundations and reaching out into nothingness." He categorically condemns such history for its emphasis on "brute factuality" and its portrayal of a depersonalized world governed by uncontrollable forces.[58] A correct approach to history requires acceptance of the view that God foresees and infuses meaning into every event. To deny this proposition is to practice false history. Such opinions are hardly exclusive to Rushdoony, but are voiced by other Christian revisionists as well.[59]

It should come as no surprise, then, that Christian history writers typically have no connection to the world of professional historians. They are part of a motley group of pastors, itinerant lecturers, and activists with little historical training but a growing audience among conservative Christians. A pioneer among them was the Californian amateur historian of early America, Verna Hall (1912–1987), a fierce opponent of FDR's New Deal and upholder of Christian values. R. J. Rushdoony was another non-professional in the field who wrote on the Christian basis of American history. Today's foremost Christian revisionists include Mark Beliles and Stephen McDowell, John Eidsmoe (*Christianity and the Constitution*), Gary DeMar (*America's Christian History: The Untold Story*), and David Barton (*The Myth of Separation* and *Original Intent*). Of these, the most prominent is Barton, a major player in the Texas Republican Party and a busy lecturer who has earned himself a place on *Time Magazine*'s list of "25 most influential evangelicals in America."

Barton and his fellow Christian revisionists present a simple, homiletic version of American history. Believing in America's special role, they focus on demonstrating the nation's Christian origins and mission. The parallel between modern America and biblical Israel is fairly obvious. The narrative they advocate is a simple one: the United States was established as a "Christian nation" founded on biblical principles with God's blessing. Over time, however, the American nation gradually betrayed its Christian heritage by departing from biblical fundamentals and embracing secular values.[60] Two of David Barton's chapter headings say it all: "The Way it Was" and "The Way it Is." History becomes a morality lesson showing Christian fidelity followed by secular decline. Religious rightists have no trouble demonstrating the second part of their thesis, i.e. that contemporary America is not faithful to orthodox biblical teaching. Much more problematic is their claim that the United States was shaped and defined by biblical Christianity in the first place.

Christian revisionist historians understand they need documentary evidence to make their case. But given their adherence to a set of unshakeable presuppositions and a "total truth" philosophy, they face the same deficiency faced by defenders of intelligent design: namely, they lack a clear method for determining the admissibility of evidence. They are unable to establish a consistent way of ascertaining facts that does not incorporate the conclusions they seek to draw from them. As with "theistic realists" like Phillip Johnson, no discussion of rules for evidence is ever advanced. Christian historians understandably prefer to adopt Johnson's courtroom approach, where evidence is selected on the basis of whether it validates one's own case and undermines one's opponent's.

Methodology aside, it can hardly be denied that Christian revisionists have shown industry in assembling a mass of Christian-themed data in agreement with their viewpoint. Much of this data consists simply of assorted quotations from documents, speeches, and letters referring to Christianity or testifying to Christian faith. Usually they are the utterances of national heroes or testimony from official decrees. Christian revisionists treat historical statements of this kind with the same kind of reverence they treat passages from their scriptural tradition. In their hands, they become a kind of substitute for sacred text. Efforts to compile Christian data relating to American history actually go back to the last century, fostered by the work of Benjamin Morris and continued in the twentieth century by stalwarts like Verna Hall, already mentioned. The collecting impulse continues today with the work of David Barton and William J. Federer. Barton is perhaps the leading user of attributed quotations to support the idea of a formative Christian nationhood. He calls such statements "organic utterances" that provide "a choir of resounding voices affirming Christianity to be the basis of our nation, government, and educational system."[61] Federer carries compilation to new heights with his 845-page reference book, *America's God and Country: Encyclopedia of Quotations* (1999), which contains testimonials to Christianity by hundreds of American notables and 125 pages of microscopic source notes.

Unfortunately, some of the material gathered from these efforts is of questionable veracity. The standard was set early on by Benjamin Morris, the great Christian embellisher par excellence. Since today's Christian history writers often rely on Morris either directly or indirectly, it is not surprising that they show the same casual approach to fact and evidence. The question of veracity became a minor scandal in recent years when some of the quotations disseminated by Barton were suspected of being phony. A number of his "organic utterances" appeared a bit too biblical to be credible, leading scholars to question their authenticity, including one showing James Madison invoking the Ten Commandments. So awkward did this problem become for Barton that in 1995 his organization WallBuilders issued a retraction of sorts, conceding that some twelve of its commonly used quotations were either demonstrably false or at least unconfirmed.[62] Barton's concession, unfortunately, has not prevented the continued deployment of many of these quotes in Christian history books and websites.[63] Barton and his associates, moreover, continue to label other highly questionable materials as authentic, such as the so-called George Washington "Prayer Journal," long ago dismissed by the Smithsonian Institution as a forgery.[64]

The issue of dummy quotations and forgeries aside, the main substantive problem with the "evidence" assembled is that it simply affirms what is already widely accepted, i.e. that Christianity was the predominant religion of settlers in North America. The quotations are, for the most part, a collection of platitudes showing prevailing religious attitudes or making random references to religion in official contexts. Such evidence mostly produces shrugs from seasoned historians. Christian history writers commonly commit the error of not distinguishing between general assertions acknowledging Christianity, which are uncontroversial, and claims for Christianity's role in the formation of the nation and Constitution. Thus, for instance, they offer the Christian affiliation of founding fathers like Washington, Jefferson, and Madison and their occasional utterances on religion as part of the "evidence" for Christian nationhood. Much of the evidence on religious affiliation is ambiguous and can be countered with conflicting evidence. Most importantly, Christian advocates fail to understand that individual religious beliefs prove little about a nation's political identity or the ideas that inspired its creation. It seems almost too obvious to point out that the founders' main political models were Greece, Rome, and England; their theoretical mentors were writers like Locke and Montesquieu; their historical assumptions were based on Whig thought; and their legal standard was the experience-based tradition of British common law.[65] If one surveys the founders' greatest contribution to political theory, *The Federalist Papers*, one finds no mention of Christianity in its pages. Historical claims for the political role of Christianity, let alone biblical or evangelical Christianity, seem guided by presuppositions rather than by facts.

In the rare instances when Christian apologists attempt to show a direct causal linkage between Christianity and the nation's founding, they run into controversy. One piece of quantitative evidence frequently offered to show biblical influence actually shows, on examination, the opposite of what is claimed. Referring to an academic article by Donald Lutz and Charles Hyneman written in 1984,[66] Christian nation proponents point to the frequent citation of the Bible in political literature between 1760 and 1805, based on a quantitative examination of 15,000 printed items, as evidence of its impact on political thinking.[67] What they fail to mention is that most of the biblical citations came from printed political sermons by preachers, many of whom were offering expedient religious justifications for the War of Independence.[68] Authors writing serious discourses on politics and nation building, by contrast, generally found the Bible of little or no use. Indeed, in the crucial period between 1787 and 1788 when the Constitution was being discussed, pro-Constitution writers cited the Bible in their writings not even once (anti-Constitution writers cited the Bible occasionally)![69]

At the center of all attempts to prove a "Christian nation" thesis are the two documents that stand at the core of the American canon, the Declaration of Independence and the U.S. Constitution. Both, however, present major challenges for Christian revisionists. While neither document shows hostility to Christianity, both convey a lofty neutrality on the subject of religion and concentrate on human goals. To fit them into a Christian framework, biblical revisionists try to take ownership of the texts by seizing on fine points and ignoring counterevidence. In the case of the Declaration, they cite several of its well-known appeals to the Almighty (e.g. "Nature's God," "Creator," "Supreme Judge") as evidence of the Signers' biblical predilections.[70] The problem is that such expressions are terms commonly used by deists of the time to refer to a God discoverable through Nature rather than Scripture.[71] Though not inconsistent with Christianity, such words signify a common-ground inclusiveness that is not typical of biblical Christianity or a Christian Worldview approach. As Alan Dershowitz points out, "The omission of any reference to Jesus Christ, or to the specific God of Christianity or of the Bible, is far more significant than the inclusion of generic words that were consistent with non-Christian beliefs."[72]

The U.S. Constitution presents an even larger challenge for Christian history advocates. Drafted in 1787 as an instrument to structure the way "political power was to be exercised,"[73] it lacks any mention of God or Christianity whatsoever. Its preamble begins with "We the people of the United States," and it adheres exclusively to the people's work. A minority of Christian Anti-Federalists, in fact, furiously opposed the Constitution in 1788 for the very reason that it was "godless."[74] They were especially angered by the ban in Article 6 on any religious test for those holding office, the original Constitution's only overt reference to religion. Christian apologists try to compensate for the lack of Christian references in the Constitution by inferring biblical influence on the basis of parallel content, rather than demonstrated cause and effect. Thus, certain revisionists claim that the idea of representative government derives from Deuteronomy 1:13 ("Take you wise men . . . known among your tribes, and I will make them rulers over you") [75] or that the concept of a tripartite division of government comes from Isaiah 33:22 ("for the Lord is our judge, the Lord is our lawgiver, the Lord is our king").[76] No evidence other than vague similarity is given for such linkages. One favorite claim is that the Christian belief in human depravity underlies the Constitution's checks and balances and other restraints on government.[77] Madison's observation in the *Federalist Papers* that men are no "angels" is cited as evidence that his idea of limited powers is influenced by the doctrine of original sin.[78] A fuller examination of Madison's statements in the *Federalist Papers*, however, indicates that his view of human nature is based on reason and observation rather than religious dogma about innate sinfulness. Madison takes the pragmatic position that negative aspects of human nature are balanced by positive ones. Indeed, he states that if humans were completely depraved in the Calvinist sense they would be insufficiently virtuous for self-government.[79]

The revisionists run into similar problems harnessing the Constitution's First Amendment, a key guarantor of religious freedom, to their pro-Christian objectives. The First Amendment's famous religion clause ("Congress shall make no law respecting an establishment of religion or prohibiting the free exercise thereof") carefully balances two related ideas: that of limiting government intrusion into religion and that of retaining full liberty for its practice. The clause's dual nature represents a creative tension that is at the core of America's distinctive contribution to religious liberty. David Barton, however, devotes two books to assailing the balanced reasoning behind the concept. Elevating Christianity to a position of primacy is acceptable, by his reading, as long as it does not involve favoring any single branch of it. Thus he stresses the words "free exercise" in the religion clause, while emasculating the words that precede them, "no law respecting an establishment," by strictly limiting the meaning of "establishment."[80]

Christian revisionists are not limited to verbal parsing, sophistry, or the use of selective facts in their quest for proof of Christian nationhood. They are also fond of citing what amounts to second-hand evidence, i.e., the secondary opinions of individuals with no personal knowledge of the issues under review. Thus the views of notables who are centuries removed from historical events are accepted as gospel when they support Christian nationalist beliefs. Advocates like David Barton and Gary DeMar, for example, focus attention on the assertion of an obscure Supreme Court justice in 1892 that the United States was a "Christian nation" by virtue of its Christian heritage.[81] Justice David Brewer, the son of a Protestant Christian missionary and an ultraconservative on the Court,[82] offered a historical justification for a Christian America drawing from the same kind of Christian documentary "evidence" now popular with today's Religious Right.[83] Brewer shared the opinions of other contemporary religious zealots interested in maintaining the cultural ascendancy of Protestant Christianity,[84] which had become a dominant force in nineteenth century America. His (and their) views of history reflected Protestant anxiety in the face of perceived threats to American identity caused by the immigration of millions of Catholics and Jews to American shores at the end of the century. It is hardly surprising that today's Religious Right, seized by its own set of anxieties, would adopt a similar form of historical nostalgia.

Nostalgia served up as history, of course, always holds a sentimental appeal. Christian revisionist historians need only to package and propagate their patriotic/sacred message for it to have a ready audience. Their public objectives, like those of intelligent design promoters, have both an educational and political focus. In the educational area, they strongly promote Christianized versions of history for use in school curricula at the state level. In Texas, for example, Christian nation advocates collaborating with the Texas Board of Education have been pivotal in reshaping the state's social science studies curriculum. Typical of their alterations are new, amplified claims of Judeo-Christian influence on American history, the downgrading of Jefferson as a political philosopher and the upgrading of John Calvin, and the elimination of any rationale for church-state separation. One of the curriculum's biggest boosters has been David Barton, a member of a panel of "experts" advising the Board.[85]

History revisionists have been active on the national political front as well. The ubiquitous David Barton has been notable among them when not preoccupied in Texas, serving as a Washington publicist and mentor to Republicans. He has an ardent circle of disciples that includes the usual suspects: Michele Bachmann, Rick Perry, Mike Huckabee, and Newt Gingrich, among others. Republican Congressman Randy Forbes of Virginia, another avid Bartonian, has sought to give Barton's theories legitimacy by introducing multiple House resolutions affirming "the rich spiritual and religious history of our Nation's founding," with the enthusiastic backing of the GOP's conservative wing.[86] Typically the resolutions include a long list of "facts" that buttress a Christianized version of history. Forbes' actions are typical of continuing efforts to "correct" the historical record and leave a trail of documents as verification. A small group of historical watchdogs on internet web sites have had their hands full debunking all of the claims.[87]

There is little doubt that Christian revisionists have made headway in advancing their message. At one time, using the term "Christian nation" was considered controversial. When, as recently as 1992, Republican governor Kirk Fordice of Mississippi referred to America as a "Christian nation" at a national conference, his words produced surprise, even shock.[88] His assertion, which received national press coverage, was quickly condemned by leading Republicans and led quickly to an apology by the governor. Even GOP conservatives were aware that the term carried with it a suggestion of exclusivity and intolerance that went down poorly with most Americans. Such was the state of public opinion in 1992. If we turn to today's political landscape, however, we observe a very different climate. Years of promotion and publicity have helped to embolden Christian nationalists and give currency to their views. Republican candidates like Mike Huckabee, John McCain, and Sarah Palin, for example, were able to employ the term "Christian nation" in the 2008 presidential campaign without undue controversy. Popular polls, moreover, suggest that the public has absorbed much of the Christian nationalist message. A poll of some 1000 Americans conducted in 2007 by New England Survey Research Associates revealed that 65 percent of respondents believed that "the nation's founders intended the U.S. to be a Christian nation."[89] Although we have no earlier baseline against which to compare these figures, and even if we concede some ambiguity attached to the words, the poll indicates how successfully the theme has been planted in the popular mind.

Christian rightists are well aware of the ways history can be used to buttress an agenda.[90] By portraying today's society as untrue to its sacred traditions, they can call it illegitimate and justify dramatic ways to transform it. The approach argues for a return to something lost, to an original purpose or "original intent" as construed by God's interpreters. The authors of *America's Providential History* underscore the sacred connection between past and present: "Today we are experiencing the fruit of secularism," they state. "To see Godly change occur in America, we must infuse the Faith of our Fathers into the life of our country."[91] How Christian worldviewers actually understand "godly change," however, is a key question. What sort of Christian America do they envision and how does it align with their worldview goals? For answers to these questions, we turn to their approach to government, economy, and law.

8

THE COMING KINGDOM

Christian Libertarianism and the War on Babel

American conservatives have always scorned what they call big government: so much so, that they have created their own distinctive way of disparaging it. Depending on the situation, the government is made to seem like it is run by faceless bureaucrats, know-it-all experts, or jack-booted federal agents. It is accused of having its hands on the people's money, their guns, and their lives. And the best way of dealing with it is to starve it or, in the words of conservative sage Grover Norquist, reduce it to a size where it can be drowned in a bathtub. The language employed is pungent and plainly secular.

More recently, however, anti-government rhetoric has taken a turn in a new direction. Thanks to the growing influence of the Christian Right, it has assumed unmistakably religious overtones. Increasingly, secular government is portrayed as a profane, evil force working for ungodly purposes. Government is no longer offensive just to human beings, but to God himself. The new religious mode of expression has become especially evident since the emergence of the Tea Party movement during the Obama years. Some of the utterances of Tea Party leaders provide lucid examples of it. Tea Party candidate Sharron Angle broke the ice in her 2010 senate campaign when she condemned the Obama administration for violations of the First Commandment (i.e., violations of the words "Thou shalt have no other gods before me"). "We have become a country entrenched in idolatry," she stated, "and that idolatry is the dependency upon our government."[1] Republican presidential hopeful Rick Perry expressed the issue as an either-or-choice between God and government: "Who do you worship?" he asked an audience in 2010. "Do you believe in the primacy of unrestrained federal government? Or do you worship the God of the universe, placing our trust in him?"[2] Jim DeMint, the recent Senator from South Carolina, expressed the tension with mathematical precision: God and government are inversely related to each other. "I've said it often and I believe it–the bigger government gets, the smaller God gets. As people become more dependent on government, [they become] less dependent on God."[3] Meanwhile, Glenn Beck contributed a biblical perspective by comparing secular government, at least of the sort practiced by President Obama, to the Tower of Babel, the biblical symbol of human overreaching and an object of God's wrath.[4]

The national media has observed such rhetoric with puzzled curiosity, hardly knowing what to make of it. Is one really to understand that God and human government are competing in a zero-sum game for the souls of the people? The notion could easily be dismissed as laughable if there were not some seriously held worldview assumptions underlying it. Human government, according to those assumptions, is an expression of rebellious human autonomy. It is justifiable only if human rulers know their place and confine themselves to serving as God's agents. When civil government involves itself in the social and economic life of the nation or attempts to improve the conditions of the people, it is straying into divine territory. Its actions in these areas are in direct competition with God and not to be tolerated,[5] since God has ordained the way things are for his own reasons. Safety nets, protective legislation, government services, and the like are forms of pandering to the people that increase dependency on government and reduce dependency on, and awe of, God.

While Christian anti-statism of the sort just expressed has surfaced with particular virulence during the first years of Obama's presidency, it is by no means a novel phenomenon in American politics. It actually existed on the political margins during the last decade or so of the twentieth century, when it took on various organizational forms under a libertarian or constitutional banner. The two main expressions of it were Howard Phillips' U.S. Taxpayers Party and the libertarian movement associated with Ron Paul, who has stood on the rightist fringe of the Republican Party for most of his political life. Because the philosophies and platforms of Phillips and Paul give us an insight into the aims of Christian anti-statism, it is useful to examine briefly these two examples.

The U.S. Taxpayers Party (USTP), later renamed the Constitution Party, has received attention in recent years because of its attraction for public figures like Sarah Palin,[6] Tom Tancredo, and others on the right. Established by Howard Phillips in 1992 as a right-wing alternative to the Republican Party, the USTP offered a program emphasizing the Constitution, small government, and biblical law. Phillips, it will be remembered, was one of the Republican operatives behind the formation of the Moral Majority in 1979. A former official under the Nixon administration, Phillips was drawn to radical theology during the late 1970s, influenced in large part by the works of R. J. Rushdoony.[7] Disillusioned with the direction of Republican politics under the first Bush administration, he left the GOP to form the USTP, bringing with him a motley group of Religious Right activists, including Randall Terry, Rus Walton, and Joseph Morecroft. In the presidential contests of 1992 and 1996, the new party was able to appeal to a niche constituency that included anti-abortion zealots, Christian dominionists, and elements of the racist right.

The platform of the 1996 USTP platform shows a direct debt to Christian Reconstructionism. It proposes that the federal government be transformed from an active entity into a shackled one under the guidance and protection of the Almighty. The nation is defined as "a republic under God, rather than a democracy," to be governed by Constitutional law "rooted in Biblical law." The "deadly hand" of today's government and the behind-the-scenes power of "Federal judges and bureaucrats" is roundly denounced. To replace the current system, the document envisions a bare-bones government limited to safeguarding life, liberty, and property. Condemning the federal government's interference in the economy, the document endorses abolishing the IRS, the Federal Reserve, the Department of Education, and other apparently redundant arms of the national government. The gaps left by a receding government are to be filled in the states and localities by God-fearing folks eager to shoulder their responsibilities. [8]

A second manifestation of Christian anti-statism was the libertarian movement espoused by Ron Paul, combining free-market and states' rights theory with a commitment to America's Christian traditions. While sharing much in common with Phillips, Paul was more inclined to promote the anti-statist cause within the confines of Republican conservative doctrine. Paul's staunch views on free markets and limited government are well known. Since the time he entered Texas politics in the 1970s, he was an avid supporter of the conservative monetary theories of Ludwig von Mises, the Austrian doyen of free market theory.[9] Paul advocated policies that would strip the federal government of most of its regulatory power, dramatically shrink its revenue source by eliminating the federal income tax, and abolish "redundant" agencies like the Federal Reserve. On constitutional matters, Paul held to an austere strict constructionism, sharing the small government views typical of his region and viewing any federal action not explicitly condoned by the Constitution as illegitimate.

Because of his primary concern with economic issues, Paul has been more reticent about tying God to politics than Phillips. Nonetheless, Paul makes clear in his writings his belief that government should be more supportive of religion. Defending America's Christian heritage, he accepts Christian rightist rhetoric about a secular "war on religion" conducted by the "Collectivist Left." The Left hates religion because churches "compete with the state for the people's allegiance,"[10] he declares, making use of a familiar theme. In line with his small government philosophy, Paul believes that the best place for government to take a stand in religion's behalf is at the state level. As a congressman, he regularly sponsored legislation to curtail the Supreme Court's jurisdiction over states in matters concerning the First Amendment's religious clause. Without the Court's oversight in this area, states would be much freer to confer unlimited rights and official recognition on Christians while reducing protection for religious minorities.[11] There is no evidence, indeed, that Paul has ever had any qualms about Christian dominance at the state level. Regarding his religious attitudes, it is perhaps no coincidence that one of his long-standing mentors–a former aide during Paul's first term to Congress in 1976–was Christian Reconstructionist Gary North. To be sure, North and Paul were drawn together more by their shared economic convictions than their views on the Book of Deuteronomy. Nonetheless, Ron Paul seems at least comfortable with some of the biblical assumptions held by North and others. Campaigning for the 2012 Republican presidential nomination in Iowa, for example, he took to quoting verses from Deuteronomy in support of sound monetary policy.[12]

For years it was possible to dismiss Ron Paul and Howard Phillips as fringe elements with little relevance to contemporary American politics. But what was fringe in the 1980s and 1990s is no longer so. One has only to look at the evolution of the Texas Republican Party to see how Christian Worldview made it into the mainstream. The process began when the Christian Coalition organized at the grassroots level in Texas to replace traditional GOP party leaders with pro-Bible conservatives. In 1993, it engineered a minor coup by electing Steven Hotze, a dominionist member of the Coalition on Revival, to the influential Houston Republican Party chairmanship. In 1994, with further grassroots support, it replaced the state GOP chairman with another one sympathetic to a more religious agenda. At this point, the victors abruptly adopted a pro-Christian posture, changing party rules that had once shown tolerance for all religious viewpoints. Christian rightist positions began to appear in party platforms, and GOP candidates were required to support them or risk being repudiated. In later contests for the legislature and State Board of Education, religiously vetted candidates were prompted to challenge and replace GOP moderates, often in bitter, internecine battles. In just a few years, the profile of the Texas GOP had changed dramatically.[13] David Barton, who took over vice-chairmanship of the party in 1997, became its public face.

In its official pronouncements, the Texas GOP combines elements of Ron Paul's states-rights libertarianism and Howard Phillips' Christian constitutionalism. Its platforms of the last decade display a vigorous anti-statism interpersed with Christian nationalist rhetoric. The Texas platform of 2012 proposes numerous ways to shrink or handcuff the federal government, including the familiar list of government downsizings and revenue retrenchments. And it renounces big government on a world scale by shrinking the United States' international duties and rescinding its membership in the United Nations. Meanwhile, calling America a Judeo-Christian nation, the platform rejects the "myth of separation of church and state" and supports "God-ordained" truths on social and cultural and social matters. Making use of Christian Worldview concepts, it justifies its attack on "humanistic" government in terms reminiscent of Kuyper and Rushdoony, under which civil government is rigorously stripped of its powers over the other spheres of society and is confined largely to its law enforcement role. Hence the platform supports "limited civil government jurisdiction under the natural laws of God, and repudiates the humanistic doctrine that the state is sovereign over the affairs of men, the family, and the church."[14]

The religiously infused libertarianism of the Texas GOP may not be typical of what all or even most Republicans endorse today. Nonetheless, the uncompromising approach associated with it has become a common platform of national Republican legislators in the post-Bush era. Righteous hostility to government under a Democratic administration became a driver of the Tea Party protest movement begun in 2009 and a central tenet of the Republican class of 2010. Since their take-over of the House in that year, congressional Republicans have carried their opposition to godless government as far as it can go, repeatedly using the threat of fiscal Armageddon as a fulcrum. Unwilling to focus on the making or modification of policy, an approach that would enable normal political interaction, they have followed an anti-government agenda with no room for deviation. It is a strategy with little subtlety or qualification, as Paul Ryan's radical budget proposals, with their bland lack of specificity, attest. For the enemy is apparently not so much this or that program any more, but government in the abstract. In line with the Christian Worldview that nourishes it, the anti-statist platform has become strictly ideological.

Anti-statism, of course, is just one pillar of the governing philosophy embraced by the today's Christian Worldview advocates. Equally important, and complementary to it, is their conviction of the hallowed role of laissez-faire capitalism in securing American freedom. The opposition of Christian rightists to human regulation of the marketplace and their trust in the redeeming activity of "job creators" unencumbered by public accountability have become articles of faith. Their devotion to a liberated capitalism is every bit as strong as their animosity toward a state that might interfere with it. What implications these attitudes have for policy will be addressed in the next section.

Biblical Economics and Biblical Responsibility

Among his many contributions, classical economist Adam Smith bequeathed to posterity one of the more memorable metaphors of economic life, the concept of the "invisible hand." Smith used the metaphor to explain the working of the capitalist economy of eighteenth century England, a country he considered a "nation of shopkeepers." As he saw it, if individuals engage in economic pursuits with no aim other than to enhance their own personal gain, they are led by an invisible hand to promote the interests of society as a whole. He argued that their self-interested efforts, taken together, confer a greater benefit on the social order than would be conferred by an enlightened government or the well-intentioned actions of idealists. The invisible hand of the market ostensibly allows the less fortunate to share in the productivity of the few through overall economic prosperity and increased employment. Smith's thesis challenged the mercantilist economic tendencies of his time, in which national governments sought to influence economic activity in order to bolster national wealth. It was, in a sense, counter-intuitive, because it seemed to outline an economy that enhanced wealth by being unplanned.

Today's Christian rightists wholeheartedly subscribe to Adam Smith's non-interventionist approach. Like him, they believe that markets perform best without the interference of human government. Coincidentally, they also seem to endorse the conceit of an invisible mechanism that lies behind their ideal marketplace. In place of Smith's invisible hand working autonomously, however, they substitute a hand with a more personal touch. They suggest that a higher intelligence upholds, or at least approves of, the implacable laws of the marketplace.

For Gary North, a long-time proponent of a biblically informed economics, the invisible hand is tantamount to the highly purposeful hand of God himself. "The operations of the market," he states, "like the operations of the atom, are ultimately guided by and upheld by God."[15] The laws of supply and demand can be understood as divine enactments sustained "on a full-time basis" by a God who has an ongoing interest in his Creation.

While not all biblical economists of the Christian Right go as far as North in identifying God with the laws of supply and demand, they would all agree that capitalism conforms with a Christian Worldview outlook. Indeed, they generally take a more absolutist approach to laissez-faire capitalism than Smith himself. Adam Smith, it will be remembered, was a child of the Enlightenment who focused on empirical phenomena and the lessons of history rather than revealed truths. While opposed to government interference in the mechanics of the marketplace, he was not an anti-government ideologue. In the final section of his *The Wealth of Nations*, Smith discussed the ways government could make a nation more secure and just through investments in social and economic infrastructure. He argued, for example, that the state should address the negative effects of industrialism by extending education to the poor.[16] Such opinions, progressive for their time, reveal a man aware of the useful role of the state in a dynamic society and economy.

Today's right-leaning biblical economists, by contrast, believe the modern secular state is essentially illegitimate. Much of their basic agenda has its roots in Christian Reconstructionism, which used biblical texts to justify a privatized economy modeled on the ancient system of the Hebrews, as discussed in an earlier chapter. A key assumption of this viewpoint is that private property has sacred underpinnings rooted in biblical principles of stewardship, while government is profane and untrustworthy.[17] In the mid-1980s Christian Worldview advocates formulated an economic platform based on these general tenets.[18] While it lacked the specificity of Rushdoony and North's model, it justified itself in broadly biblical terms. Most Christian rightists since then have supported this template, sometimes with minor adjustments.[19]

The reader is already familiar with the importance biblical conservatives attach to the Dominion Mandate in conveying God's economic expectations for humanity. God requires mankind to take dominion over the earth, namely, to "be fruitful, and multiply, and replenish the earth, and subdue it" (Genesis 1:26–28). He expects humans, acting as his servants, to exercise control not by conquest or theft, but through the individual ownership and use of property, "in line with God's requirements" of course.[20] And throughout much of the Bible, especially in the Book of Proverbs, humans are exhorted to demonstrate thrift, diligence, and enterprise. Biblical economists carry these themes a further step by arguing that human industry is best given scope in an environment devoid of official restraint, one where government plays a minimal role in economic activity. People fulfill their mandated economic roles most dutifully when they are directly responsible to God rather than to government entities.

God's stake in all of this should be self-evident. Planet earth is his special project, and setting humans on a course of fruitful endeavor helps to make that project a success. Through their productive efforts, humans glorify his Creation. But God's concerns extend beyond his role as cosmic architect and engineer. He also serves as supreme judge, concerned about the conduct and fidelity of his creatures. In the eyes of biblical economists, the topic of economy has always been closely allied to questions of morality.[21] Thus how individuals handle their ethical and covenantal responsibilities within the economic framework becomes vital. Economic necessity presents a way for God to measure humans' worthiness as Christians. Because of their natural inclination toward sin and sloth, God provides positive and negative incentives to guide them, bestowing blessings for faithfulness and good management, and withholding them in the event of negligence. The framework is one where individuals either respond positively and succeed, or fail. It presents a simple model in which all are given an opportunity to show biblical responsibility, prove themselves morally worthy, and "work out their salvation."[22]

Biblical responsibility takes on a specific meaning in this God-centered system: it signifies accountability to God and compliance with

God's commands. R. John Rushdoony, whose theology sums up the responsibility ethic in its most exacting form, stresses the idea that "man's primary responsibility is to God" and only secondarily "to his fellow men."[23] Alert to the dangers of human autonomy, he calls for a code of action that demands discipline and strictly conforms to God's laws. The duties it emphasizes focus primarily on the individual and the traditional family, while duties outside of these areas are narrowly constructed. Rushdoony gives voice to this limited view when he condemns stepping beyond the explicit commands of Scripture in the performance of duties. He calls generous acts not directly guided by God's commands examples of "presumptuous responsibility" and scoffs at the idea of attempting to serve as "my brother's keeper."[24] In his view, humanitarians and government agencies that aim to address broad human needs fail to understand the dark side of human nature or to draw distinctions between recipients of aid based on standards of "holiness and righteousness."[25] In sum, Rushdoony rejects outright the modern concept of responsibility, which includes within its scope not just personal duties but also societal ones that welcome, if not require, the participation of state and community.[26]

Today's right-wing advocates for biblical economics generally adhere to the narrow model of responsibility outlined above, focusing on the individual and shunning collective action. They are quick to condemn comprehensive measures taken in behalf of the citizenry and the environment, seeing them as examples of human overreaching. Because modern secular government is usually the agent of last resort in addressing broader problems, it is the main object of their disapproval. Its activity warrants special censure because it conflicts with God's jurisdictional authority. Specifically, it commits the egregious sin of attempting to alter the world as God has presented it. By compensating for the harsh edges of the economic order, an active government short-circuits God's providential mechanics and hinders his will from prevailing as generally intended, that is, on an individual-by-individual basis. Broad attempts to improve conditions are unacceptable since the world's structural inequalities and inconsistencies exist for reasons that conform with God's purposes.[27] The main economic tasks of humans should be limited to glorifying God's Creation through strenuous effort and attending to one's immediate responsibilities.

By offering a righteous stand against government action and casting economic issues in terms of personal responsibility, biblical economics has become a useful tool in the hands of Christian rightists. Because it harmonizes nicely with Republican nostrums about small government and morality, it provides an added justification for a conservative agenda. Two articulate supporters of a biblical approach, Marvin Olasky and E. Calvin Beisner, have been especially prominent in advancing the idea of an unrestricted marketplace in conjunction with a Bible-based concept of responsibility. In recent years these men have focused on social welfare and the environment as fertile areas in which to put God's principles into practice. We turn now to consider their views and advocacy efforts.

Marvin Olasky has long been a key voice in right wing political as well as religious circles. His views have had a lasting impact on Republican policy in areas of social legislation. Raised in a secular Jewish family, Olasky became a young convert to Calvinistic Christianity after a brief flirtation with Marxism. Finding his vocation in journalism, Olasky was determined to use his communication skills to disseminate Christian orthodoxy to the masses. As a professor of journalism at the University of Texas, Olasky became an outspoken advocate of the Christian Right and the author of many books on biblical approaches to modern problems. The book that made his name in conservative circles and catapulted him into the national spotlight, however, was one he wrote on the history and practice of welfare in America: *The Tragedy of American Compassion* (1992). The work accentuates both the evils of state intervention and the merits of a laissez-fair economy under God's watchful eye. Quickly recognizing its usefulness in the welfare debate, Republican House Speaker Newt Gingrich made the book required reading for the newly elected GOP freshmen class of 1994.[28] As its title suggests, the book attempts to offer a kind of post-mortem on American welfare policy. It argues that modern governments have diminished the meaning of personalized compassion through their large-scale attempts to assist the poor and unemployed. Showing nostalgia for a Puritan small-town America that was once supposedly able to handle its poor citizens through community efforts, the author sees federal aid as impersonal and unwieldy. He regards the secular programs of modern government as futile since they do not address the individual's spiritual affliction and are not equipped to teach biblical standards of responsibility.

As with all biblical traditionalists, Olasky begins with the axiom of mankind's innate sinfulness. Humans can do nothing to address the effects of this fundamental condition other than to put themselves on the right side of God through hard work and obedience. By following his commands and putting them into practice, they can benefit from God's bounty and blessing while, at the same time, advancing his earthly kingdom. Personal responsibility, biblically defined, becomes the royal road to approval in the eyes of God.

Given such assumptions, it is no surprise that Olasky takes heed of God's stern requirements when addressing social problems. Believing that any social aid should be modeled on how the Old Testament God would administer it,[29] Olasky holds that those deemed worthy by God's standards should receive merciful treatment while those deemed unworthy should be left to suffer on their own. Negative incentives for the poor, especially the withholding of assistance unless there is unquestioned proof of redemptive behavior, are a standard element of the biblical approach, even though children would be left to suffer for the faults of their parents (God would presumably have his own ways of counteracting the collateral damage). Olasky, like any true Calvinist, has little trouble with the idea that some mortals are naturally destined for heaven and others for hell.[30] His book, in essence, is an argument for *selective* deliverance in the earthly domain. Human government has no business substituting its judgment for God's in such matters. Instead, families, churches, and private charities should be the central actors in the administering of social assistance, since they are presumably more qualified to sift the deserving from the undeserving and better positioned to use their proselytizing skills to turn individuals around. Applying God's rules and preaching about "God's expectations" become means of infusing biblical responsibility in those who have lost their way.[31]

Olasky, of course, is not unique in espousing the cause of personal responsibility, a cause that resonates with people of all political persuasions when stripped of its Calvinistic sermonizing. Liberals as well as conservatives have rightly acknowledged the key role of personal responsibility in ending dependency and enabling people to become contributing members of society. Democrats Jesse Jackson and Patrick Moynihan have been prominent among them. What distinguishes Olasky is his refusal to recognize collective responsibility as a natural or necessary accompaniment of personal responsibility in dealing with entrenched national problems such as this one. His stance is colored by an uncritical assessment of the prevailing economic system. Olasky holds, essentially, that a pure form of capitalism is consistent with what he calls "biblical anthropology."[32] It is in line with what God favors. Capitalism with minimal regulations or government intervention assures, in his view, that humans have the freedom to prove themselves and show their adherence to biblical principles. Olasky says little, however, about the un-level playing field that exists under such a system and the risks citizens confront over which they have little control. Nor does he adequately address the vulnerability of children, who bear no responsibility for the decisions of adults. While hailing old-fashioned methods of private charity, he is silent on the complexities of modern industrial society and the demonstrated inability of local and private organizations to handle large-scale economic problems, made obvious during times of economic distress.

Olasky's views were soon to have an important impact on national policy. His book was a big boost for the GOP's "war on welfare" and contributed to its legislative outcome: the so-called Personal Responsibility and Work Reconciliation Act of 1996, shaped by a Republican Congress and signed into law reluctantly by President Clinton. The Act was ostensibly intended to reform a welfare system that all sides admitted was inefficient and infused with perverse incentives. Unfortunately, theology rather than reason or experience lay behind a major assumption of the Act, i.e. that the simple threat of deprivation would solve the problems of decades. Critics of the program included moderate Democrat Patrick Moynihan and conservative columnist

George Will, who both strongly objected to its punitive measures, undiscriminating approach, and potentially devastating effects on children.[33] The Act pushed single mothers into largely low wage and temporary jobs without considering the adequacy of such jobs for a basic living or the availability of child-care for working mothers.

The new program gave the appearance of achieving some of its goals in its first years. Shortly after passage, the Act's draconian requirements brought about a reduction in federal welfare expenditures and a diminishment of welfare recipients. The booming economy of the late 1990s helped make jobs available for many of them. But in the longer term, the program fell seriously short of achieving a sustainable system that could enable people to climb out of poverty and dependency. Critics viewed it as simply a way of sweeping America's growing economic inequalities under the rug and pushing the problem into the laps of regional authorities with limited resources. Years after the passage of the Act, low-wage jobs fail to make families independent, and inequalities between rich and poor continue to grow.[34]

Calvin Beisner is another key advocate of biblical responsibility, although one who focuses on environmental rather than social policy. Beisner was a founding member of the Coalition on Revival (COR) in the 1980s, and has been a leading economic theorist and apologist for the movement ever since. Most recently, he has served as one of the Christian Right's key spokesmen on the environment. Beisner is founder and national spokesman of the Cornwall Alliance for the Stewardship of Creation, a coalition of orthodox Christians initiated in 2000 with the goal of applying biblical principles to environmental problems.[35] The organization ostensibly endorses "stewardship" over the earth, a principle taken seriously by most Christians. But there is a wide range of interpretation among Christians about what stewardship means in practice. Mainstream Christians and moderate evangelicals generally interpret it to mean much more than nominal oversight. The Evangelical Environmental Network, for example, conducts an active campaign of "creation care" to uphold the sustainability of God's earth, lobbying for action addressing species extinction, deforestation, resource degradation, and climate change.[36] Beisner's Cornwall Alliance, in contrast, rejects this moderate position in favor of one that adheres to a narrow reading of the biblical text. Finding fault with any kind of large-scale conservation efforts, it sees stewardship as personal, local, and limited.

Beisner and his allies would concede that some form of environmental responsibility is needed in the modern developing world. Nonetheless, they hold that their conservative theological principles must govern any approach. As believers in God's Dominion Mandate, they stress at the outset humans' role as producers, resource developers, and populaters. While calling on such subduers of the earth to act as responsible stewards, they downplay the concerns of environmental and wildlife organizations about human-produced problems. Interpreting stewardship in light of ancient maxims about husbandry, they tend to see stewardship in terms of private property management. Their argument is that unleashing "people's natural incentive to care for their own property" addresses almost all problems. Since the Bible is silent on how to deal with broad economic and environmental challenges, biblical economists look to its pages for simpler remedies to simpler problems. The issues they address are generally those susceptible to easy diagnosis, e.g., ones dealing with inadequate sanitation, improper disposal of wastes, and the like. Matters such as multiple-source pollution and global warming, which involve complex causes and indefinite moral responsibility, go far beyond the biblical model. As such, they are glossed over or minimized by traditionalists. To the extent that collective measures can be considered at all, biblical economists like Beisner hold that they must occur "at the most local level possible."[37]

Traditionalists shy away from large-scale public measures for the same reasons Rushdoony did. First, they believe that government actions taken without biblical guidance go beyond the proper limits of responsibility, constituting a form of "autonomy." For example, they would consider efforts to protect certain species from human encroachment or to ban the extraction of oil from sensitive areas as romantic efforts to "deify" nature, [38] a form of modern day paganism. Second, they are convinced that God, as creator and overseer of the cosmos, has provided a reliable system that insulates planet earth from any existential danger. As Beisner recently stated to a congressional committee, "the biblical worldview sees Earth and its ecosystems as the effect of a wise God's creation and . . . therefore robust, resilient, and self-regulating, like the product of any good engineer."[39] Scientific claims of global warming, overpopulation, or species loss are accordingly not only baseless and "greatly exaggerated,"[40] but an implicit affront to the Almighty. Beisner's confidence in God's craftsmanship, based on the analogy of the purposeful intelligent designer rather than on empirical data, becomes a major prop for complacency when he is confronted with systemic threats. As in Olasky's case, theology takes precedence over fact and science, and righteousness trumps demonstrated need.

Their aversion to environmental regulation, of course, makes Christians like Beisner natural allies of industrial polluters and property-rights advocates, not exactly exemplars of enlightened responsibility. The Cornwall Alliance, for example, is closely tied to the oil giants through collaborative networks. Right-wing organizations like the Committee for a Constructive Tomorrow (CFACT), a group heavily funded by Exxon Mobil, regularly work in unison with religious rightists to undermine broadly accepted climate science.[41] The tight relationship between biblical Christians and the anti-regulation lobby is a long-standing one, having begun in the 1990s with collaboration between the Wise Use Movement, a faux populist movement underwritten by industrial interests, and like-minded religious activists.[42] The modern Republican Party, having abandoned its former support of cap-and-trade and climate science, has become an integral part of this anti-environmental network. The policy ramifications were evident during the Bush II administration, which saw the Department of Interior under Gale Norton and Dirk Kempthorne regularly aligning itself with private interests.[43] Today Republican stalwarts in Congress attack environmentalism with culture-war religiosity. The public face of the new attitude is Oklahoma Senator Inhofe of the Environment and Public Works Committee, who augments his environmental "skepticism" with anti-scientific harangues and biblical platitudes. Little is heard about responsibility in that context since social responsibility is the sort the senator knows little about.

The two policy areas just discussed provide clear evidence of how a biblically based responsibility ethic pervades the Republican perspective on economics and society. In recent years this ethic, presented in non-religious language, has undoubtedly worked well for the GOP as an effective justification for privatization and government retrenchment. Because the general theme of responsibility is in tune with values held by virtually all Americans, it is small wonder that in matters involving public belt tightening, the theme has struck a chord that often translates into support for conservative policies. Unfortunately, our two examples suggest that the cost of such policies, if permanently adopted, will likely be severe. They highlight the obvious dangers of a responsibility ethic that is constricted and dogmatic, and show that a refusal to acknowledge the role of collective responsibility in tandem with individual responsibility can lead to a numbing passivity toward the most severe problems, with potentially devastating effects for society and the environment. An ethic that sneers at the idea of "presumptuous responsibility" and condemns autonomy, flexibility, and open-mindedness is hardly a serious prescription for today's challenges.

Law and Theocracy

In July of 2001, an Alabama justice made one of the most startling symbolic statements in American legal history. Chief Justice Roy Moore of the Alabama Supreme Court installed a two and one-half ton granite monument honoring the Ten Commandments in the rotunda of the Alabama State Judicial Building. Justice Moore made it clear from the outset what his purpose was. At the public unveiling of the monument, he declared that the action "mark[ed] the restoration of the moral foundation of law to our people and the return to the knowledge of God in our land."[44] The event was actually a replay of Moore's placement of a similar but smaller display six years earlier in his circuit courthouse in Etowah County, Alabama. This time around, however, Justice Moore was no small-town county judge, but the recently elected Supreme Court Justice for the state of Alabama, a man who had campaigned as the "Ten Commandments Judge" and received wide attention. His installation of the eye-catching block immediately put the issue of separation of church and state in the national spotlight. The ACLU filed suit to have the monument removed, arguing that the monument was an official endorsement of religion in violation of the First Amendment's Establishment Clause. The case (Glassroth v. Moore) was heard in Federal District Court in October, 2002.

As expected, Moore and his legal team attempted to refute the idea that his action violated the Constitution. Their argument was unusually bold, ignoring federal court precedents on church-state matters and evoking Christian nationalist themes to justify Moore's conduct. At the same time, they stressed the innocence of his motives. They argued that rather than endorsing religion, Justice Moore was merely bringing to public notice what was ostensibly self-evident, i.e. that the Ten Commandments were the "moral foundation of American law" and that God was sovereign over the affairs of mankind. Moore's action was simply a form of secular public instruction designed to set the record straight. Moore's lawyers even suggested that he could have gone much further in his instructional activities. In their view, for instance, he had the authority to decorate the courthouse with crosses and similar symbols, adorn the walls of the courtroom with biblical murals, and have proselytizing messages played over the public address system.[45]

These arguments did not much impress the court. Moore's claim of secular motivation is undermined by his own trial testimony, in which he admitted that his purpose was to acknowledge officially the sovereignty of the biblical God "over the affairs of men."[46] His view that the biblical God was a "foundation of legal doctrine" through the traditions of the English common law[47] is simply not supported by historical evidence.[48] Moreover, the official recognition of that God and the official use of biblical symbols, which Moore endorses, are clearly indicative of favoritism toward a specific religious tradition. It legitimizes the Judeo-Christian God's claims vis-a-vis other deities and suggests that all citizens fall under the umbrella of his scriptural pronouncements. The state establishments that Jefferson and Madison found so offensive at the time of the Revolution were timid affairs by comparison. They were religious establishments that gave preferential treatment to a particular Christian denomination, but at least expressed a degree of respect for competitors.

By contrast, the framework favored by Moore and his defenders is modeled more after the theocracies of early Puritan New England, which looked to the Bible as a guide to their lawmaking and stressed religious orthodoxy.

Given the ambitious claims of the defendants, the district court's ruling was a foregone conclusion. It found that Moore's action was unconstitutional by endorsing not just religion in general, but one brand of religion over others. When its decision was confirmed on appeal at the circuit court level in the summer of 2003, Moore was directed to remove the monument. This led to a tense standoff. Taking his orders from a "higher authority" and backed by a core of ardent supporters, Moore refused to comply. The rest is history. The monument was wheeled away, and the Alabama Chief Justice was soon removed from office by a state ethics board for failing to uphold the law.

Moore's campaign to "acknowledge" God, however, cannot be dismissed as the obsession of a lone zealot. While his tactics and timing were a matter of personal choice, his approach to government matches that of most Christian worldviewers, who hold as a matter of course that the God of Scripture is the ultimate sovereign of nations. Rather than a social contract between human beings, they see government as an entity authorized by God and accountable to him. The idea, originally expressed in Romans 13 ("the powers that be are ordained of God") and embraced by traditional Calvinists, is a central component of Christian Worldview.[49] While this notion of divine authorization conforms readily with seventeenth century Puritan ideas of government, it has little in common with the principles outlined in the American Constitution some 150 years later. In 1789 it was not God, but "We the people" who "ordained" and "established" America's constitutional system as stated clearly in the Constitution's preamble.[50]

The will of the people, however, has not always sat well with the supporters of God's earthly sovereignty. In their eyes, the people's prerogatives are secondary to God's. Indeed, the idea of putting God at the apex of the political system has appealed to the orthodox in all eras of American history. The original authors of the U.S. Constitution had just finished their labors, for example, when Calvinist clergymen mounted an attack upon it for having omitted any reference to God. They especially assailed the Constitution for its famous Article VI, which forbids any religious test for those seeking federal office. In the state conventions, numerous constitutional opponents (anti-Federalists) clamored to add changes to the text that would explicitly acknowledge God. Ultimately, of course, their efforts were defeated by those supporting a religiously neutral document.[51]

Even after the ratification of the Constitution by the states, a small number of religious holdouts continued to critique the work of the Founders. In the ninteenth century, some seized upon America's growing sectional crisis as evidence of God's displeasure with America's "atheistic" Constitution. The American Civil War brought these feelings to a head, at which time defenders of biblical Christianity, especially conservative Presbyterians, began a major effort to insert theistic wording into the Constitution's preamble. Organizing under the name of the National Reform Association in 1863, they proposed an amendment acknowledging God as the "source of all authority and power in civil government" and Jesus Christ as "Governor among the Nations."[52] Needless to say, the organizers were unsuccessful in garnering enough support to see their amendment passed. Still, the efforts of the National Reform Association continued undaunted over some 80 years, eventually petering out at the end of World War II as God's supporters turned their attention to America's Pledge of Allegiance and other vehicles for expressing official reverence towards the Almighty.

In more recent years, conservative Christians have embraced a new strategy for advancing God's authority. They have looked for ways of establishing proof of his hidden presence and influence in America's constitutional origins. One of the popular ways of accomplishing this was to stress the "original intent" of founders and lawmakers, and then to construe that intent in biblical Christian terms. As already discussed, religious rightists like David Barton promoted this sort of interpretation, reframing American history for popular audiences. Still others delved directly into the history of the law itself, hoping to be able to claim that biblical morality and notions of divine sovereignty were imbedded in Anglo-American legal traditions. One of the key spokesmen for this legal approach was none other than Roy Moore's chief attorney in the Ten Commandments case, Herbert Titus. Titus, an avid Christian constitutionalist, has come to play a central role in advancing the Religious Right's biblical approach to the law.

Ironically, Herb Titus began his career doing the devil's work as an attorney for the ACLU in the 1960s. He continued in that line until experiencing a dramatic conversion to Christianity in 1975. Studying with Francis Schaeffer and then finding himself drawn to the radical ideas of Christian Reconstructionism, Titus came to believe that the Bible was foundational for American constitutional law. In the late 1980s, he was hired by Pat Robertson as Dean of Regent University Law School, where he actively promoted a biblically oriented curriculum.[53] His growing reputation as a Christian constitutionalist served him well, earning him a place on the U.S. Taxpayers Party ticket in 1996 as the vice-presidential running mate of Howard Phillips.

In his work as writer and educator, Titus took on the challenging task of trying to demonstrate Christianity's role in the development of British and American law. He sought to show that the law at the time of the American Revolution and for at least a century afterward reflected a biblical perspective. The American Founders and those who came after them, Titus argues, assumed that behind all human law were "laws of nature" that embodied God's will as taught in the Bible.[54] Their supposed assumptions were ostensibly buttressed by the views of William Blackstone in his popular legal treatise, the *Commentaries on the Laws of England*. Mr. Titus holds up Blackstone (1723–1780) as a model of jurisprudence, both for his own time and for ours. Blackstone was an eighteenth century English Tory and strong proponent of the existing order who apparently held that the principles underlying the English common law were God-given and unchanging. According to Titus, this Blackstonean approach prevailed in American legal practice and education with beneficial effects until some time after the Civil War, at which time it began to be replaced by a secular approach. Increasingly law was seen as a human product that evolved over time, and a new empirical method, i.e., the case method, was introduced to teach it in American law schools.[55] These trends, Titus argues, led to the modern-day removal of God from courtrooms and legislatures and the consequent loss of public confidence in the American judicial system.

Titus' take on legal history is questionable, to say the least. One well-known conservative scholar shows that Blackstone was actually more a legal relativist than an absolutist, a practical student of legal history who understood that most law was evolving and a function of social norms.[56] In spite of his references to God in the introduction to the *Commentaries*, Blackstone the scholar showed scant interest in the law of the Bible, devoting almost all of his attention to Greece, Rome, and other pagan societies.[57] As a jurist, he is best described as a legal positivist, supporting the preeminent law-making authority of a human entity, namely the British Parliament. His modern adulators understandably gloss over the fact that he was a firm supporter of Parliament's authority over the American colonies, and would surely have viewed it as overriding any divinely endowed "rights" of the colonists (he left Parliament, however, six years before the Declaration of Independence). And while Blackstone's legal views clearly influenced American law after the Revolution, they hardly instilled the unchanging divine principles that Titus claims.[58] In spite of all this, Titus has promoted without embarrassment his simplistic portrayal of Blackstone as a biblical conservative and champion of legal absolutes. This portrait, which conforms nicely with Christian Worldview orthodoxy, has been embraced by Christian rightist intellectuals.

Bolstered by Blackstonean assumptions, Christian constitutionalists have worked strenuously to push American constitutional law in a direction more congenial to their views. Far from marking an end to the fight, the litigation over Justice Moore represented the opening volley. Following Moore's removal from the bench, the Religious Right quickly elevated the ex-justice to the status of martyr and used the "Ten Commandments case" as a key exhibit in an attempt to limit federal judicial authority. Its main targets were the human judges who, we are told, placed themselves above God in their adherence to the principle of church-state separation and the modern understanding of the Constitution. Socially conservative Republicans in the House and Senate, aiming to shield God and religion from human oversight, explored the utilization of an obscure clause of the Constitution, located in Section 2 of Article III, which gave Congress the power to make "exceptions" to the court's appellate jurisdiction. Although the clause had never been invoked for anything but minor jurisdictional applications in the past, it was advanced in this case to negate the Supreme Court's jurisdiction over one of the prime cornerstones of America's liberties, the religion clause of the First Amendment. The vehicle for this bold strategy was a piece of national legislation called the Constitution Restoration Act (CRA).

The CRA is a striking example of the scope of the Religious Right's political objectives. Drafted specifically for the Republican leadership by Titus and Moore, the legislation limits federal court jurisdiction in cases where state and local officials have invoked God as the ultimate source of authority. It fully shelters such divine appeals, and any implied endorsement of biblical Christianity they include, from federal judicial review. Actions by state officials like Justice Moore would be made acceptable practice, and religious minorities with complaints would be stripped of protection under the U.S. Constitution. At the very least, the bill would throw into confusion whole areas of constitutional law dealing with the powers of different branches of government and the separation of church and state.

Such potential for mischief, however, hardly deterred congressional Republicans from embracing the CRA when it was introduced in 2004. With strong Religious Right support, the legislation actually passed the Republican-led House, and was popular enough in the Senate to gain the support of powerful senators like Trent Lott, Sam Brownback, and Lindsay Graham.[59] Although the bill eventually died in the Senate in the absence of a filibuster-proof Republican majority, further efforts to protect the "public acknowledgement" of God are likely if Republicans take full control of Congress. The Supreme Court would no doubt weigh in on any such legislation if it passed, enhancing the possibility of a major showdown between branches of government and raising the threat of a constitutional crisis. Ultimately, the secular identity of the United States could be put in jeopardy, made vulnerable to a legislative end-run around the Constitution, with not even a nod to the constitutional amendment process.

What would happen if acts of religious establishment at the state level were no longer subject to federal court review? In the event of such a development, it is quite possible that islands of theocracy would begin to emerge, unchecked, within America's borders. Legislators in scattered statehouses across the nation, generally in "red" states of the south and west, would be tempted to move quickly to recognize the God of the Ten Commandments as the ultimate source of law. Following that, official acknowledgements of God, Christian oaths for office-holders, and government-sponsored religious displays would soon be the order of the day. State officials could easily require Christian prayer in public schools and the recognition of God in classrooms, science labs, and at sporting events. Judges might soon be interpreting law with reference to Scripture and encouraging juries to do likewise when deliberating on cases, assuring that punishments would be more consistent with biblical standards of justice. Theocracy in principle, if not in name, could become prevalent in large swaths of the country.[60]

Nothing better reflects the authoritarian core of the Christian Worldview than the sort of theocracy implicit in Titus and Moore's misguided legislation. Whether state or federal, the Ten Commandments regime it would seem to favor makes the jealous, Old Testament God the symbol of ultimate authority and makes obedience to his commands a civic ideal. The Commandments that would presumably be engraved in courthouse foyers and plastered on public school classroom walls are defined, to a large extent, by the stark pronouncements of Commandments One and Two, the biblical God's demands for exclusive recognition. The sentence "Thou shalt have no other gods before me" exemplifies the First Commandment, while "Thou shalt not bow down thyself to them [i.e. the images of other gods]" illustrates the Second. These explicit renunciations of the concept of religious freedom are accompanied by a gratuitous display of God's vengeful justice at the tail end of Commandment Two: "I . . . am a jealous God, visiting the iniquity of the fathers upon the children unto the third and fourth generation" (Exodus 20:5), a statement that evokes images of collective retribution, typical of totalitarian regimes. Such calls for submission, religious conformity, and vengeful justice describe to perfection the creed of the theocrats who hope one day to shape the government Americans live under.

Needless to say, if such tendencies were allowed to go unchecked, they would alter the face of America's open and pluralistic democracy. Official neutrality in religious matters, the United State's great contribution to religious freedom as enshrined in the First Amendment, would effectively be repudiated. A form of biblical Christianity would be recognized as the dominant religion, trumping all other religions and value systems and placing American government in a theistic shell. The Bible would take its place next to the Constitution as a guide for governance, while God's intentions would become the plaything of politicians. Most readers of this book can hope that such developments will never be accepted by a majority of Americans.

9

A PROPER DIAGNOSIS

9/11 was a wake-up call for Americans. Clearly the attack showed how vulnerable and how inseparably linked with the rest of the world America was. The U.S. could no longer exist as if it were a gated community among nations. In a more immediate sense, it provided a grisly lesson on the dangers of religious fanaticism. It demonstrated the power of deep resentments, both religious and political, to push individuals toward desperation and extremism. It showed how a set of tenets, incorporating those resentments, could motivate individuals to do the unthinkable, to throw their lives away in attacking what they considered a vile enemy. In a baptism of fire, Americans suddenly became intimately acquainted with the ideology of Islamic fundamentalism. For reasons of self-interest, if for no others, they soon realized that they needed to come to grips with that ideology and combat it effectively.

In spite of their first-hand experience of Islamic extremism, however, Americans have spent little time considering a similar kind of extremism within their own borders. In some ways this internal form of the disease, while not as obvious or dramatic, is arguably as insidious as the external kind. The impact of homegrown religious extremism is evidenced, not in sensational acts of destruction, but in the gradual transformation of our body politic into a cultural war zone. Instead of airplanes, its preferred weapon is inflammatory rhetoric, which it uses to attack core values of our democracy, including pluralism, tolerance, and mutual respect. The extremism of the Christian Right, expressed in the language of its distinctive ideology, has been with us now for some 30 years and shows little sign of receding. While we have examined its ideology here in the light of its own cultural background, it is useful to remind ourselves that it shares many traits with its foreign Islamic cousin. Christian Worldview is an outgrowth of Christianity in much the same way that Islamic fundamentalism is an outgrowth of Islam. Both ideologies demonstrate a remarkable alienation from the world around them, and both react to that world by steering their traditional faiths in new and militant directions. It is striking, but not really surprising, that their thought processes are so much alike.

Certainly a key characteristic of Christian Worldview and Islamic fundamentalism is their dedication to a form of jihad or struggle, as mentioned in Chapter Six. Both thought systems see the world as a dualistic theatre of conflict where there exist no shades of gray and where civilization hangs in the balance. They each externalize the idea of an intractable enemy, often identified as the agent of Satan, and define it in apocalyptic terms. Both harbor a keen sense of resentment, picturing themselves as victims of a mighty conspiracy aimed at the heart of their respective religions. Only the conviction that God and absolute truth are on their side sustains their belief in ultimate victory.

The two ideologies, to be sure, define the immediate enemy in different terms. Sayyid Qutb (1906–1966), often considered the most influential ideologue of radical Islamism, pictures the enemy as the "Zionist, Crusader and imperialist," i.e., those worldly forces most responsible for humiliating and undermining Islamic societies. Such forces represent an alien Western civilization at odds with the sacred values of Islam.[1] The corresponding Christian ideologue sees the enemy generally in domestic rather than foreign terms. The enemy is personified by the existing cultural and political elite, the dedicated followers of humanism, Darwinism, and New Age philosophies, who seek to trivialize and undermine the Christian religion. Taken in the abstract, however, the ultimate enemy for both ideologies is the same. It is secularism and the modern spirit. The core of secularism for all fundamentalists is the "rebellion of man against God."[2] Secular society exemplifies this rebellion because it largely accepts the validity of "man-centered values" and denies the absolute truth of an all-powerful God.[3]

Because they are both "man-centered," reason and science are natural targets for fundamentalists of all stripes. Islamist extremists, like

Christian Worldviewers, deem any knowledge filtered through the mind to be unreliable and consider rational argument futile. Faith, informed by God's revelation, is the only reliable guide to truth. For both Islamists and Christian presuppositionalists, religious belief is clearly a necessary precondition for true knowledge.[4] To understand the real world, one must reject the worldview of human science, which talks of material causes and effects in rational language. Instead, one must understand the cosmos as a living product of the Creator. Not the laws of causality, but the God who creates those laws by an act of will, is what governs the universe. In the words of Sayyid Qutb, "Nothing happens in this world without God's authority."[5] His view of God's providential role is little different from that of Christian Worldview.

Both fundamentalist outlooks essentially merge religion, politics, and society into a single "totalistic" ideology, blending sacred with secular. The sacralization of worldly activities, indeed, has always been a central factor in both the Calvinist and Islamic outlook. God is the pole star around which one is required to live one's earthly life, while human authority is meant to be limited and accountable to God.[6] In both ideologies, civil government risks losing its legitimacy if it is not submissive to God's moral law. Finally, in order to provide legitimacy for their God-centered agendas, each ideology looks to a golden age in the not too distant past as a model for its ideal order. While the Christianist sees it in the image of the Founding Fathers donned in Christian robes, the Islamist envisions it in the idea of the Ottoman Caliphate, the empire that ruled and united the world's Muslims for some 500 years.[7]

Obviously, Religious rightists are uncomfortable with any analysis that lumps them with the assassins of September 11. When the *Economist* came out with an issue warning of the dangers of religious extremism wherever it might appear in the world, including the United States, Christian worldviewers like Chuck Colson bristled. Colson rejected any comparison of American religionists with foreign extremists, arguing that American Christians did not resort to "political violence,"[8] as he put it. Colson overlooks the fact that elements of his own movement are indeed guilty of violence, most notably the bombings of clinics and assassinations of abortion providers. The killing of Dr. George Tiller in

2009 is but the latest example. Although such selective assassinations may not match the record of Islamic fundamentalists, they amount to a form of what most people call terrorism, associated with continuous threats against medical personnel and accompanied by internet "wanted" postings and death decrees.

In spite of its controversial history, the Religious Right refuses to see itself as a source of dysfunction in today's society. On the contrary, it prefers to portray itself as a force for truth that has been unjustly persecuted and ostracized. In its view, Christianity has been excluded from the "public square" in the name of separation of church and state. Richard Neuhaus, a conservative Lutheran pastor who later converted to Catholicism, was the originator of this theme back in the 1980s. Even after his death, his arguments continue to frame America's present-day debates about the role of religion in society. Neuhaus blamed modern secularism for the "nakedness" of the public square. Like his allies on the Religious Right, he saw secularism as an ominous trend characterized by anti-religious antipathy and judicial activism.[9] Secularist values produced, in his opinion, an amoral political culture resulting in a vacuum at the center of American public life.[10] Neuhaus contended that this vacuum needed to be filled by religion in the form of a rejuvenated orthodox Christianity. He evoked the image of a "sacred canopy" that would provide an overall moral framework for society and offer a "transcendent" point of reference.[11]

Such arguments, which resonate with conservative Christians, have gained wide acceptance in the culture at large. Part of their allure can be attributed to the adroitness of Neuhaus' metaphors. Thus the "naked public square" vividly suggests the idea of something stripped of what it has a natural right to be clothed with. Who, after all, could be against allowing religious voices to be fully heard in public life? Aren't such voices entitled to free rights of expression like everyone else? It would seem, however, that the proponents of a more religious public square protest a bit too much. Can one seriously claim that religion and its concerns are really banned from the public forum? Politicians freely advance religious views, hold prayer rallies in stadiums, and enlist religionists in articulating platforms and policy. Religious viewpoints are openly expressed on the airwaves, in the workplace, in the military, and in the public schools.[12] To be sure, some religious symbols are prohibited from official venues, but only to guarantee a level playing field for all religions and to prevent religious majoritarians from securing official recognition. In sum, secularism is hardly the gendarme at the public gate that conservative religionists would have us believe.

A second metaphor, the so-called "sacred canopy," suggests the image of a tent under which religiously based values would serve as a moral guideline for most citizens. Surely, however, this is a fanciful notion in our changing world. The danger of claustrophobia under such a tent is strikingly revealed when Neuhaus has it take the form of a biblical value system that would bring "all institutions and belief systems . . . under judgment," meaning the judgment of the wrathful Old Testament God.[13] By most assessments, Neuhous' canopy would have difficulty accommodating the views of most Christians, let alone most citizens. It would privilege the biblical God's moral pronouncements while devaluing alternative moral points of view, challenging the very idea of a democracy dedicated to freedom of speech and conscience.

Neuhaus attempts to strengthen his argument for a robust Christian role in national life by citing historical opinion and evidence. He refers, for instance, to Alexis de Tocqueville's testimony on Christianity's central place in American life.[14] He reminds us that the French commentator saw religiously based values as "points of reference for public moral discourse." Those values not only underlay the everyday American "construction of reality," but inspired movements in behalf of social justice, such as the cause of abolition, and most recently, civil rights.[15] He hails Martin Luther King as an example of the religious leader who, in recent times, put Christian values to use in a just cause. He even makes parallels between Martin Luther King and Jerry Falwell, hailing their similar "appeal to religiously based moral values."[16]

History shows, however, that Tocqueville and King practiced a different species of Christianity than the one promoted by today's Religious Right. The benign religion observed by Tocqueville bears little resemblance to the doctrinaire creed that would put believers and nonbelievers alike under the judgment of a biblical God. Tocqueville held a traditional, non-political view of religion, believing that its salutary influence on society was exerted through customs and "mores."[17] He pointed out that when it became involved in politics, its beneficial influence and very existence as an independent entity were undermined.[18] Nor is muscular religion in the public sphere at all comparable to the inclusive religion of Martin Luther King, whose outlook was pluralistic and ecumenical: pluralistic because he acknowledged the worth of those he disagreed with and saw them as reachable; ecumenical because he recognized that people of diverse religions and secular backgrounds could share and work for the same ideals. It is significant that two of King's main spiritual guides, Gandhi (Hindu)and Thoreau (transcendentalist), were non-Christian. King, of course, used his religion to address current issues of civil rights, justice, and peace, and sought to influence public opinion and the actions of politicians. But, like Tocqueville, he was sensitive to the dangers of mixing religion and politics. King refused to align himself with establishment forces and had no interest in seeking power or asserting it over others. By speaking truth to power and often finding himself the victim of power, he never lost his integrity as a religious leader. The same can hardly be said for the politically connected leaders of today's Christian Right.

As shown in earlier chapters, the Religious Right today behaves more like an ideological party attempting to enforce a dogma than a religious movement simply advancing its point of view in the public square. With obvious political skill, it has ridden a wave of conservative Christian discontent and leveraged it to attain a position of enviable national power. Having successfully infiltrated one of America's two major political parties and imposed much of its ideological agenda upon it, it now poses a genuine threat to America's pluralist traditions.

The Christian Right, to be sure, has not gone unopposed. Supporters of a different kind of America have spent years in the trenches in defense of abortion rights, church-state separation, fact-based science, and other major issues, seeking to hold the line against right-wing pressure to turn back the clock. While exhausting and time-consuming, these efforts have often proven fruitful as well, resulting in the breaking of new ground. Major progress, in particular, has been shown in the matter of gay rights, which Christian traditionalists have fought vociferously. Gay people can now serve openly in the military, marry legally in many states, and count on greater security in workplaces. These substantial gains over a short period of time have not happened by chance. They have occurred because affected groups did their homework, took the initiative, and made it clear that they were being deprived of key rights for specious reasons and that their cause was just. They faced down religious rightist propaganda and showed that they could fight and discredit it. The fight, of course, is far from over.

Such lessons should not be lost on those looking for effective ways of challenging the Religious Right and its agenda. In this author's opinion, defenders of our open system need to expose and dissect fully the movement's ideology. As stated earlier in this book, for all the bluster of its advocates, the Christian Worldview is highly vulnerable to critique. Its value system is dogmatic, intolerant, and counter to America's historic commitment to rights and freedoms. Its attacks on a long list of enemies in the name of God and antithesis have no place in a heterogeneous democracy. While it hides behind the language of religious freedom, its actions betray its attachment to Christian supremacy, its contempt for minority religions, and its desire to impose its version of truth on the whole of society.

Up until now, the Christian Right has made every effort to recast America's values in ways that confirm its absolutist assumptions. It has adroitly used language and rhetoric to make it seem like secular civilization, rational thinking, and open-mindedness are fatally flawed. Level headed Americans need to retake the initiative by unmasking these premises and redefining the issues at stake. Secularism is not hatred of religion, pluralism is not anarchy, tolerance is not indulgence, autonomy is not rebellion. Culture war is not the norm, and truth is not the possession of any single creed or point of view. Instead of a naked public square, we need to speak of our open public square. Instead of a sacred canopy, we should speak of the freedom to disagree on ultimate things. Rather than ungodly government, we should speak of the people's government. In sum, by resetting the parameters of the debate, we can argue forcefully for what we stand for.[19]

Today we are confronted with a novel kind of movement that focuses on bogus enemies and offers radical solutions to overcome them. Setting the agenda for much of our public discourse, it has sucked oxygen out of our political system and contributed to cultural conflict. The mainstream media and liberal opinion-makers, unfortunately, have mostly treated the Religious Right as a nuisance, an unruly distraction. They have broadly underestimated its long-term danger to civil society. As in the case of any dysfunctional phenomenon, what is desperately needed is a proper diagnosis, followed by a commitment to act. This book, together with the efforts of other critics, attempts the first of these steps in the hopes of facilitating the second. It asks Americans urgently to examine and confront something that is alien to most of them: an organized political movement driven by an absolutist ideology. The time for exposing the full nature of the Christian Right and refuting its worldview is long past due.

Glossary

AMILLENNIALISM
A disbelief in the future establishment of a millennial kingdom as predicted in biblical prophesy.

ANTITHESIS
A central concept of Neo-Calvinism, holding that within every individual and every society there exists a core conflict between light and darkness, especially between the tendency to be faithful to God and the tendency to rebel against him.

APOLOGETICS
A branch of theology whose purpose is to defend Christianity and Christian doctrine through the use of argument.

AUTONOMY
A term used by Neo-Calvinists and Reconstructionists to characterize human rebellion against God. It literally conveys the meaning of "living by one's own law."

BABEL
The city referred to in Genesis where humans built a famous tower to celebrate their unity and achievement. The project was halted by God who, viewing it as an expression of human over-reaching, scattered the city's inhabitants to the corners of the earth and confused their tongues.

BIBLICAL ECONOMICS
A branch of economics that is ostensibly founded on biblical tenets. It is often identified with the ultra laissez-faire economics advanced by Reconstructionists like Gary North.

CALVINISM
The theology of John Calvin and his followers, centered on the idea of an all-powerful God, the moral and cognitive depravity of human beings, and the doctrine of predestination (the predetermination by God of the fate of human souls after death).

CHARISMATICS
Christians who engage in and experience "gifts of the spirit," such as spiritual healing and speaking in tongues. In this respect they are similar to Pentecostals, although usually belong to mainstream denominations.

CHRISTIAN RECONSTRUCTIONISM
A theology developed by R. John Rushdoony and his followers in the 1960s and '70s that calls for replacing the secular order with one based on biblical law.

CHRISTIAN REVISIONIST HISTORY
A version of history that emphasizes the role and significance of biblical Christianity. In the case of the United States, Christian revisionists offer arguments for the nation's biblical Christian origins, God's providential role at key moments, and the nation's modern decline under secular influence.

CHRISTIAN RIGHT
A social and political movement of conservative evangelical Christians begun in the late 1970s calling for an America faithful to biblical principles.

CHRISTIAN WORLDVIEW
A way of perceiving the world that is based on a biblically Christian point of view, at least according to its advocates. Founded on Calvinist and Neo-Calvinist doctrine, it makes unique claims to truth and accuracy. As understood further by Christian rightists, it shares no common ground with non-Christian worldviews and offers a comprehensive agenda for transforming the socio-political order.

CREATION
God's productive acts as described in the first book of Genesis. Also used to refer to the the planet earth and its inhabitants when understood as the special object of God's attention.

CULTURAL MANDATE. See DOMINION MANDATE.

Glossary

DOMINION MANDATE
God's command to humans in the first book of Genesis to be fruitful, multiply, subdue the earth, and have dominion over every living thing.

DOMINION THEOLOGY. See DOMINIONISM.

DOMINIONISM
A theology that interprets the Dominion Mandate as a mandate specific to Christians and that calls on them to assert control over all sectors of national life.

EPISTEMOLOGY
The study or theory of the grounds, limits, and reliability of knowledge.

EVANGELICALS
Christians who believe in the uniqueness of the Bible as a guide to life and have a highly personal faith in the transforming power of Jesus Christ.

EVIDENTIALISM
The method of argument utilized in traditional Christian apologetics. It assumes that evidence and logic are sufficient to make a convincing case for the truth of Christianity.

FUNDAMENTALISM
The belief in the literal truth of one's sacred texts and the commitment to an anti-modernist form of religion. It is best known in Christian and Muslim forms.

HUMANISM
In its modern form, a philosophy that rejects the supernatural, endorses the use of reason, and stresses self-realization and the dignity of the individual.

IDEOLOGY
An integrated package of doctrines that finds expression in a socio-political program.

KINGDOM NOW
A charismatic movement begun in the 1980s under the leadership of Earl Paulk holding that Christians should bring about the Kingdom of God on earth now rather than waiting for Christ's return. It maintains that Christians should exercise dominion over all of society.

LAWS OF NATURE
According to writers like the eighteenth century jurist William Blackstone, the laws of nature are implanted in human minds by God and confirm in a general way the truths of Scripture. Some conservative Christians distinguish such laws from natural law, which they see as having no reference to God and thus as lacking authority.

NEO-CALVINISM
A movement formed in the late nineteenth century under the leadership of the Dutch theologian, Abraham Kuyper, to revive Calvinism and modify it to compete with modernism and secularism.

NEW APOSTOLIC REFORMATION (NAR)
A late twentieth century movement in the Pentecostal tradition following the teachings of C. Peter Wagner. The movement stresses spiritual warfare against the enemies of Christianity.

PENTECOSTALS
Members of a branch of evangelical Christianity who seek a deep spiritual experience in their worship and emphasize spiritual healing and speaking in tongues.

PIETISM
A private form of worship that does not actively engage society and is often dismissed as ineffective by today's Christian rightists.

PLURALISM
A state of society in which diverse social, religious, and ethnic groups are extended full freedom and equal treatment.

POSTMILLENNIALISM
The millennial belief that Christ's Second Coming will come *after* a thousand year kingdom on earth in which humans will be full participants under Christ's *spiritual* leadership. It is optimistic in recognizing that humans can contribute to the gradual improvement of society prior to Christ's actual return.

PREMILLENNIALISM
The millennial belief that Christ's Second Coming will *precede* the establishment of a thousand year kingdom on earth. It is pessimistic in assuming that humans will be unable to make lasting improvements to society prior to Christ's return.

PRESUPPOSITIONALISM
A school of Christian apologetics developed by Abraham Kuyper and Cornelius Van Til arguing that all humans are predisposed in their beliefs by their core assumptions about God and the world. It maintains that assumptions based on biblical Christianity are the only sure foundation for a consistent and rational understanding of reality.

PROVIDENCE
The notion of God as the overseer and sustainer of Creation and the creatures within it.

PURITANISM
A life philosophy based on Calvinist and Presbyterian theology, originally developed in sixteenth and seventeenth century England and later transferred to the American colonies. It emphasized an austere way of life centered on the absolute authority of God.

RECONSTRUCTIONISM. See CHRISTIAN RECONSTRUCTIONISM.

REFORMED
Referring to those Christian denominations that accept the principles of the Protestant Reformation as expressed in the theology of Calvinism. Included among them are the Dutch Reformed Church, the Protestant Reformed Church of France (the Huguenots), and orthodox branches of the Presbyterian Church.

REGENT CONSTITUTIONALISTS
A group of constitutional theorists concentrated at Regent University who subscribe to a legal and constitutional system based on Christian principles, as suggested in certain statements by William Blackstone and others. They believe that English common law and the American Declaration of Independence incorporate the idea of a transcendent divine law.

RELIGIOUS RIGHT. See CHRISTIAN RIGHT.

SECULAR HUMANISM. See HUMANISM

SPHERE SOVEREIGNTY
A notion of sovereignty advanced by Abraham Kuyper that distinguishes the numerous spheres or groupings that constitute society, most notably the family, the school, the church, the workplace, and the state, and notes that these spheres owe their primary allegiance to God rather than to any human authority.

THEISTIC REALISM
A concept of science premised on the absolute conviction of God's existence. It has been recently advanced by Philip Johnson as a substitute for a science based on human reason.

THEOCRACY
Rule or government by God, in which God's laws and authority take precedence over human ones, and in which God's rule extends to all individuals and pertains to all aspects of life.

THEONOMY
Literally, God's law. The term is meant to refer to a civil order in which the laws of God, as laid out in the first five books of the Old Testament, govern society.

VOLUNTARISM
A metaphysical philosophy that confers a greater role to the will than to reason and the intellect.

WESTMINSTER CONFESSION
A set of religious tenets arrived at during a famous convocation of English and Scottish divines asked by Parliament to provide guidelines for the Church of England. After years of discussion, the convocation produced a document in 1646 (later revised in 1648) that encapsulated the doctrines of orthodox Presbyterianism then being advanced by the country's Puritans. These doctrines were based on Calvinist principles.

WORLDVIEW
A set of perceptions about the world expressing the point of view of a particular religion or social group based on its unique assumptions and experiences.

Endnotes

INTRODUCTION

[1] Brannon Howse. "Code Blue: Hearts and Minds at Risk." DVD recorded live at the 2007 Branson Worldview Weekend Family Reunion. We also borrow from his book, *One Nation under Man? The Worldview War between Christians and the Secular Left* (Nashville, Tenn.: Broadman & Holman Publishers, 2005).

[2] David K. Naugle, *Worldview: The History of a Concept* (Grand Rapids, Mich.: William B. Eerdmans Publ. Co., 2002), 280.

[3] *Merriam-Webster's Collegiate Dictionary*, 11th ed. (Springfield, Mass.: Merriam-Webster, Inc., 2007), 616.

[4] Francis Schaeffer, *A Christian Manifesto* (Westchester, Il.: Crossway Books, 1981), 89–110. While Schaeffer repudiated theocracy in one famous instance (*A Christian Manifesto*, 120–121), his opinions on divine law suggest sympathy with theocratic principles. See discussion in Chapter 5, i.

[5] Schaeffer, *A Christian Manifesto*, 90–91.

[6] Charles Colson & Nancy Pearcey, *How Now Shall We Live?* (Wheaton, Il.: Tyndale House Publishers, 1999), 13.

1 MOVEMENT ON A MISSION

[1] Dinesh D'Souza, *Falwell Before the Millennium: A Critical Biography* (Chicago: Regnery Gateway, 1984), 109–111.

[2] Weyrich had actually met Falwell earlier that year at a conference in Dallas, where the possibility of political engagement was informally discussed. Sara Diamond, *Spiritual Warfare: The Politics of the Christian Right* (Boston: South End Press, 1989), 56; Dan Gilgoff, *The Jesus Machine: How James Dobson, Focus on the Family, and Evangelical America are Winning the Culture War* (N.Y.: St. Martin's Press, 2007), 80–81.

[3] William Martin, *With God on Our Side: The Rise of the Religious Right in America* (N.Y.: Broadway Books, 1996), 156–159.

[4] D'Souza, *Falwell*, 110–111; Sara Diamond, *Spiritual Warfare*, 60; Gilgoff, *The Jesus Machine*, 79.

[5] Frederick Clarkson. "The Religious Right Ain't Over in the GOP." *Daily Kos*. September 18, 2007. http://www.dailykos.com/story/2007/09/19/387084/-The-Religious-Right-Ain-t-Over-in-the-GOP

[6] George M. Marsden, *Understanding Fundamentalism and Evangelism* (Grand Rapids, Mich.: William B. Eerdmans, 1991), 65.

[7] "Fundamentalists" are generally characterized as embracing an anti-modernist form of Christianity distinct from the mainstream denominations; "neo-evangelists" practice a more mainstream evangelicalism often associated with Billy Graham; Reformed Christians are more doctrinally conscious, hewing to a strict form of Calvinism; Pentecostals seek a deep spiritual experience in their worship and emphasize healing and speaking in tongues; "charismatics" also seek to experience the "gifts of the spirit", but are usually from mainstream denominations. The fluid definitions of such terms as "fundamentalist" and "evangelical" are discussed by Marsden in *Understanding*, 232–236.

[8] Gilgoff, *The Jesus Machine*, 78–79.

[9] George M. Marsden, *Fundamentalism and American Culture*, 2nd ed. (N.Y.: Oxford University Press, 2006), 242.

[10] Martin, *With God*, 193–194.

[11] Among those who spent time at l'Abri and later achieved prominence are the Christian worldview writer Nancy Pearcey; Neo-Calvinist intellectual Os Guiness, who taught there; Kathleen Harris, the Florida Secretary of State during the controversial 2000 election; and two members of the anti-abortion movement with a later violent history, Michael Bray and James Kopp.

[12] Francis A. Schaeffer, *How Should We Then Live? The Rise and Decline of Western Thought and Culture* (Old Tappan, N.J.: Fleming H. Revell, 1976), 205–246; Jerry Falwell, *Listen, America!* (N.Y.: Bantam Books, 1980), 6.

[13] Ronald A. Wells, "Schaeffer on America," in Ronald W. Ruegsegger, ed., *Reflections on Francis Schaeffer* (Grand Rapids, Mich.: Academie Books, 1986), 234.

[14] Francis A. Schaeffer, *A Christian Manifesto* (Westchester, Il.: Crossway Books, 1981), 74.

[15] D'Souza, *Falwell*, 130.

[16] The Human Life Statute, sponsored by Jesse Helms and Henry Hyde in 1981, held that "human life shall be deemed to exist from conception." The Family Protection Act, introduced in 1981, included 31 provisions that would have banned abortion, re-instated school prayer, provided tax credits for private schooling, and given local groups veto power over public school texts, among other measures. The School Prayer Amendment, which reached a vote in the Senate in 1984, would have allowed individual and group prayer in public schools, made prayer ostensibly voluntary, but remained silent on government-initiated prayer. See Martin, *With God,* 226–233.

[17] Chip Berlet & Matthew Lyons, *Right-Wing Populism in America: Too Close for Comfort* (N.Y. & London: Guilford Press, 2000), 256.

[18] Ralph Reed, *Active Faith* (N.Y.: Free Press, 1996), 109–111, 121–122.

[19] Diamond, *Spiritual Warfare*, 72–76.

[20] Berlet & Lyons, *Right-Wing Populism*, 256.

[21] Reed, *Active*, 109.

[22] Reed, *Active*, 128, 157.

[23] Frederick Clarkson, *Eternal Hostility: The Struggle Between Theocracy and Democracy* (Monroe, Maine: Common Courage Press, 1997), 22.

[24] Robert Boston, *The Most Dangerous Man in America? Pat Robertson and the Rise of the Christian Coalition* (Amherst, N.Y.: Prometheus Books, 1996), 91. Ralph Reed actually coined the term "stealth candidates." See http://www.answers.com/topic/stealth?cat=entertainment

[25] Clarkson, *Eternal Hostility*, 20–26; Erin Saberi, "From Moral Majority to Organized Minority: Tactics of the Religious Right," *Christian Century*, August 11, 1993.

[26] Gilgoff, *The Jesus Machine*, 99.

[27] Esther Kaplan, *With God on their Side: George W. Bush and the Christian Right* (N.Y. & London: The New Press, 2004), 73.

[28] Kaplan, *With God*, 7.

[29] Gilgoff, *The Jesus Machine*, 117–118.

[30] Gilgoff, *The Jesus Machine*, 106–113.

[31] Gilgoff, *The Jesus Machine*, 114–117.

[32] Kaplan, *With God*, 83–85.

[33] For example, Monica Goodling, a key player in the firing of federal prosecutors under Alberto Gonzales, was one of many Regent Law School

graduates brought into the Civil Rights Division of the Justice Department. See Tim Mitchell. "Jilting Justice for Jesus." *Talk to Action.* May 21, 2007. http://www.talk2action.org/story/2007/5/21/8329/01731. For the role of Patrick Henry graduates as staff personnel at the White House, see Hanna Rosin. "Bush's Real Legacy: Faithful Conservatism." *USA Today–Opinion.* http://blogs.usatoday.com/oped/2007/10/bushs-real-lega.html

34 Kaplan, *With God*, 108–114, 173–177.

35 Kaplan, *With God*, 123–128, 91–122, 135–136, 66–67, 186–190, 7, 252. On the reshaping of the Civil Rights Division at Justice, see Tim Mitchell. "Jilting Justice for Jesus."

36 Two useful treatments of the faith-based initiative are Kaplan, *With God*, 39–63, and Michelle Goldberg, *Kingdom Coming: The Rise of Christian Nationalism* (N.Y.: W.W. Norton, 2006), 106–133.

37 Bush administration sources place the amount of money dispensed somewhere in the low billions per year (Goldberg, *Kingdom Coming*, 108). Taking an opposing view is David Kuo, a former faith-based official in the White House and now a critic, who feels the amount has been exaggerated to inflate the administration's faith-based accomplishments and lure certain constituencies to the Republican Party. See David Kuo, *Tempting Fate: An Inside Story of Political Seduction* (N.Y.: Free Press, 2006), 209–210, 239–242, 248–249, 251–254. In fact, the amount is extremely difficult to assess, as it has been distributed throughout the bureaucracy with little accounting.

38 Kaplan, *With God*, 40.

39 Kaplan, *With God*, 54.

40 Amy Sullivan. "Faith Without Works." *Washington Monthly.* October 2004. http://www.washingtonmonthly.com/features/2004/0410.2sullivan.html. See also Goldberg, *Kingdom Coming*, 107–109, 115–117.

41 Amy Sullivan. "Faith Without Works." Sullivan points out that Bush often emphasized "results" when selling his faith-based initiative, but never monitored performance once the funds were handed out, a curious oversight on the part of a chief executive who called himself the "accountability president" when it came to government programs.

42 Goldberg, *Kingdom Coming*, 121.

43 Gilgoff, *The Jesus Machine*, 121–122, 178–183.

44 Kaplan, *With God*, 248–249.

45 The desire to "federalize" the case was brazenly inconsistent, since Christian rightists had long been trying to remove federal court jurisdiction over family and religious issues, not reinstate it. See Barry W. Lynn, *Piety and*

Politics: The Right-Wing Assault on Religious Freedom (N.Y.: Harmony Books, 2006), 192–193.

[46] See Goldberg, *Kingdom Coming*, 177, 169, and 154–179 for a good summary of the issues.

[47] Article III, section 2 of the Constitution does empower the Congress to make "exceptions" and "regulations" pertaining to the Supreme Court's appellate jurisdiction. But as one commentator has pointed out, the recently proposed bills go well beyond making "exceptions." They "authorize Congress to pass laws curtailing constitutional rights and exempt those laws from Supreme Court review. This would leave Congress as the sole arbiter of the constitutionality of the laws it enacts, in effect amending the Constitution without following the constitutional processes for doing so." See Mark Agrast. "Judge Roberts and the Court-Stripping Movement." *Center for American Progress.* http://www.americanprogress.org/issues/2005/09/bl023255.html

[48] Schaeffer, *A Christian Manifesto*, 100–102, 117–130.

[49] Schaeffer, *A Christian Manifesto*, 93.

[50] An argument can be made that the Bible actually condones abortion under certain circumstances and does not regard abortion, at least in early pregnancy, as murder. See Numbers 5:11–31 and Exodus 21:22–25, and T. Murray. "More Biblical Precedent for Allowing Abortion." *Talk to Action.* May 18, 2008. http://www.talk2action.org/story/2008/5/18408/44176

[51] James Risen & Judy L. Thomas, *Wrath of Angels: The American Abortion War* (N.Y.: Basic Books, 1998), 56–57, 46–49.

[52] On Planned Parenthood and King, see Planned Parenthood. "The Reverend Martin Luther King Jr." http://www.plannedparenthood.org/about-us/who-we-are/the-reverend-martin-luther-king-jr.htm (March 25, 2013). On Randall Terry and King, see Steve Aquino. "Pro-Lifer Links Movement to MLK, Damns Slain Abortion Doctor." *Mother Jones.* June 1 2009. http://motherjones.com/mojo/2009/06/pro-lifer-links-movement-mlk-damns-slain-abortion-doc

[53] Risen & Thomas, *Wrath*, 66, 69.

[54] Risen & Thomas, *Wrath*, 102–104, 113–114, 117.

[55] See Schaeffer, *A Christian Manifesto*, 98–100. "Higher law" is commonly interchangeable with God's law as revealed in the Bible. See Whitehead, *The Second American Revolution* (Westchester, Il.: Crossway Books, 1982), 75.

[56] Risen & Thomas, *Wrath*, 240–248.

[57] Risen & Thomas, *Wrath*, 206–207, 221–223.

[58] Risen & Thomas, *Wrath*, 257.

[59] Randall K. O'Bannon. "Abortion Totals, Rates, Ratios Drop to Lowest Levels in Decades." http://www.nrlc.org/news/2003/NRL02/randy.html (March 25, 2013)

[60] Clarkson, *Eternal Hostility*, 140–143, 148–50, 157. Extremists Michael Bray, Paul Hill, Gary North, and probably Randall Terry himself, viewed the rescue movement as having revolutionary potential for bringing about a biblical society.

[61] Bomber Michael Bray, and assailants Shelly Shannon, Michael Griffin, and Paul Hill were all Protestant evangelicals. Gunmen James Kopp and John Salvi, on the other hand, were Catholics.

[62] Risen & Thomas, *Wrath*, 80–81, 368–370; Clarkson, *Eternal Hostility*, 137; "Dedication & Some Introductory Notes." *Army of God Manual.* Third Edition. http://www.armyofgod.com/AOGsel1.html (March 18, 2008)

[63] Frederick Clarkson. "The Lingering Effects of Anti-Abortion Terrorism." *Talk to Action.* April 1 2008. http://www.talk2action.ort/story/2008/4/1/18738/ 59227. Clarkson has kept close track of the anti-abortion crusade over the years. See also his other articles on Talk to Action.

[64] Both quotations are from Nancy Pearcey, *Total Truth: Liberating Christianity from its Cultural Captivity* (Wheaton, Il.: Crossway Books, 2004), 18–19.

[65] Pearcey, *Total Truth*, 47.

[66] Pearcey, *Total Truth*, 19.

[67] Frederick Clarkson, "The Culture Wars Are Not Over: The Institutionalization of the Christian Right." *The Public Eye* 15, 1 (Spring, 2001). http://www.publiceye.org/magazine/v15n1/State_of_Christian_Rt.html

[68] See Dan Gilgoff, *The Jesus Machine*, especially 18–42.

[69] HSLDA. "About HSLDA." http://www.hslda.org/about/default.asp

[70] Helen Cordes. "Battling for the heart and soul of home-schoolers." *Salon.* October 2, 2000. http://archive.salon.com/mwt/feature/2000/10/02/homeschooling_battle/index.html; Mitchell L. Stevens, *Kingdom of Children: Culture and Controversy in the Homeschooling Movement* (Princeton: Princeton University Press, 2001), 118–128, 148–177.

[71] Sheldon Culver & John Dorhauer, *Steeplejacking: How the Christian Right is Hijacking Mainstream Religion* (Brooklyn, N.Y.: Ig Publishing, 2007), 38–46, 74–78. See chapters 1 and 2 for a good historical summary of the IRD and the renewal movement.

[72] James Tonkovich. "About IRD." The Institute on Religion and Democracy.

http://www.ird-renew.org/site/pp.asp?c=fvKVLfMVIsG&b=308891 (Aug. 21, 2007).

73 Institute on Religion and Democracy. "Reforming America's Churches: 2001–2004 Executive Summary." http://www.theocracywatch.org/internal_document_ird.html (March 25, 2013). This document is no longer available on the IRD website

74 See Diamond, *Spiritual Warfare*, 51, 111–112.

75 During the 1980s and early '90s, a phenomenon called "shepherding," in which members of cell groups were placed under the authority of higher-ups, led to intense ideological indoctrination and forms of psychological control and abuse. See Sara Diamond, *Spiritual Warfare*, 111–127; Clarkson, *Eternal Hostility*, 101–102; Berlet & Lyons, *Right-Wing Populism*, 253.

76 See Martin, *With God*, 91.

77 Sara Diamond, *Spiritual Warfare*, 51.

78 Martin, *With God*, 91–93.

79 Anne C. Loveland, *American Evangelicals and the U.S. Military 1942–1993* (Baton Rouge: Louisiana State University Press, 1996), 5.

80 Loveland, *American Evangelicals*, 16–32.

81 Loveland, *American Evangelicals*, 27–32. On support for evangelical religion from higher officers, see especially chapters 4, 5, 8, and 13.

82 Regular reports on such abuses by journalists Chris Rodda, Bruce Wilson, and others can be found on the website www.talk2action.org

83 For in-depth information on the import of these trends, with striking illustrations from the Air Force Academy, see Michael L. Weinstein & Davin Seay, *With God on Our Side: One Man's War against an Evangelical Coup in America's Military* (N.Y.: Thomas Dunne Books, 2006).

84 Christian Embassy. "Statement of Faith." http://www.christianembassy.com

85 Loveland, *American Evangelicals*, 206–207.

86 Bruce Wilson. "Turning US Military Members into 'Government Paid Missionaries' for Christ." *Talk to Action.* October 9, 2007. http://www.talk2action.org/story/2007/10/9/8599/55674

87 The Family was founded in 1935 by a Swedish-American pastor, Abraham Vereide, who sought to promote a kind of Christian fundamentalism among the corporate and political elite. He supported spiritual struggle against the forces of evil in the world, which he identified with communism, trade unionism, and the New Deal. The Family became influential in Washington as early as World War II. Later, it endorsed an aggressive

foreign policy and identified itself with a number of repressive right-wing dictators, e.g., General Suharto of Indonesia and General Costa e Silva of Brazil. See Jeff Sharlet, *The Family: The Secret Fundamentalism at the Heart of American Power* (N.Y.: HarperCollins, 2008), 87–113, 218–224.

88 Sharlet, *The Family*, 18–20.

89 Sharlet, *The Family*, 216–217.

90 Sharlet, *The Family*, 44–47.

91 Clarkson, *Eternal Hostility*, 188, 198–200; Martin, *With God On Our Side*, 349–353.

92 Bill Berkowitz. "Promise Keepers try to regain the offensive." *Talk to Action.* July 16, 2007. http://www.talk2action.org/story/2007/7/16/162016/464

93 The Association of Classical and Christian Schools (ACCS) was founded in the 1990s to support and promote this educational movement. Some idea of its approach can be found at its website, http://www.accsedu.org

94 Bruce Barron, *Heaven on Earth? The Social and Political Agendas of Dominion Theology* (Grand Rapids, Mi.: Zondervan Publishing House, 1992), 53–66; Tim Mitchell. "Jilting Justice for Jesus." *Talk to Action.* May 21, 2007. http://www.talk2action.org/story/2007/5/21/8329/01731; Hanna Rosin. "Bush's Real Legacy: Faithful Conservatism." *USA Today–Opinion.* http://blogs.usatoday.com/oped/2007/10/bushs-real-lega.html

95 Barron, *Heaven on Earth?*, 61.

96 E.g., see Tim Mitchell. "Jilting Justice for Jesus." *Talk to Action.* May 21, 2007. http://www.talk2action.org/story/2007/5/21/8329/01731

97 Barbara Forrest & Paul R. Gross, *Creationism's Trojan Horse: The Wedge of Intelligent Design* (N.Y.: Oxford University Press, 2007), 207–210.

98 David K. Naugle, *Worldview: The History of a Concept* (Grand Rapids, Mich.: William B. Eerdmans, 2002), 279–281.

99 Pearcey, *Total Truth*, 23.

2 THE ANSWER TO MODERNISM

1 Francis A. Schaeffer, *A Christian Manifesto* (Westchester, Il.: Crossway Books, 1981), 17–18, 25–26, 44–45. For Schaeffer on modernism, see Schaeffer, *How Should We Then Live? The Rise and Decline of Western Thought and Culture* (Old Tappan, N.J.: Fleming H. Revell, 1976), 152, 160, 164, & Chapts. 9–11.

2 See David K. Naugle, *Worldview: The History of a Concept* (Grand Rapids,

Mich.: William B. Eerdmans Publ. Co., 2002), 6–13.

[3] James Orr, *A Christian View of God and the World as Centering in the Incarnation* (Edinburgh: Andrew Eliot, 1893), 4. Quoted in David K. Naugle, *Worldview: The History of a Concept* (Grand Rapids, Mich.: William B. Eerdmans Publ. Co., 2002), 7–8.

[4] See Naugle's discussion in *Worldview*, 256–259, 266–267.

[5] Naugle, *Worldview*, 8.

[6] Naugle, *Worldview*, 8.

[7] Naugle, *Worldview*, 12.

[8] Naugle, *Worldview*, 17–18, 20.

[9] Glen G. Scorgie, *A Call for Continuity: The Theological Contribution of James Orr* (Vancouver: Regent College Publishing, 2004 [1988]), 44–46, 50–51.

[10] See the discussion of evangelicalism's relationship to the American Enlightenment in George M. Marsden, *Understanding Fundamentalism and Evangelicalism* (Grand Rapids, Mich.: William B. Eerdmans Publ. Co., 1991), 122–124, 126–127.

3 CREDO: EVERY SQUARE INCH FOR GOD

[1] Quoted in Abraham Kuyper, *Lectures on Calvinism* (Grand Rapids, Mich.: William B. Eerdmans, 1931), 14.

[2] James Orr, "Calvinism," in James Hastings, ed., *Encyclopaedia of Religion and Ethics*, 13 vols. (N.Y.: Charles Scribners, 1951), 3:146.

[3] Kuyper, *Lectures*, 11.

[4] John T. McNeill, *The History and Character of Calvinism* (Oxford: Oxford University Press, 1954), 226.

[5] Kuyper, *Lectures*, 69.

[6] John Calvin, *Institutes of the Christian Religion* , ed. John T. McNeill, 2 vols. (Louisville, Ky.: Westminster John Knox Press, 1960), 1:198–199, 200, 202 (I.xvi.2–4).

[7] Especially Ephesians 1, Romans 8 and 9.

[8] Calvin, *Institutes*, 2:955 (III.xxiii.7).

[9] Calvin, *Institutes*, 2:947–948 (III.xxiii.1), 968–969 (III.xxiv.4). Paul's metaphor is from Romans 9:21.

[10] J.B. Schneewind, *The Invention of Autonomy: A History of Modern Moral Philos-*

ophy (Cambridge: Cambridge University Press, 1998), 8. For a discussion of voluntarism and intellectualism, the two philosophical ways of conceiving God in relation to morality, see Schneewind, *The Invention*, 8–9. Plato famously juxtaposed the clash of outlooks in the *Euthyphro* by having Socrates ask whether God loved the good because it was good, or whether it was good because God loved it. Socrates pointed out the philosophical problems with the second, voluntarist position.

11 See Michael Martin, *The Case against Christianity* (Philadelphia: Temple University Press, 1991), 229–251.

12 Calvin, *Institutes*, 2:949 (III.xxiii.2).

13 Even on issues as basic as murder and killing, biblical standards of morality are ambiguous and dependent on God's arbitrary ruling. The mass killings under God's eye of Canaanites, Philistines, Moabites, and others are typically fraught with irony.

14 Guenther H. Haas, "Calvin's Ethics," in Donald K. McKim, *The Cambridge Companion to John Calvin* (Cambridge: Cambridge University Press, 2004), 93.

15 Attaining a knowledge of God, to be sure, is not simply a cognitive exercise as the words might imply, but one that requires the full commitment of both affective and intellectual faculties. See Calvin, *Institutes*, 1:583–4 (III.ii.36).

16 Calvin, *Institutes*, 1:44–45 (I.iii.1, I.iii.2).

17 Calvin, *Institutes*, 1:43–44 (I.iii.1).

18 Calvin, *Institutes*, I:47–48 (I.iv.1–2)

19 Many biblical scholars would call a simple, literal interpretation of Romans 1 misleading and one-sided. While the passage is scathing on the moral failings of pagans, the following chapter (Romans 2) provides a different perspective, focusing on the parallel failings of the Jews and offering a more positive view of pagan morality. Quoting Romans 1 in isolation risks distorting seriously the Apostle's message. See, for instance, John Knox, Exegesis to the "Epistle to the Romans," *The Interpreter's Bible*, vol. 9 (N.Y.: Abingdon-Cokesbury Press, 1954), 400, 410–411.

20 Naugle, *Worldview*, 274.

21 See, for example, Kuyper, *Lectures*, 52, 137; Herbert Schlossberg & Marvin Olasky, *Turning Point: a Christian Worldview Declaration* (Westchester, Il.: Crossway Books, 1987), 134–135; Charles Colson & Nancy Pearcey, *How Now Shall We Live?* (Wheaton, Il.: Wheaton House Publishers, 1999), 56, 196; Nancy Pearcey, *Total Truth: Liberating Christianity from its Cultural*

Captivity (Wheaton, Il.: Crossway Books, 2004), 40–42, 313–314; Cindy Jacobs, *The Reformation Manifesto* (Minneapolis, Minn.: Bethany Publishers, 2008), 98, 111, 119.

22 For example, Rev. Gordon Klingenschmitt uses an extended quotation from Romans 1 to disparage scientific critic Ed Brayton in an internet dispute. See Ed Brayton. "Fisking Klingenschmitt, Part 2." *Dispatches from the Culture Wars.* July 17, 2007. http://scienceblogs.com/dispatches/2007/07/fisking_klingenschmitt_part_2.php

23 Calvin, *Institutes*, 1:724–725 (III.x.6).

24 Calvin, *Institutes*, 2:1487 (IV.xx.2).

25 For a general discussion, see William R. Stevenson, Jr., "Calvin and Political Issues," in McKim, *Cambridge Companion*, 175–177.

26 McNeill, *The History and Character*, 225.

27 Jan de Bruijn, "Calvinism and Romanticism: Abraham Kuyper as a Calvinist Politician," in Luis E. Lugo, *Religion, Pluralism, and Public Life* (Grand Rapids, Mich.: Wm. B. Eerdmans Publ. Co., 2000), 52–54.

28 Naugle, *Worldview*, 16.

29 James D. Bratt, *Dutch Calvinism in Modern America: A History of a Conservative Subculture* (Grand Rapids, Mich.: William B. Eerdmans Publishing Co., 1984), 16.

30 Abraham Kuyper, *Lectures*, 46.

31 Bratt, *Dutch Calvinism*, 17–18.

32 Herman Dooyeweerd, *Roots of Western Culture: Pagan, Secular, and Christian Options* (Toronto: Wedge Publishing Foundation, 1979), 1–4. Dooyeweerd traces the idea of antithesis to Kuyper and Groen Van Prinster, but the concept was apparently formulated by Franz Baader (1765–1841), a maverick German Catholic connected with the mystical tradition. See J. Glenn Friesen, "Franz Xavier von Baader." *Studies relating to Franz von Baader.* 2003–2006. http://members.shaw.ca/jgfriesen/mainheadings/Baader.html

33 Kuyper, *Lectures*, 11.

34 Kuyper, *Lectures*, 91–93.

35 Kuyper, *Lectures*, 82, 88.

36 Kuyper, *Lectures*, 82–90; Bratt, *Dutch Calvinism*, 26.

37 Kuyper, *Lectures*, 90–92 and passim.

38 A major influence on Kuyper was the Dutch anti-revolutionary leader,

Groen van Prinsterer (1801–1876). A critic of the "idolatrous philosophy" of the French Revolution, Groen argued for shrinking the secular state and enhancing the independence of church and family. He used the phrase "sovereignty within its own sphere." Dooyeweerd, *Roots*, 53–54.

39 Dooyeweerd, *Roots*, 54–55. Dooyeweerd points out that Kuyper wasn't entirely consistent since he included among his "sovereign spheres" not merely social units but units that were governmental extensions of the state, e.g. municipalities and provinces.

40 Bratt, *Dutch Calvinism*, 19.

41 Kuyper, *Lectures*, 123.

42 Dooyeweerd refers to the dualities of spirit and matter ("form-matter"), sacred and profane ("grace-nature"), reason and nature ("freedom-nature"), implicit in the Greek-Roman, medieval, and modern worldviews, respectively. He uses the term "ground motive" (meaning roughly "spiritual orientation') to classify these underlying tendencies. See Dooyeweerd, *Roots*, 14–22, 28–36, 111–121, 148–174.

43 Dooyeweerd, *Roots*, 35, 118.

44 Dooyeweerd, *Roots*, 30.

45 For instance, see John M. Frame, *Cornelius Van Til: An Analysis of His Thought* (Phillipsburg, N.J.: P & R Publishing, 1995), 374.

46 See Francis Schaeffer, *Escape from Reason* in *Francis Schaeffer Trilogy* (Wheaton, Il.: Crossway Books, 1990), 209–236; Brian J. Walsh & J. Richard Middleton, *The Transforming Vision: Shaping a Christian World View* (Downers Grove, Il.: IVP Academic, 1984), 107–129; Pearcey, *Total Truth*, 74–87, 100–109.

47 Bratt, *Dutch Calvinism*, 18.

48 Greg Bahnsen, ed., *Van Til's Apologetic: Readings and Analysis* (Phillipsburg, N.J.: P&R Publishing, 1998), 566, 627. Van Til quotes from Romans 1:25.

49 Frame, *Cornelius Van Til*, 34–37.

50 Frame, *Cornelius Van Til*, 29–34.

51 Frame, *Cornelius Van Til*, 3.

52 Bahnsen, *Van Til's Apologetic*, 530.

53 R.C. Sproul, John Gerstner, Arthur Lindsley, *Classical Apologetics: A Rational Defense of the Christian Faith and a Critique of Presuppositional Apologetics* (Grand Rapids, Mich.: Zondervan Publishing House, 1984), 185.

54 Quotations from Van Til in R. John Rushdoony, *By What Standard?: An*

Analysis of the Philosophy of Cornelius Van Til (Vallecito: Ross House Books, 1995 [1958]), 22.

55 Rushdoony, *By What Standard?*, 23.

56 Frame, *Cornelius Van Til*, 89–92, 382.

57 A number of critics have been openly sarcastic about Van Til's circularity. For example, Sproul et. al in *Classical Apologetics* (188): "Yes, indeed, he [Van Til] declares, but what a glorious circle! What a divine circle. . . . Presuppositionalists travel only in the very best circles." See also John Warwick Montgomery's Swiftian critique of Van Til in his "Once Upon an A Priori," in E. R. Geehan, ed., *Jerusalem and Athens: Critical Discussions on the Philosophy and Apologetics of Cornelius Van Til* (Phillipsburg, N.J.: Presbyterian & Reformed Publishing Co., 1971), 380–392.

58 Bahnsen, *Van Til's Apologetic: Readings and Analysis* (Phillipsburg, N.J.: P&R Publishing, 1998), 2.

59 For an abbreviated example of this sort of circular argumentation, see Frame, *Cornelius Van Til*, 409. Frame, a Reformed theologian in the Vantillian tradition, rejects out of hand any reasoning that does not embrace the assumption that God is naturally revealed to all. Rather than defending his point logically, he simply states that such reasoning is "intolerable to the Bible-believer."

60 Bahnsen, *Van Til's Apologetic*, 518–520.

61 Bahnsen, *Van Til's Apologetic*, 409.

62 Bahnsen, *Van Til's Apologetic*, 469–472, 482–496.

63 See Cornelius Van Til, "My Credo," in E.R. Geehan, ed., *Jerusalem and Athens*, 17–20.

64 Van Til's argumentative inconsistency along these lines is well demonstrated in Sproul et. al., *Classical Apologetics*, 234–239.

65 See the 1996 debate between rationalist Michael Martin and presuppositionalist John Frame. Frame, adopting Van Til's apologetic method, claims that God must first be assumed to exist for logic to exist and hence must be immune from human arguments based upon it, but provides no justification outside of Scripture. Michael Martin, "The Transcendental Argument for the Nonexistence of God." http://www.infidels.org/library/modern/michael_martin/ martin-frame/tang.html. (March 28, 2013); John Frame, "A Brief Response..." http://www.reformed.org/apologetics/martin/frame_contra_ martin.html (March 28, 2013)

4 BLUEPRINT: GOD'S LAW

1 This is a mantra used throughout North's works. See, for instance, Gary North, *Political Polytheism: The Myth of Pluralism* (Tyler, Texas: Institute for Christian Economics, 1989), 8–9, and passim.

2 R. John Rushdoony, *The Roots of Reconstruction* (Vallecito, California: Ross House Books, 1991), 545–546.

3 Reconstructionists R. J. Rushdoony, Greg Bahnsen, and Gary North have all been associated with the OPC, the first two as ordained ministers, while Gary DeMar and Kenneth Gentry are members of the PCA.

4 The OPC split away from the mainstream Presbyterian Church of the U.S.A. (PCUSA) in 1936 under the leadership of J. Gresham Machen over doctrinal disagreements. The PCA, only slightly less conservative than the OPC, was founded in 1973 when it broke away from the southern-based Presbyterian Church in the U.S. (PCUS).

5 The Puritan stress on Old Testament law and covenant is due, in large part, to the influence of John Tyndale (1492?–1536), the early Protestant translator and interpreter of the Bible. Tyndale in his treatises and introductions places the Old and New Testament on the same level, and closely ties Jesus' message to covenantal obligations and the laws of Moses. See Henning Graf Reventlow, *The Authority of the Bible and the Rise of the Modern World* (Philadelphia: Fortress Press, 1985), 105–108. See also Richard T. Hughes, *Myths America Lives By* (Urbana & Chicago: University of Illinois Press, 2003), 21–23. For Reconstructionist views on the covenantal idea, see R. John Rushdoony, *The Institutes of Biblical Law* (The Presbyterian and Reformed Publishing Co., 1973), 693–697. Also North, *Political Polytheism*, 31–35 and passim.

6 Calvin is commonly viewed as an amillennialist, i.e. one who takes biblical predictions of the millennium in a symbolic rather than literal sense. See, for instance, W. Robert Godfrey, "Calvin and Theonomy," in William S. Barker & W. Robert Godfrey, eds., *Theonomy: A Reformed Critique*, eds. (Grand Rapids, Mich.: Academie Books, 1990), 312. Predictably, Christian Reconstructionists tend to see latent postmillennialism in Calvin's thought. See Gary North, *Westminster's Confession: The Abandonment of Van Til's Legacy* (Tyler, Tx.: Institute for Christian Economics, 1991), 349–356.

7 For a good portrayal of "Sunbelt" conservatism, see Chip Berlet & Matthew Lyons, *Right-Wing Populism in America: Too Close for Comfort* (N.Y. & London: Guilford Press, 2000), 218.

8 See Chip Berlet, "Christian Economics, the John Birch Society, and Chris-

tian Reconstructionism." *Talk to Action.* March 5, 2007. www.talk2action.or/story/2007/3/5/172426/4273. See also Chad Bull, "Stalwarts of Freedom: An Inside Look at the John Birch Society." *Chalcedon Foundation.* Sept/Oct 2006. www.chalcedon.edu/articles/article.php? ArticleID=2334. Also Rushdoony, *The Institutes*, 746–747. Gary North had links with the JBS as well. See Sara Diamond, *Spiritual Warfare: The Politics of the Christian Right* (Boston: South End Press, 1989), 139.

9 Gary North & Gary DeMar, *Christian Reconstruction: What It Is, What It Isn't* (Tyler, Texas: Institute for Christian Economics, 1991), ix–x; Gary North. "R.J. Rushdoony, R.I.P." *LewRockwell.com.* http://www.lewrockwell.com/north/north33.html; Gary North, *An Introduction to Christian Economics* (The Craig Press, 1973), v.

10 Max Blumenthal, *Republican Gomorrah: Inside the Movement that Shattered the Party* (N.Y.: Nation Books, 2009), 17.

11 British Centre for Science Education. "In extremis–Rousas Rushdoony and his connections." (Nov.4, 2007). http://www.bcseweb.org.uk/index.php/Main/RousasRushdoony

12 Even the OPC eventually proved insufficiently stringent for Rushdoony, as he came to regard Calvin himself as not completely faithful to Scripture. He was to take particular exception to Calvin's defense of natural law and his "weak views" on the application of Biblical law. See Rushdoony, *Institutes*, 9–10, 651, 659.

13 R. John Rushdoony, *The Foundations of Social Order: Studies in the Creeds and Councils of the Early Church* (Phillipsburg, N.J.: Presbyterian and Reformed Publishing Co., 1968), 63–64, 82.

14 Rushdoony, *Roots of Reconstruction*, 545–546.

15 North. "R.J. Rushdoony, R.I.P."

16 Howard Ahmanson, heir to a savings and loan fortune, alone contributed over $700,000 to Chalcedon as of 1996. See Clarkson, *Eternal Hostility: The Struggle between Theocracy and Democracy* (Monroe, Maine: Common Courage Press, 1997), 111; also Blumenthal, *Republican Gomorrah*, 32–35.

17 Within five to ten years, most of Rushdoony's early books were seeing second printings. *Institutes* went through several.

18 On Bahnsen, see Kenneth L. Gentry, Jr., "Appointed for the Defense of the Gospel: The Life and Ministry of Greg L. Bahnsen." http://www.anthonyflood.com/bahnsen.htm (March 28, 2013)

19 Several of Rushdoony's students later became noted Reconstructionists, namely Kenneth Gentry, David Chilton, James Jordan, and Gary DeMar.

[20] North, *Westminster's Confession*, 41–47.

[21] See Greg L. Bahnsen & Kenneth L. Gentry, Jr., *House Divided: The Break-up of Dispensational Theology* (Tyler, Tx.: Institute for Christian Economics, 1989) and Greg L. Bahnsen, *No Other Standard: Theonomy and its Critics* (Tyler, Tx.: Institute for Christian Economics, 1991).

[22] Greg Bahnsen, ed., *Van Til's Apologetic: Readings and Analysis* (Phillipsburg, N.J.: P & R Publishing, 1998).

[23] On North, see North & DeMar, *Christian Reconstruction*, ix–xv; North, *Rapture Fever: Why Dispensationalism is Paralyzed* (Tyler, Texas: Institute for Christian Economics, 1993), xxvii–xxviii.

[24] North & DeMar, *Christian Reconstruction*, xi.

[25] North and DeMar, *Christian Reconstruction*, ix–xiv.

[26] Gary North, Editor, *Foundations of Christian Scholarship: Essays in the Van Til Perspective* (Vallecito, Ca.: Ross house Books, 1976), vii–viii, 3–24; North & DeMar, *Christian Reconstruction*, 41–43; North, *Rapture Fever*, 6–8.

[27] According to Kuhn, only when there is a shift to a new paradigm, as in the case of the Newtonian and later the Darwinian view of the world, does knowledge truly advance, forcing researchers to address new problems with new solutions. See Thomas S. Kuhn, *The Structure of Scientific Revolutions*, 2nd ed. (Chicago: University of Chicago Press, 1970), especially chapters 6, 7, 8 & 13.

[28] For North's version of events, see North, *Westminster's Confession*, 334–337.

[29] Gary North, *Baptized Patriarchalism: The Cult of the Family* (Tyler, Tx.: Institute for Christian Economics, n.d.[ca. 1994]), 66, 69.

[30] North, *Baptized Patriarchalism*, 24–26.

[31] North, *Baptized Patriarchalism*, 27–63. North maintains that Rushdoony's unorthodox views were discernible as early as *The Institutes*, but were not fully outlined until later.

[32] North, *Baptized Patriarchalism*, 70.

[33] North, *Baptized Patriarchalism*, 65.

[34] Gary North, *Theonomy: An Informed Response* (Tyler, Tx.: Institute for Christian Economics, 1991), 257.

[35] North, *Political Polytheism*, 675–703.

[36] North, *Westminster's Confession*, 12.

[37] Gary North attests to having been "graciously provided with sufficient funds" for his foundation and business, apparently sometime in the 1980s.

See Bahnsen & Gentry, *House Divided*, xlii.

[38] Abraham Kuyper, *Lectures on Calvinism* (Grand Rapids, Mich.: Wm. B. Eerdmans Publishing Co., 1931), 92; R. John Rushdoony, *This Independent Republic: Studies in the Nature and Meaning of American History* (Nutley, N.J.: The Craig Press, 1964), 146, 148; Gary North, *The Dominion Covenant: Genesis: An Economic Commentary on the Bible, Volume I* (Tyler, Tx.: Institute for Christian Economics, 1982), 150–155; North, *Political Polytheism*, 85, 106.

[39] Gary North quoting Rushdoony in North, *The Dominion Covenant*, 151.

[40] See Rushdoony, *This Independent*, 10, 146–147.

[41] Rushdoony, *This Independent*, 148.

[42] Rushdoony, *This Independent*, 148–150.

[43] R. J. Rushdoony, *By What Standard? An Analysis of the Philosophy of Cornelius Van Til* (Vallecito, Ca.: Ross House Books, 1995 [1958]), 39–40.

[44] North, *Political Polytheism*, 334.

[45] Newton was not himself a deist. He was a professed Christian, although his view of the Christian God was unconventional and non-Trinitarian, as noted in Gary North, *Political Polytheism*, 340–341, 345–347. By removing the idea of the Trinity, Newton was attempting to eliminate irrational elements from Christianity. For a detailed discussion, see Richard S. Westfall, "Isaac Newton," in Gary B. Ferngren, ed. *Science and Religion: A Historical Introduction* (Baltimore: Johns Hopkins University Press, 2002), 153–162.

[46] North, *Political Polytheism*, 335–339.

[47] Rushdoony, *By What Standard?*, 49.

[48] Rushdoony, *By What Standard?*, 48–49.

[49] R. John Rushdoony, *Politics of Guilt and Pity* (Nutley, N.J.: Craig Press, 1970), 122–123. For Kuyper's perspective on the fallen or "abnormal" condition of the universe, see his *Lectures*, 131–136.

[50] J. B. Schneewind, *The Invention of Autonomy: A History of Modern Moral Philosophy* (Cambridge: Cambridge University Press, 1998), 8, 511.

[51] Schneewind, *The Invention*, 490, 511.

[52] J. B. Schneewind believes that religious conflict was "largely responsible for stimulating the rethinking of morality" in the centuries that followed, overshadowing even the influence of philosophy. Schneewind, *The Invention*, 6–7.

[53] Kant's categorical imperative is the principle that one should act only on a

maxim that one could will as a universal law for all other persons.

54 Rushdoony, *Politics of Guilt and Pity*, 148, 153–154.

55 R. John Rushdoony, *The Nature of the American System* (Fairfax, Va.: Thoburn Press, 1978 [1965]), 16; Rushdoony, *Politics of Guilt and Pity*, 298.

56 Rushdoony, *Politics of Guilt and Pity*, 320; Rushdoony, *This Independent Republic*, 122.

57 Rushdoony, *This Independent Republic*, 123, 125–133; Rushdoony, *The Nature*, 27–29; Rushdoony, *Politics of Guilt and Pity*, 321–322.

58 Rushdoony, *The Nature*, 30.

59 Rushdoony, *This Independent Republic*, 9–11, 15–16, 21–22.

60 Rushdoony, *The Nature*, 2; Rushdoony, *This Independent Republic*, 21–22.

61 Rushdoony, *The Nature*, 17; 11–17.

62 Rushdoony, *The Nature*, 82. See generally 17–20, 78–112.

63 R. J. Rushdoony, *The Messianic Character of American Education: Studies in the History of the Philosophy of Education* (Nutley, N.J.: Craig Press, 1963), 18–32.

64 Rushdoony, *The Messianic Character*, 18.

65 Rushdoony, *The Nature*, 49–51.

66 Rushdoony, *The Biblical Philosophy*, 6–7; Rushdoony, *Politics of Guilt and Pity*, 315. Rushdoony overstresses the role of chance, which merely provides the raw material in the form of random mutations that are then subject to the orderly work of natural selection.

67 Gary North, "From Cosmic Purposelessness to Humanistic Sovereignty" in North, *The Dominion Covenant*, 245–321. North calls Darwinism "an enormously successful sleight-of-hand operation" (267). Advocates of evolution are evidently tricksters who first diminish man's importance only later to blow it out of all proportion.

68 Rushdoony, *The Nature*, 15–22.

69 Rushdoony, *The Nature*, 113–121.

70 Rushdoony, *Politics of Guilt and Pity*, 75, 73, 76.

71 Rushdoony, *Politics of Guilt and Pity*, 91, 92–93, 96.

72 Greg L. Bahnsen, *Theonomy in Christian Ethics*, 3rd ed. (Nacogdoches, Tx.: Covenant Media Press, 2002), 35. Note: the pagination for the third edition is different from earlier editions.

73 Rushdoony, *Institutes*, 7–8.

[74] Bahnsen, *Theonomy*, 141, 253–254; Rushdoony, *Institutes*, 1–14.

[75] Bahnsen, *Theonomy*, 424–425.

[76] Rushdoony, *Institutes*, 571.

[77] Bahnsen, *Theonomy*, 424; Rushdoony, *Institutes*, 216.

[78] Bahnsen, *Theonomy*, 425, 431.

[79] Rushdoony, *Institutes*, 12–14, 515.

[80] Bahnsen, *Theonomy*, 425.

[81] Bahnsen, *Theonomy*, 426.

[82] Bahnsen, *Theonomy*, 69–74. For a linguistic analysis, see Gerhard Kittel & Gerhard Friedrich, *Theological Dictionary of the New Testament*, trans. and ed. Geoffrey W. Bromley, vol. 6 (Grand Rapids, Mi.: Wm. B. Eerdmans, 1968), 290–298, especially 294. The entry under "pleroo" by Gerhard Delling shows that the word means to "actualize" or "fulfill God's promise" and does not imply endorsement of a legal system, as Bahnsen would have it. According to Delling, "The goal of the mission of Jesus is . . . to actualize the will of God made known in the OT [Old Testament]. . . . How this is done is illustrated in vv. 21–48 [i.e. the verses in Matthew that follow the quotation in question and in which Jesus interprets the law in broad moral terms]."

[83] E.g., Bahnsen marginalizes Jesus' words to "turn the other cheek" (Matthew 5:38–42), attributing them to "hyperbole." Bahnsen, *Theonomy*, 119. Gary North, for his part, postulates that Jesus' words are tactical and insincere. Gary North, "In Defense of Political Bribery," in Rushdoony, *Institutes*, 845–846. Biblical arch-literalists tend to treat passages they don't like non-literally.

[84] For a traditional interpretation, see Sherman E. Johnson, Exegesis to the "Gospel According to St. Matthew," *The Interpreter's Bible*, vol. 7 (N.Y.: Abingdon-Cokesbury Press, 1951), 291–305. Specific critiques of the theonomist interpretation of Jesus' words can be found in Sinclair B. Ferguson, "An Assembly of Theonomists? The Teaching of the Westminster Divines on the Law of God," in Barker & Godfrey, eds., *Theonomy*, 334–337; and House & Ice, *Dominion Theology: Blessing or Curse? An Analysis of Christian Reconstructionism* (Portland, Oregon: Multnomah Press, 1988), 103–122.

[85] For instance, in one of many references to the Mosaic codes Calvin states: "There are some who deny that a commonwealth is duly framed which neglects the political system of Moses . . . . Let other men consider how perilous and seditious this notion is; it will be enough for me to have proved it false and foolish." Calvin, *Institutes*, 2:1502 (IV.xx.14). Recon-

structionists either angrily disagree with Calvin on this point (Rushdoony, *Institutes*, 9–10) or claim, as does North, that he showed ambivalence on the issue in his more obscure writings. See Gary North, "Publisher's Preface," in John Calvin, *The Covenant Enforced: Sermons on Deuteronomy 27 and 28* (Tyler, Tx.: Institute for Christian Economics, 1990), vii–xxv.

86 Ferguson, "An Assembly of Theonomists?, 346–348.

87 E.g., North, *Westminster's Confession*, 48–72, 237–245; Bahnsen, *Theonomy*, 495–524.

88 Rushdoony, *Institutes*, 123.

89 Rushdoony, *Institutes*, 24.

90 Rushdoony, *Politics of Guilt*, 331–332; Gary DeMar, *God and Government: A Biblical and Historical Study*, Vol. 1 (Atlanta, Ga.:American Vision Press, 1982), 3–38.

91 DeMar, *God and Government*, Vol. 1, 7–11, 21–26.

92 Rushdoony, *Roots of Reconstruction*, 68.

93 DeMar, *God and Government*, Vol. 1, 36; see also Rushdoony, *Institutes*, 739–741.

94 Rushdoony, *Institutes*, 282. Christian Identity cultists who refused to pay income tax in the 1980s often cited Rushdoony as an authority on biblical views of taxation. See Gary North, *Tools of Dominion: The Case Laws of Exodus* (Tyler, Tx.: Institute for Christian Economics, 1990), 912.

95 North, *Political Polytheism*, 584–585; North, *Tools of Dominion*, 906–912.

96 Gary DeMar, *God and Government: Issues in Biblical Perspective*, Vol. 2 (Brentwood, Tn.: Wolgemuth & Hyatt, 1989), 101–103.

97 DeMar, *God and Government*, Vol. 2, 144–145, 156, 78, 156; David Chilton, *Productive Christians in an Age of Guilt Manipulators: A Biblical Response to Ronald Sider* (Tyler, Texas: Institute of Christian Economics, 1981), 28–30, 33.

98 Gary North, *An Introduction to Christian Economics* (Craig Press, 1973), 211. See also North's critical comments on Kuyper's social policies in North, *Westminster's Confession*, 126–129.

99 North, *The Dominion Covenant*, ix–x; Gary North, "Free Market Capitalism," in Robert G. Clouse, *Wealth and Poverty: Four Christian Views of Economics* (Downers Grove, Il.: InterVarsity Press, 1984), 28–31; Gary North, *An Introduction*, 215–216; Rushdoony, *Institutes*, 523–524.

100 North, *An Introduction*, 215.

[101] Edd S. Noell, "A Reformed Approach to Economics: Christian Reconstructionism," *Bulletin, Association of Christian Economists*, Spring, 1993: 10.

[102] North, *An Introduction*, 4, 8.

[103] Chilton, *Productive Christians*, 34.

[104] Gary North, *Honest Money: The Biblical Blueprint for Money and Banking* (Nashville, Tenn.: Thomas Nelson, 1986), 107, as quoted in Noell, "A Reformed Approach," 12.

[105] North, *An Introduction*, 4, 8–15; Noell, "A Reformed Approach," 12, 14.

[106] See the comments of William E. Diehl and Art Gish, who reflect mainstream Christian sentiment, in response to Gary North's essay on free-market capitalism in Clouse, ed., *Wealth and Poverty*, 66–72 and 73–79.

[107] Christopher J.H. Wright, *God's People in God's Land: Family, Land, and Property in the Old Testament* (Grand Rapids, Mi.: William B. Eerdmans Publ. Co., 1990), 176–180.

[108] Reconstructionists understandably attempt to construe the Jubilee principle as narrowly as possible. See Chilton, *Productive Christians*, 127–132.

[109] Wright, *God's People*, 56.

[110] R. John Rushdoony, *The Roots of Reconstruction* (Vallecito: Ross House Books, 1991), 63–64.

[111] Gary DeMar, *God and Government: The Restoration of the Republic*, Vol. 3 (Atlanta, Ga.: American Vision, 1986), 92.

[112] DeMar, *God and Government*, Vol. 3, 93.

[113] North, *Political Pluralism*, 87.

[114] North, *Political Pluralism*, 249.

[115] North, *Political Pluralism*, 75, 87.

[116] North, *Political Polytheism*, 111, 227, 265; Gary North & Gary DeMar, *Christian Reconstructionism: What It Is, What It Isn't* (Tyler, Tx.: Institute for Christian Economics, 1991), 143.

[117] North & DeMar, *Christian Reconstructionism*, 141.

[118] North, *Political Polytheism*, 585–586.

[119] Gary North, *Backward, Christian Soldiers* (Tyler, Tx.: Institute for Christian Economics, 1984), 47, 57.

[120] Early books by Diamond and Clarkson dealing with aspects of Christian Reconstructionism received less attention than they deserved. They are still useful. See Sara Diamond, *Spiritual Warfare: The Politics of the Christian*

Right (Boston: South End Press, 1989) and Clarkson, *Eternal Hostility.*

121 Barron, *Heaven,* 40–41.

122 Clarkson, *Eternal Hostility,* 107.

123 Martin, *With God,* 354.

124 Martin, *With God,* 354.

125 Frederick Clarkson. "Theocratic Dominionism Gains Influence: No Longer Without Sheep." *PublicEye.org.* March/June 1994. http://www.publiceye.org/magazine/v08n1/chrisre3.html

126 Frederick Clarkson. "Theocratic Dominionism Gains Influence."

127 Anthony Williams. "'Dominionist' Fantasies." *FrontPageMagazine.com.* May 4, 2005. http://www.frontpagemag.com/Articles/Read.aspx?GUID= 86BEC0B4-D01C-40A0-A060-33D9FB999057

128 Christian rightists shared the podium with Christian Reconstructionists, for example, at the Confronting the Judicial War on Faith Conference of April 2005. See Michelle Goldberg, *Kingdom Coming: The Rise of Christian Nationalism* (N.Y.: W. W. Norton, 2006), 164–170, 175.

5 MISSION: RECLAIMING AMERICA

1 Ronald W. Ruegsegger, "Schaeffer's System of Thought," in Ronald W. Ruegsegger, ed., *Reflections on Francis Schaeffer* (Grand Rapids, Mich.: Academie Books, 1986), 33–34.

2 Francis A. Schaeffer, *How Should We Then Live? The Rise and Decline of Western Thought and Culture* (Old Tappan, N.J.: Fleming H. Revell, 1976), 20.

3 Clark H. Pinnock, "Schaeffer on Modern Theology," in Ruegsegger, ed., *Reflections,* 177.

4 Major critics include Cornelius Van Til and Gary North. See Gary North, *Political Polytheism: The Myth of Pluralism* (Tyler, Texas: Institute for Christian Economics, 1989), 170–172.

5 Schaeffer discussed Rushdoony's controversial history text, *This Independent Republic* (1964). See Ronald A. Wells, "Schaeffer on America," in Ruegsegger, *Reflections,* 234–235, 242.

6 Francis Schaeffer, *A Christian Manifesto* (Westchester, Il.: Crossway Books, 1981), 28–29, 134–137. For comparison, see R. J. Rushdoony, *This Independent Republic: Studies in the Nature and Meaning of American History* (Nutley, N.J.: The Craig Press, 1964), 90–120.

[7] North, *Political Polytheism*, 194–196, 218.

[8] Schaeffer, *A Christian Manifesto*, 90–91.

[9] Schaeffer, *A Christian Manifesto*, 120–121.

[10] See North, *Political Polytheism*, 165–220.

[11] Wells, "Schaeffer on America," 229–231, 240.

[12] Richard V. Pierard, "Schaeffer on History," in Ruegsegger, *Reflections*, 212–215. Rutherford was not, as Schaeffer claims, the inspirer of John Locke and John Witherspoon, neither of whom apparently were even familiar with his writings.

[13] In addition to Richard Pierard and Ronald Wells, George M. Marsden in Chapter 6 of *The Search for Christian America* (Westchester, Il.: Crossway Books, 1983) and Gary North in Chapter 4 of *Political Polytheism* have attacked Schaeffer's historical accuracy.

[14] Wells, "Schaeffer on America," 235–236.

[15] Schaeffer, *A Christian Manifesto*, 29.

[16] I believe James Skillen is generally correct in differentiating what he calls "cautious and critical conservatives" from "pro-American conservatives," their more boisterous counterparts on the Religious Right. He lists Colson as one of the former and Falwell et. al. among the latter. See James W. Skillen, *The Scattered Voice: Christians at Odds in the Public Square* (Alberta, Canada: Canadian Institute for Law, Theology and Public Policy, 1996 [1990]), 33–74.

[17] Jerry Falwell, *Listen America!* (N.Y.: Bantam Books, 1980), 224.

[18] John W. Whitehead, *The Second American Revolution* (Westchester, Il.: Crossway Books, 1982), 73.

[19] Whitehead, *The Second*, 179–180.

[20] Pat Robertson with Bob Slosser, *The Secret Kingdom* (N.Y.: Bantam Books, 1984), 200.

[21] For similar definitions, see Bruce Barron, *Heaven on Earth? The Social & Political Agendas of Dominion Theology* (Grand Rapids, Mich.: Zondervan Publishing House, 1992), 14; and Chip Berlet & Matthew N. Lyons, *Right-Wing Populism in America: Too Close for Comfort* (N.Y. & London: Guilford Press, 2000), 247.

[22] Sociologist Sara Diamond originally used the term "dominion theology" to refer to the Reconstructionist idea that "Christians are biblically mandated to 'occupy' all secular institutions." See Sara Diamond, *Spiritual*

Warfare: The Politics of the Christian Right (Boston: South End Press, 1989), 138. Frederick Clarkson and Chip Berlet were the first to use the more general term "dominionism." See Chip Berlet, "How We Coined the Term 'Dominionism.'" *Talk to Action.* Sept.1, 2011. http://www.talk2action.org/story/2011/8/31/17047/5683

23 R. John Rushdoony, *The Institutes of Biblical Law* (Presbyterian and Reformed Publishing Co., 1973), 448.

24 Rushdoony, *The Institutes*, 14, 724, 729–730. See also Barron, *Heaven on Earth?*, 18, 24.

25 Gary North, *Unconditional Surrender: God's Program for Victory* (Tyler, Texas: Institute for Christian Economics, 1988), 368–369. North justifies the connection between teaching and dominion through several steps of logic: teaching is a type of discipline, discipline implies a set of rules, and rules lead to law enforcement and "a chain of authority."

26 Quoted in House & Ice, *Dominion Theology: Blessing or Curse? An Analysis of Christian Reconstruction* (Portland, Oregon: Multnomah, 1988), 153. For a discussion of the Reconstructionists' use of the Great Commission to broaden their dominionist claims, see the above work, 150–162, and Barron, *Heaven on Earth?*, 152–154.

27 Berlet & Lyons, *Right-Wing Populism*, 247.

28 Barron, *Heaven on Earth?*, 98–100.

29 Barron, *Heaven on Earth?*, 86–87.

30 William Martin, *With God on Our Side: The Rise of the Religious Right in America* (N.Y.: Broadway Books, 1996), 259–260.

31 Barron, *Heaven on Earth?*, 64.

32 Barron, *Heaven on Earth?*, 74–79. The Latter Rain revival erupted in Saskatchewan, Canada, in 1948, but later faded after its ostracism by the mainstream Pentecostal community. The Latter Rain reference to "apostles and prophets" comes from Ephesians 4:11–13 in the New Testament.

33 Barron, *Heaven on Earth?*, 67–74.

34 Frederick Clarkson, *Eternal Hostility: The Struggle Between Theocracy and Democracy* (Monroe, Maine: Common Courage Press, 1997), 97–98.

35 Coalition on Revival. "The 17 Worldview Documents." http://www.church-council.org/Reformation_net/Pages/COR_Docs_Worldview_Docs.htm (7/26/2008). The 17 documents can be accessed from this site in .pdf format.

36 Bruce Barron, *Heaven on Earth?*, 101–104.

[37] Clarkson, *Eternal Hostility*, 99, 103, 242–243 footnote 17.

[38] Clarkson, *Eternal Hostility*, 103.

[39] Clarkson, *Eternal Hostility*, 99.

[40] Barron, *Heaven on Earth?*, 54–58. For more discussion of Christian views on legal history, see our Chapter 8, especially 205–206 and 264n.48. Because their approach does not "formally Christianize the state" or "compel religious belief in their leaders," Barron declines to call the Regent constitutionalists genuine dominionists. See Barron, *Heaven on Earth?*, 66.

[41] David A. Noebel, *Understanding the Times: The Religious Worldviews of Our Day and the Search for Truth* (Eugene, Or.: Harvest House Publishers, 1991), 4.

[42] D. James Kennedy & Jerry Newcombe, *Lord of All: Developing a Christian World-and-Life View* (Wheaton, Il.: Crossway Books, 2005), 19.

[43] D. James Kennedy & Jerry Newcombe, *What If America were a Christian Nation Again?* (Nashville, Thomas Nelson, 2003), 240.

[44] See Kennedy & Newcombe, *What If America*, passim.

[45] For Colson's opinions on the Reconstructionists and their methods, see Charles Colson with Ellen Santilli Vaughn, *Kingdoms in Conflict* (Zondervan & William Morrow, Publishers, 1989), 117, 291, 305.

[46] Pearcey has been a Senior Fellow at the Center for the Renewal of Science and Culture (CRSC), the headquarters for the ID movement.

[47] Nancy Pearcey, *Total Truth: Liberating Christianity from Its Cultural Captivity* (Wheaton, Il.: Crossway Books, 2004), 17, 22.

[48] Charles Colson & Nancy Pearcey, *How Now Shall We Live?* (Wheaton, Il.: Wheaton House Publishers, 1999), 296–297.

[49] Colson & Pearcey, *How Now Shall We Live?*, 400–404, 412–413.

[50] Colson & Pearcey, *How Now Shall We Live?*, 295–296.

[51] For their recent comments on dominionism, see, for example, Nancy Pearcey. "Dangerous Influences: The New Yorker, Michele Bachmann, and Me." *Human Events.* August 12, 2011. http://www.humanevents.com/article.php?id=45467; Chuck Colson. "Ayatollahs on the Prairie? Theocracy and Secular Hysteria." June 22, 2007. *Breakpoint.* www.breakpoint.org/commentaries/2653-ayatollahs-on-the-prairie

[52] Combining aspects of personal evangelism with the Christian Worldview perspective, the curriculum de-emphasizes some of the worldview's more caustic elements. It does, however, make God's sovereignty in human affairs an important priority.

[53] Prophets and apostles, mentioned in Ephesians 2:20 and 4:11, are understood by Wagner to have distinct roles in fulfilling God's divine purpose. Prophets receive God's revelation and convey it to apostles, while apostles are ministers sent by God to further the work of the church. See C. Peter Wagner, *Apostles and Prophets: The Foundation of the Church* (Ventura, Ca.: Regal Books, 2000), 88–106; C. Peter Wagner, *Apostles Today* (Ventura, Ca.: Regal Books, 2006), 27.

[54] Jacobs, *The Reformation Manifesto* (Minneapolis, Minn.: Bethany House, 2008), 83.

[55] Jacobs, *The Reformation*, 85.

[56] Jacobs, *The Reformation*, 87.

[57] Jacobs, *The Reformation*, 92–93.

[58] Jacobs, *The Reformation*, 9–11.

[59] C. Peter Wagner, *Dominion! How Kingdom Action Can Change the World* (Grand Rapids, Mich.: Chosen, 2008), 59–60.

[60] Jacobs, *The Reformation*, 106–107, 112–121, 127–129, 167–171.

6 CHRISTIAN JIHAD

[1] See, for instance, Javed Ahmad Ghamdi. "The Islamic Law of Jihad." *Studying Islam.* http://www.studying-islam.org/articletext.aspx?id=771

[2] Patrick J. Buchanan. "The Houston Syndrome." May 11, 1994. http://buchanan.org/blog/the-houston-syndrome-157 (March 28, 2013))

[3] Chip Berlet & Matthew N. Lyons, *Right-Wing Populism in America: Too Close for Comfort* (N.Y. & London: Guilford Press, 2000), 7, 10.

[4] Richard Hofstadter, *The Paranoid Style in American Politics and Other Essays* (N.Y.: Alfred A. Knopf, 1965), 39.

[5] Hofstadter, *The Paranoid Style*, 29.

[6] Rushdoony, *The Nature of the American System* (Fairfax, Va.: Thoburn Press, 1978 [1965]), 140. From Rushdoony's chapter, "The Conspiracy View of History."

[7] Rushdoony, *The Nature*, 139.

[8] Rushdoony, *The Nature*, 140.

[9] Rushdoony, *The Nature*, 140.

[10] Rushdoony, *The Nature*, 48, 142; Gary North, *Political Polytheism: The Myth*

of Pluralism (Tyler, Texas: Institute for Christian Economics, 1989, 468, 482–485.

[11] Rushdoony, *The Nature*, 148, 150; 116, 121. 122

[12] Gary North, *Conspiracy: A Biblical View* (Fort Worth, Tx.: Dominion Press, 1986), 5–6.

[13] North, *Conspiracy*, 3.

[14] North, *Conspiracy*, 6, 10.

[15] Rushdoony, *The Nature*, 142.

[16] North, *Conspiracy*, 10–11, 33.

[17] Rushdoony, *The Nature*, 84–85.

[18] See Pat Robertson, *The New World Order* (Dallas, Tx.: Word Publishing, 1991).

[19] Schaeffer, *A Christian Manifesto* (Westchester, Il.: Crossway Books, 1981), 41–62.

[20] Schaeffer, *A Christian Manifesto*, 56.

[21] Schaeffer, *How Should We Then Live? The Rise and Decline of Western Thought and Culture* (Old Tappan, N.J.: Fleming H. Revell, 1976), 228–245.

[22] Schaeffer, in particular, provided La Haye with a historical background for the so-called struggle between humanism and Christianity. See Tim LaHaye, *The Battle for the Mind* (Old Tappan, N.J.: Fleming H. Revell, 1980), 27–40.

[23] LaHaye tends, however, to lump generic humanists, including humanists with religious backgrounds, together with secular humanists. He uses religious references from the more general Manifesto I to claim that secular humanism, more representative of the later Manifesto II, is a form of religion. See LaHaye, *The Battle*, 125–127, 130.

[24] LaHaye, *The Battle*, 57–58.

[25] LaHaye, *The Battle*, 59–78.

[26] LaHaye, *The Battle*, 129–130, 147, 179.

[27] LaHaye, *The Battle*, 10.

[28] Tim LaHaye, *Mind Siege: The Battle for Truth in the New Millennium* (Nashville, Tenn.: Word Publishing, 2000), 35–36.

[29] Peter S. Heslam, "The Meeting of the Wellsprings: Kuyper and Warfield at Princeton," in Luis Lupo, Ed., *Religion, Pluralism, and Public Life: Abraham Kuper's Legacy for the Twenty-First Century* (Grand Rapids, Mich.: William B.

Eerdmans Publ. Co., 2000), 31.

[30] R. John Rushdoony, *Politics of Guilt and Pity* (Nutley, N.J.: Craig Press, 1970), 315–317.

[31] Schaeffer, *A Christian Manifesto*, 25–27, 48.

[32] Pearcey, *Total Truth: Liberating Christianity from its Cultural Captivity* (Wheaton, Il.: Crossway Books, 2004), 106–115.

[33] Pearcey, *Total Truth*, 142–146, 227–247.

[34] Samuel L. Blumenfeld, *NEA: Trojan Horse in American Education* (Boise, Id.: Paradigm Co., 1984), 53. The citation comes from a chapter entitled "Turning Children into Animals." Blumenfeld's educational conspiracy theories turn up in works by Pat Robertson (*The New Millennium*), Melvin & Norma Gabler (*What Are They Teaching Our Children?*), and others.

[35] "Tom Delay's Speech to House after Columbine." *Theocracy Watch.* http://www.theocracywatch.org/schools_delay_primordial_mud.htm (March 28, 2013)

[36] D. James Kennedy & Jerry Newcombe, *Lord of All: Developing a Christian World-and-Life View* (Wheaton, Il.: Crossway Books, 2005), 23, 29–30.

[37] See Gary North, *None Dare Call it Witchcraft* (New Rochelle, N.Y.: Arlington House Publishers, 1976), 184–185.

[38] Pat Robertson, *The New Millennium* (Dallas, Tx.: Word Publishing, 1990), 74.

[39] David A. Noebel, *Understanding the Times: The Religious Worldviews of Our Day and the Search for Truth* (Eugene, Oregon: Harvest House Publishers, 1991), 852.

[40] Barbara B. Gaddy, T. William Hall, & Robert J. Marzano, *School Wars: Resolving Our Conflicts over Religion and Values* (San Francisco: Jossey-Bass, 1996), 40.

[41] See, for instance, Constance Cumbey, *The Hidden Dangers of the Rainbow: The New Age Movement and the Coming Age of Barbarism* (Lafayette, La.: Huntington House, 1983); David Hunt, *Peace, Prosperity, and the Coming Holocaust* (Eugene, Or.: Harvest Books, 1983); Texe Marrs, *Dark Secrets of the New Age: Satan's Plan for a One World Religion* (Wheaton, Il.: Crossway Books, 1987); Johanna Michaelson, *Like Lambs to the Slaughter* (Eugene, Or.: Harvest Books, 1989); Randall Baer, *Inside the New Age Nightmare* (Lafayette, La.: Huntington House, 1989); Eric Buehrer, *The New Age Masquerade: The Hidden Agenda in Your Child's Classroom* (Brentwood, Tn.: Wolgemuth & Hyatt, 1990).

[42] Gaddy et. al., *School Wars*, 39–40, 45.

[43] Gaddy et. al., *School Wars*, 45.

[44] Bruce Wilson. "Burning Buddhas, Books, and Art: Meet the New Apostolic Reformation." *Talk to Action.* Sept. 14, 2011. http://www.talk2action.org/story/2011/9/14/192516/418/

[45] Bruce Wilson. "NAR Apostle Cindy Jacobs Leads Hispanic Groups in Anti-Catholic Prayer Initiative." *Talk to Action.* Sept. 28, 2011. http://www.talk2action.org/story/2011/9/28/14855/2836; Rachel Tabachnik. "Phony Ex-Terrorist Kamal Saleem in Reconciliation Ceremony at The Call Detroit." *Talk to Action.* Nov. 13, 2011. http://www.talk2action.org/story/2011/11/13/142342/27

[46] See Clarkson, *Eternal Hostility: The Struggle Between Theocracy and Democracy* (Monroe, Maine; Common Courage Press, 1997), 164–177.

[47] James Davison Hunter, *Culture Wars: The Struggle to Define America* (N.Y.: Basic Books, 1991), 42–43.

[48] Hunter, *Culture Wars*, 35–39, 42.

[49] Hunter, *Culture Wars*, 42–43, 62.

[50] Hunter, *Culture Wars*, 44.

[51] Hunter, *Culture Wars*, 124.

[52] Hunter, *Culture Wars*, 46.

[53] Hunter, *Culture Wars*, 156.

[54] Hunter, *Culture Wars*, 57–59.

[55] Hunter, *Culture Wars*, 52, 58.

[56] See Frederick Clarkson's analysis in *Eternal Hostility*, 164–171.

[57] Hunter, *Culture Wars*, 261.

[58] Clarkson, *Eternal Hostility*, 174–175.

[59] Gaddy, et. al., *School Wars*, 263.

[60] Hunter, *Culture Wars*, 44.

[61] One needs to remember that *Roe v. Wade*, which is defended by progressives, makes no hallowed assertions about abortion. It is a nuanced decision that considers abortion allowable under specific conditions and not under others.

[62] This is a classic example of how framing an issue affects how the issue is perceived. On framing, see George Lakoff, *Don't Think of an Elephant: Know your Values and Frame the Debate* (White River Junction, Vermont: Chelsea Green Publishing, 2004).

7 TOTAL TRUTH

[1] Walter Kaufmann, *Critique of Religion and Philosophy* (Princeton, N.J.: Princeton University Press, 1958), 311, 278.

[2] "For the invisible things of him from the creation of the world are clearly seen, being understood by the things that are made, even his eternal power and Godhead." Romans 1: 20

[3] Greg Bahnsen, ed., *Van Til's Apologetic: Readings and Analysis* (Phillipsburg, N.J.: P & R Publishing, 1998), 163.

[4] Bahnsen, ed., *Van Til's Apologetic*, 156.

[5] R. John Rushdoony, *The Biblical Philosophy of History* (Phillipsburg, N.J.: Presbyterian & Reformed Publishing Co., 1979 [1969]), 72.

[6] R. John Rushdoony, *By What Standard? An Analysis of the Philosophy of Cornelius Van Til* (Vallecito, Cal.: Ross House Books, 1995 [1958]), 23.

[7] Rushdoony, *By What Standard?*, 28.

[8] Rushdoony, *By What Standard?*, 26–27. Van Til was actually the first to use the term "brute facts."

[9] Rushdoony, *By What Standard?*, 23.

[10] Rushdoony, *The Biblical Philosophy of History*, 72–73.

[11] Francis Schaeffer, *The God Who is There*, in *Francis A. Schaeffer Trilogy* (Wheaton, Il.: Crossway Books, 1990), 156–17; Clark H. Pinnock, "Schaeffer on Modern Theology," in Ronald W. Ruegsegger, ed., *Reflections on Francis Schaeffer* (Grand Rapids, Mich.: Academie Books, 1986), 182.

[12] Schaeffer believed that if any biblical fact were to be open to question, then logically no other biblical fact could be considered "safe." See Pinnock, "Schaeffer," 178.

[13] "God has spoken, in a linguistic propositional form, truth concerning Himself and truth concerning man, history, and the universe." Schaeffer, *The God Who Is There*, 100.

[14] See, for instance, Schaeffer, *Escape from Reason*, in *The Francis Schaeffer Trilogy*, 218; and Schaeffer, *He is There and He is Not Silent*, in *The Francis Schaeffer Trilogy*, 311.

[15] See Schaeffer, *Escape from Reason*, Chapters 2–7; Pearcey, *Total Truth: Liberating Christianity from its Cultural Captivity* (Wheaton, Il.: Crossway Books, 2004), 74–95. The notion of a split in thinking is derived from Dooyeweerd's analysis of modernist thought, discussed earlier.

16 Schaeffer eschews "rationalism" because of its human orientation, but values "rationality" under proper direction. See "Appendix A: The Question of Apologetics," in *The Francis Schaeffer Trilogy*, 183–185; also Pinnock, "Schaeffer," 182, 190, on Schaeffer's rationalism.

17 Pearcey, *Total Truth*, 247.

18 Pearcey, *Total Truth*, 247.

19 Phillip E. Johnson, *The Wedge of Truth: Splitting the Foundations of Naturalism* (Downers Grove, Il.: IVP Books, 2000), 13–14.

20 Phillip E. Johnson, *Reason in the Balance: The Case against Naturalism in Science, Law, & Education* (Downers Grove, Il.: InterVarsity Press, 1995), 49.

21 Johnson, *Reason*, 108.

22 Barbara Forrest & Paul R. Gross, *Creationism's Trojan Horse: The Wedge of Intelligent Design* (N.Y.: Oxford University Press, 2004), 17.

23 Center for the Renewal of Science & Culture, Discovery Institute, "The Wedge Strategy." http://www.antievolution.org/features/wedge.html (March 28, 2013). See also discussion of Wedge Document in Forrest & Gross, *Creation's Trojan Horse*, 25–33.

24 Both R. J. Rushdoony and Gary North, for instance, see a connection between the elimination of God in the evolutionary process and the intervention of autonomous man as a new kind of messiah to take God's place. Rushdoony, *Politics of Guilt and Pity* (Nutley, N.J.: Craig Press, 1970), 104–105, 315; Gary North, *The Dominion Covenant: Genesis: An Economic Commentary on the Bible, Volume I* (Tyler, Tx.: Institute for Christian Economics, 1982), 245–321.

25 Discovery Institute, "The Wedge Strategy."

26 For ties between the two approaches, see Forrest & Gross, *Creationism's Trojan Horse*, 273–296.

27 Forrest & Gross, *Creationism's Trojan Horse*, 37–47.

28 Robert T. Pennock, *Tower of Babel: The Evidence against the New Creationism* (Cambridge: MIT Press, 1999), 52, 54. See 49–55, 352–356 for a fuller discussion.

29 Pennock, *Tower*, 181–185, 188

30 Pennock, *Tower*, 186–188

31 Kenneth R. Miller, *Finding Darwin's God: A Scientist's Search for Common Ground between God and Evolution* (N.Y.: HarperCollins, 1999), 91–92.

[32] Phillip E. Johnson, *Darwin on Trial* (Downers Grove, Il.: InterVarsity Press, 1991), 117.

[33] Johnson, *Darwin*, 9, 126–127.

[34] Pennock, *Tower*, 189–192. For how Johnson construes the issue, see Johnson, *Reason*, 205–218.

[35] Pennock, *Tower*, 195.

[36] Curiously, Johnson initially seemed to accept the distinction between metaphysical and methodological naturalism. For instance, in a lecture in 1992, he stated: "*Methodological* naturalism–the principle that science can study only the things that are accessible to its instruments and techniques–is not in question." Science, he said, "can study only what science can study." More recently he has attempted to explain away the inconsistency (see Johnson, *Reason*, 212).

[37] Johnson, *Darwin*, 120–123.

[38] Pennock, *Tower*, 208–209.

[39] Johnson, *Darwin*, 85, 118; 123.

[40] Pennock, *Tower*, 210–211.

[41] Pennock, *Tower*, 197–198, 202.

[42] Johnson, *Reason*, 49.

[43] Johnson, *Reason*, 107–109; Pennock, *Tower*, 203.

[44] Johnson, *Darwin*, 123; also Johnson, *Reason*, 195.

[45] Johnson, *Reason*, 205–206.

[46] Miller, *Finding Darwin's God*, 232–239; Pennock, *Tower*, 192, 200.

[47] For a discussion of the Dover case, see Forrest & Gross, *Creationism's Trojan Horse*, 325–334.

[48] Forrest & Gross, *Creationism's Trojan Horse*, 337.

[49] H.R. 910, labeled the "Energy Tax Prevention Act of 2011," was passed in the Republican-controlled House on April 7, 2011 by a vote of 255–172 with unanimous Republican support.

[50] Mark A. Beliles & Stephen K. McDowell, *America's Providential History* (Charlottesville, Va.: Providence Foundation, 1989), 171–173; David Barton, *The Myth of Separation* (Aledo, Tx.: Wallbuilder Press, 1992), 108–110; William J. Federer, *America's God and Country: Encyclopedia of Quotations* (St. Louis, Mo.: Amerisearch, Inc., 1999); Tim LaHaye, *Faith of Our Founding Fathers* (Brentwood, Tn.: Wolgemuth & Hyatt, 1987), 57–58. Some details

in these accounts differ slightly.

51 Jim Allison. "The Franklin Prayer Myth." *The Constitutional Principle: Separation of Church and State.* http://candst.tripod.com/franklin.htm (March 29, 2013). For historical events, Allison mostly uses James Madison's notes, edited by Max Farrand and published as *Records of the Federal Convention of 1787* (New Haven, Ct.: Yale University Press, 1911), and a manuscript of Franklin's speech in the Library of Congress with added comments. See also Chris Rodda's useful commentary in *Liars for Jesus: The Religious Right's Alternate Version of American History* (Published by the author, 2006), 251–279.

52 Jim Allison. "The Franklin Prayer Myth."

53 Beliles & McDowell, *America's Providential History*, vii.

54 Abraham Kuyper, *Lectures on Calvinism* (Grand Rapids, Mich.: Wm B. Eerdmans, 1931), 25, 199.

55 Kuyper, *Lectures*, 84.

56 Most Christian revisionists incorporate providential themes in their history, following in the footsteps of Verna M. Hall and Rosalie J. Slater, who produced Christian documentary materials on the American founding in the 1960s and 70s. They include the author teams of Marshall Foster and Mary-Elaine Swanson, Mark A. Beliles and Stephen K. McDowell, and Peter Marshall and David Manuel. Authors Harold O. J. Brown, Jerry Falwell, and D. James Kennedy are likewise strong providentialists. David Barton, Gary DeMar, and John W. Whitehead hold similar opinions, but less prominently. Francis Schaeffer and John Eidsmoe are not explicit (to my knowledge) about God's direct role, at least in print. See Verna M. Hall, *The Christian History of the Constitution of the United States of America* (San Francisco: FACE, 1960); Rosalie J. Slater, *Teaching and Learning America's Christian History, the Principle Approach* (San Francisco FACE, 1965); Marshall Foster & Mary-Elaine Swanson, *The American Covenant: The Untold Story* (Mayflower Institute, 1983); Mark A. Beliles and Stephen K. McDowell, *America's Providential History*; Peter Marshall and David Manuel, *The Light and the Glory* (Grand Rapids, Mich.: Fleming H. Revell, 1977); Harold O. Brown, *The Reconstruction of the Republic* (Milford, Mich.: Mott Media, 1981), 219–228; Jerry Falwell, *Listen America!* (N.Y.: Bantam Books, 1981), 217–221; D. James Kennedy, *What If America were a Christian Nation Again?* (Nashville, Tenn.: Thomas Nelson, 2003), 6–19, 222–231; Barton, *The Myth*, 257–260; Gary DeMar, *God and Government, Volume 1: A Biblical and Historical Study* (Atlanta: American Vision Press, 1982), 121–125; John W. Whitehead, *The Second American Revolution* (Westchester, Il.: Crossway Books, 1982), 158–160, 164; Schaeffer, *A Christian Manifesto*; John Eidsmoe,

Christianity and the Constitution: The Faith of our Founding Fathers (Grand Rapids, Mich.: Baker Book House, 1987).

57 Barton, *The Myth*, 258.

58 R. John Rushdoony, *The Biblical Philosophy of History*, 8, 17, 14.

59 For arguments along similar lines, see Slater, *Teaching and Learning*, 54–55; Foster & Swanson, *The American Covenant*, 35–36; David A. Noebel, *Understanding the Times: The Religious Worldviews of Our Day and the Search for Truth* (Eugene, Oregon: Harvest House Publishers, 1991), 722–723.

60 On this typical narrative, see also Mark Noll, Nathan Hatch, George Marsden, *The Search for Christian America* (Westchester, Il.: Crossway Books,1983), 129.

61 Barton, *The Myth*, 83–84.

62 See Rob Boston, "Consumer Alert! Wallbuilders Shoddy Workmanship," *Church and State* 49, 7 (July/August 1996), 11–13.

63 William Federer, for example, continues to feature the quotations in his compilation, *America's God and Country.*

64 Barton, *Original Intent: The Courts, the Constitution, and Religion* (Aledo, Tx.: WallBuilder Press, 2002 [1996]), 280; Federer, *America's God and Country*, 657–660. For background on the "Prayer Journal," see Chris Rodda. " 'Revisionism: A Willing Accomplice'–The Remarkable Hypocrisy of David Barton (Part 1)." *Talk to Action.* April 29, 2007. http://www.talk2action.org/story/2007/4/29/11251/5051/Front_Page/_quot_Revisionism_A_Willing_Accomplice_quot_The_Remarkable_Hypocrisy_of_David_Barton_Part_1

65 For the intellectual origins of the American Revolution and the U.S. Constitution, see such works as Bernard Bailyn, *The Ideological Origins of the American Revolution* (Cambridge, Mass.: Harvard University Press, 1967) and Forrest McDonald, *Novus Ordo Seclorum: The Intellectual Origins of the Constitution* (Lawrence, Ks.: University Press of Kansas, 1985).

66 Donald Lutz & Charles Hyneman, "The Relative Influence of European Writers on Late Eighteenth-Century American Political Thought," *The American Political Science Review* 78 [1984], 189–197.

67 Eidsmoe, *Christianity and the Constitution*, 51–53; Beliles & McDowell, *America's Providential*, 186; Barton, *The Myth*, 195–196.

68 Mark A. Noll, Nathan O. Hatch, George M. Marsden, *The Search for Christian America* (Westchester, Il.: Crossway Books, 1983), 81–82.

69 See Jim Allison & Tom Peters. "How Often Did the Founders Quote the

Bible?" *The Constitutional Principle: Separation of Church and State.* http://candst.tripod.com/tnppage/arg9.htm (March 28, 2013).

70 See Barton, *The Myth*, 97–98, 200–201; Kennedy, *What If America*, 33; Gary T. Amos, *Defending the Declaration: How the Bible and Christianity Influenced the Writing of the Declaration of Independence* (Brentwood, Tenn.: Wolgemuth & Hyatt, 1989), 20–23.

71 The words were favorite terms with writers like Lord Bolingbroke, the British deist. Jefferson, the main author of the Declaration, happened to be a devoted reader of Bolingbroke and copied extensive extracts of his works into his commonplace book. See Allen Jayne, *Jefferson's Declaration of Independence: Origins, Philosophy, and Theology* (Lexington: University of Kentucky Press, 1998), 20, 19–40.

72 Alan Dershowitz, *Blasphemy: How the Religious Right is Hijacking our Declaration of Independence* (Hoboken, N.J.: John Wiley & Sons, 2007), 12.

73 Forrest McDonald, *E Pluribus Unum: The Formation of the American Republic* (Indianapolis: Liberty Press, 1979), 310.

74 Isaac Kramnick & R. Laurence Moore, *The Godless Constitution: The Case against Religious Correctness* (N.Y.: W. W. Norton, 1997), 28–37.

75 Beliles & McDowell, *America's Providential*, 264; Slater, *Teaching and Learning*, 241.

76 Beliles & McDowell, *America's Providential*, 191.

77 Eidsmoe, *Christianity and the Constitution*, 369–372. See also Whitehead, *The Second*, 201, 204, 206, 209; Beliles & McDowell, *America's Providential*, 188; LaHaye, *Faith*, 71–72.

78 See Eidsmoe, *Christianity and the Constitution*, 369, which refers to Madison's *Federalist Paper* No. 51.

79 In *Federalist Paper* No. 55, Madison states: "As there is a degree of depravity in mankind which requires a certain degree of circumspection and distrust, so there are other qualities in human nature which justify a certain portion of esteem and confidence. Republican government presupposes the existence of these qualities in a higher degree than any other form." The most appropriate form of government for an innately depraved humanity, he opines, would be "despotism."

80 For Barton, "an establishment of religion" is restricted to the notion of legitimizing a particular denomination of Christianity, such as the Anglican Church in England. Barton, *Original Intent*, 29, 44–48.

81 Barton, *The Myth*, 47–51, 137–139; Barton, *Original Intent*, 49–52; Gary DeMar, *America's Christian History* (Atlanta, Ga.: American Vision, Inc.,

1993), 9–13; Beliles & McDowell, *America's Providential*, 178.

[82] Brewer was one of the few U.S. officials in high position at the time to support the aims of the National Reform Association, a religious fringe group. The Association's aims included inserting religious language into the Constitution's preamble. See Morton Borden, *Jews, Turks, and Infidels* (Chapel Hill: University of N. Carolina Press, 1984), 73.

[83] Brewer's assertion about America's Christian nationhood was made in the 1892 case, *Church of the Holy Trinity v. the United States.* It was an observation not material to the Court's holding and attached to the end of the opinion.

[84] Elisha Mulford, Josiah Strong, and Daniel Dorchester were three such Christian writers with a strong Protestant bias in matters of history. See Joseph Moreau, *School Book Nation: Conflicts over American History Textbooks from the Civil War to the Present* (Ann Arbor: University of Michigan Press, 2003), 99–101.

[85] Bruce Maiman. "Conservatives on Texas school board revising curriculum, change history." *Examiner.com.* March 14, 2010. http://www.examiner.com/populist-in-national/conservatives-on-texas-school-board-revising-curriculum-change-history

[86] In the 111th Congress (2009–2010), Forbes' resolution was designated House Resolution 397 and named "America's Spiritual Heritage Week."

[87] Chris Rodda at talk2action.org and Jim Allison and Susan Batte at candst.tripod.com, have been untiring defenders of historical accuracy.

[88] Stephen L. Carter, *The Culture of Disbelief: How American Law and Politics Trivialize Religious Devotion* (N.Y.: Basic Books, 1993), 86.

[89] First Amendment Center. "'07 Survey Shows Americans' Views Mixed on Basic Freedoms." *First Amendment Center.* Sept. 24, 2007. http://www.firstamendmentcenter.org/news.aspx?id=19031

[90] Religious rightist Doug Phillips reminded his audience at a 2007 Worldview Conference that "those who control history define the culture." See Jeremy Leaming. "Fringe Festival." *Church and State* 60, 7 (July/August 2007), 10–13.

[91] Beliles & McDowell, *America's Providential*, viii.

8 THE COMING KINGDOM

[1] Stephanie Condon. "Sharron Angle: Democrats Making 'Government Our God.'" *CBS News.* Aug.4, 2010. http://www.cbsnews.com/8301-503544_162-20012649-503544.html

[2] Christy Hoppe. "Perry says nation's soul is at stake in election." *Dallasnews.com.* June 11, 2010. http://www.dallas news.com/news/state/headlines/20100611-Perry-says-nation-s-soul-is-7990.ece

[3] Scott Keyes. "Jim DeMint's Theory of Relativity: 'The Bigger Government Gets, The Smaller God Gets.'" March 15, 2011. *ThinkProgress.* http://think progress.org/politics/2011/03/15/150676/demint-big-govt/

[4] Glen Beck. "The Tower of Babel like you've never heard it before." Nov. 17, 2010. http://www.glenbeck.com/content/articles/article/198/48240/

[5] The notion of "intolerable" competition between God and government is fully ingrained in today's Christian Worldview. It has been present since its mention in the Religious Right's earliest worldview statement on government in 1986. See Gary DeMar & Colonel Doner. "The Christian World View of Government." http://65.175.91.69/Reformation_net/COR_Docs/Christian_Worldview_Government.pdf, 5.

[6] Palin and her husband once had ties with a local affiliate of the U.S. Taxpayers Party in Alaska. Michael Finnegan. "Palin ties to Alaskan party downplayed." Sept. 3, 2008. *Los Angeles Times.* http://articles.latimes.com/2008/sep/03/nation/na-aip3

[7] Phillips befriended Rushdoony, calling him "the smartest man I've ever met," and accepted the basic tenets of Christian Reconstructionism. See Michelle Goldberg, *Kingdom Coming: The Rise of Christian Nationalism* (N.Y.: W. W. Norton & Co., 2006), 166.

[8] *U.S. Taxpayers Party Platform: Excerpts from Preamble and Each Article* [1996]. 8-sided folder in author's possession.

[9] Christopher Caldwell, "The Antiwar, Anti-Abortion, Anti-Drug-Enforcement-Administration, Anti-Medicare Candidacy of Dr. Ron Paul," *New York Times Magazine,* July 22, 2007.

[10] Ron Paul. "The War on Religion." *LewRockwell.com.* December 30, 2003. http://www.lewrockwell.com/paul/paul148.html. By all accounts, Ron Paul is the actual author of articles on LewRockwell.com, unlike those in his famous newsletters, which he disavows.

[11] Ron Paul. "The First Amendment Protects Religious Speech." *LewRockwell.com.* April 2, 2003. http://www.lewrockwell.com/paul/paul85.html; Jeremy Leaming. "Bad Bills on the Hill: Church-State Wall Under Fire in New Congress." Jan. 22, 2007. *The Wall of Separation.* http://www.au.org/blogs/wall-of-separation/bad-bills-on-the-hill-church-state-wall-under-fire-in-new-congress

[12] See Chris Moody. "Saint Paul: Inside Ron Paul's effort to convince Chris-

tian conservatives that he's their man." *Yahoo! News.* Dec.9, 2011. http://news.yahoo.com/blogs/ticket/saint-paul-inside-ron-paul-effort-convince-Christian-150637605.html

13 Texas Freedom Network. "The Anatomy of Power: Texas and the Religious Right in 2006." http://www.tfn.org/site/PageServer?pagename=publications_state_of_the_religious_right#state%20of%20the%20Religious%20Right:%202006

14 Republican Party of Texas. "2012 Report of Platform Committee." http://www.texasgop.org/about-the-party

15 Gary North, *The Dominion Covenant: Genesis* (Tyler, Tx.: Institute for Christian Economics, 1982), 10.

16 Jerry Z. Muller. *Adam Smith in His Time and Ours: Designing the Decent Society* (N.Y.: The Free Press, 1993), Chapter XI: "The Visible Hand of the State," 140–153.

17 David Chilton, *Productive Christians in an Age of Guilt Manipulators* (Tyler, Tx.: Institute for Christian Economics, 1981), 28–29.

18 E. Calvin Beisner & Daryl S. Borquist, Chairman & Co-Chairman, "The Christian World View of Economics." http://65.175.91.69/Reformation_net/COR_Docs/Christian_Worldview_Economics.pdf (June 7, 2011). This is one of several Christian Worldview position papers issued by the Coalition on Revival in 1986, as discussed in our Chapter Five.

19 Some religious rightists like Charles Colson and Nancy Pearcey, while supporting the pro-capitalist thrust of Christian Worldview theology, leave themselves room to criticize the most obvious defects of capitalism and argue for more Christian morality in the marketplace. See Charles Colson & Nancy Pearcey, *How Now Shall We Live?* (Wheaton, Il.: Tyndale House, 1999), 383–39.

20 Chilton, *Productive Christians*, 28–32.

21 In the words of Gary North: "Biblical justice, biblical law, and economic growth are intimately linked." See Gary North, "Free Market Capitalism," in Robert G. Clouse, Ed., *Wealth and Poverty: Four Christian Views of Economics* (Downers Grove, Il.: InterVarsity Press, 1984), 27.

22 North, *The Dominion*, 146; also 24, 42, 108, 439. See Philippians 2:12.

23 R. John Rushdoony, *The Institutes of Biblical Law* (Presbyterian & Reformed publishing Co., 1973), 270.

24 R. John Rushdoony, *Politics of Guilt and Pity* (Nutley, N.J.: Craig Press, 1970), 44–46. Rushdoony makes much of the fact that the phrase is taken from the words of Cain, not God.

[25] Rushdoony, *Politics of Guilt and Pity*, 73, 86–87

[26] I am indebted to George Lakoff for his treatment of narrowly and broadly constructed concepts of responsibility and, more generally, his discussion of conservative and progressive moral worldviews. See George Lakoff, *Whose Freedom? The Battle Over America's Most Important Idea* (N.Y.: Picador, 2006), 74–76, 81–88, 103–106.

[27] Chilton, *Productive Christians*, 124. Chilton quotes American clergyman Samuel Willard, a Puritan who speaks critically of corrective action by human authorities: "It implies a fault found with His [God's] Government of the World," he states, "as if He dealt Unjustly, and did not distribute His Favours, either in Wisdom or Righteousness." See also Beisner & Borquist, "The Christian World View of Economics," 7.

[28] Michelle Goldberg, *Kingdom Coming*, 112.

[29] He states: "The only question might be how would we want God to deal with us?" Marvin Olasky, *The Tragedy of American Compassion* (Washington, D.C.: Regnery Publishing, Inc., 1992), 8.

[30] Olasky, *The Tragedy*, 123.

[31] Olasky, *The Tragedy*, 8–9.

[32] Olasky, *The Tragedy*, 10; Trevin Wax. "From Marxism to Christ: Interview with Marvin Olasky (1)." Oct. 19, 2009. http://thegospelcoalition.org/blogs/trevinwax/2009/10/19/from-marxism-to-christ-interview-with-marvin-olasky-1/

[33] See, for instance, Daniel Patrick Moynihan, *Miles to Go: A Personal History of Social Policy* (Cambridge, Mass.: Harvard University Press, 1996), 26–63.

[34] For different assessments of the program ten years after passage, see Ron Haskins & Mark Greenberg, "Welfare Reform, Success or Failure?" *Policy & Practice*, March 2006: 10–12.

[35] A coalition of conservative Christian leaders, including well-known figures James Dobson and Charles Colson, endorsed a statement of principles called the Cornwall Declaration on Environmental Stewardship in 2000. In November of 2005 the Interfaith Stewardship Alliance (ISA) was formed to publicize and apply the principles. The group changed its name to the Cornwall Alliance for the Stewardship of Creation in May 2007. The organization's board of advisors has included David Barton, D. James Kennedy, John Neuhaus, Louis P. Sheldon, and James Tonkowich, among others. Cornwall Alliance. "About the Cornwall Alliance–Dominion. Stewardship. Conservation." http://www.cornwallalliance.org/about/ (March 29, 2011)

[36] David Kenneth Larson, "Evangelical Environmental Network." http://

www.clas.ufl.edu/users/bron/PDF–Christianity/Larson-Evangelical %20Enviro%20Newtork.pdf (May 18, 2011).

37 Cornwall Alliance. *Cornwall Declaration on Environmental Stewardship.* http://www.cornwallalliance.org/articles/read/the-cornwall-declaration-on-environmental-stewardship/ (March 29, 2011)

38 Cornwall Alliance. *Cornwall Declaration.*

39 Agence France-Presse. "Climate change debunkers take stage in US Congress." *The Raw Story.* March 26, 2009. http://rawstory.com/news/2008/Climate_change_debunkers_take_stage_in_326.html

40 Cornwall Alliance. *Cornwall Declaration.*

41 CFACT, which lists Beisner as a board member, has also been instrumental in helping to publicize the Cornwall Declaration. See Lee Fang. "The Oily Operators behind the Religious Climate Change Denial Front Group, Cornwall Alliance." Think Progress. *Wonk Room.* June 15, 2010. http://wonkroom.thinkprogress.org/2010/06/15/cornwall-alliance-frontgroup/

42 Stephanie Hendricks, *Divine Destruction: Wise Use, Dominion Theology, and the Making of American Environmental Policy* (Hoboken, N.J.: Melville House Publishing, 2005), 35–38.

43 See David Helvarg, *The War Against the Greens*, Revised and Updated (Boulder, Co.: Johnson Books, 2004), 315–343.

44 Roy Moore with John Perry, *So Help Me God: The Ten Commandments, Judicial Tyranny, and the Battle for Religious Freedom* (Nashville, Tenn.: Broadman & Holman Publishers, 2005), 145.

45 *Glassroth v. Moore*, 335 F. 3rd 1282 (11th Circuit, 2003), 27.

46 *Glassroth v. Moore*, 10.

47 Moore relies on the arguments of the Regent constitutionalists, who saw Christianity as the basis of English common law and, by way of William Blackstone, American law. See Moore, *So Help Me God*, 188–189.

48 Arguments to support the thesis that the Ten Commandments, or some form of Christianity, served as the foundation of English common law are notoriously vague when attempted at all. For examples of the genre, see John C. H. Wu, *Fountain of Justice: A Study in the Natural Law* (London: Sheed & Ward, 1955); Herbert W. Titus, *God, Man, and Law: The Biblical Principles* (Oak Brook, Il.: Institute in Basic Life Principles, 1994), 4–5, 31–38, 42–47, and passim; and John Eidsmoe, "Operation Josiah: Rediscovering the Biblical Roots of the American Constitutional Republic," in H. Wayne House, ed., *The Christian and American Law: Christianity's*

Impact on America's Founding Documents and Future Direction (Grand Rapids, Mich.: Kregel Publications, 1998), 83–106. For a mainstream scholarly treatment that emphasizes Christian influence but is fairly nuanced, see Harold J. Berman, *Law and Revolution: The Formulation of the Western Legal Tradition* (Cambridge: Harvard University Press, 1983). Common law refers to the body of law derived from custom and traced to the decisions of the English common law courts since the early Middle Ages. By any measure, that law was unsystematic, experienced-based, and overwhelmingly secular. Prior to the eleventh century, Christianity played an "essentially passive" role in the face of an entrenched English folk law, as Berman points out (*Law and Revolution*, 75). After the Norman Conquest in 1066, church authorities imported Christian canon law, a well-codified system modeled on the old Roman law, into England. This canon law, which itself was a blend of Christian and pagan influences, affected the English common law only indirectly since it was practiced in ecclesiastical courts separate from the king's common law courts. Legal historian Harold J. Berman, a Christian evangelical, makes the best case for such tangential influence during those early centuries, mainly in areas of concern to church authorities such as family and marriage law. But, as Berman acknowledges for the most part, this Christian influence was limited. For general background, see the classic work, Frederick Pollock & Frederic William Maitland, *The History of English Law Before the Time of Edward I*, Vol. 1 (London: Cambridge Univ. Press, 1895), Chapters 4 & 5.

[49] See, for instance, Schaeffer, *A Christian Manifesto* (Westchester, Il.: Crossway, 1981) , 89–91.

[50] The Preamble to the Constitution states: "We the people of the United States . . . do ordain and establish this Constitution for the United States of America."

[51] Isaac Kramnick & R. Lawrence Moore, *The Godless Constitution: The Case Against Religious Correctness* (N.Y.: W.W. Norton, 1996), 32–45.

[52] Kramnick & Moore, *The Godless*, 144–149.

[53] Concerning Titus' role at Regent University, see Bruce Barron, *Heaven on Earth? The Social and Political Agendas of Dominion Theology* (Grand Rapids, Mich.: Zondervan, 1992), 53–66.

[54] See Herbert W. Titus, *God, Man, and Law: The Biblical Principles* (Oak Brook, Il.: Institute in Basic Life Principles, 1998 [1994]), 4–5 and passim.

[55] The case method involved the empirical classification of judges' opinions in particular cases and the study of their reasoning in order to extract generalized rules of law. Inspired by the rise of the inductive sciences and Darwin's theory of evolution, it was gradually adopted in law schools

starting with Harvard in the 1870s. Christopher Columbus Langdell, the Harvard dean who pioneered the case method, and Oliver Wendell Holmes, whose skeptical attitude toward legal absolutes helped to undermine traditional legal views, are cast as the main villains. Titus, *God, Man, and Law*, 3–7.

56 See Albert W. Alschuler, "Rediscovering Blackstone. (William Blackstone's 'Commentaries')," *University of Pennsylvania Law Review* 145, 1 (November, 1996). Alschuler shows that Blackstone tended to view the right to property, for example, as a right created by society rather than one dictated by divinely determined natural law. Laws of inheritance Blackstone saw as nothing more than man-made contrivances.

57 Gary North notes that in the four volumes of the *Commentaries*, there are only about a dozen references to the Bible, all insignificant, whereas the laws of Greece, Rome, and other pagan countries are referenced liberally throughout. See Gary North, *Political Polytheism: The Myth of Pluralism* (Tyler, Tx.: Institute for Christian Economics, 1989), 321-322.

58 Early American law was very much a function of economic and political realities, as in later times. See Morton J. Horwitz's hard-headed analysis, *The Transformation of American Law, 1780–1860* (Cambridge: Harvard University Press, 1977).

59 Michelle Goldberg, *Kingdom Coming: The Rise of Christian Nationalism* (N.Y.: W. W. Norton, 2006), 46–48.

60 See Goldberg, *Kingdom Coming*, 174–175, for further analysis of the likely effects of the CRA.

9 A PROPER DIAGNOSIS

1 John Calvert, *Sayyid Qutb and the Origins of Radical Islamism* (N.Y.: Columbia University Press, 2010), 204.

2 David Zeidan, *The Resurgence of Religion: A Comparative Study of Selected Themes in Christian and Islamic Fundamentalist Discourses* (Leiden: Brill, 2003), 93. For a comparative analysis of the anti-secular theme, see 93–127.

3 Zeidan, *The Resurgence*, 93.

4 Calvert, *Sayyid Qutb*, 208, 213.

5 Calvert, *Sayyid Qutb*, 209.

6 Zeidan, *The Resurgence*, 165.

7 Zeidan, *The Resurgence*, 206.

8 Chuck Colson. "Wars of Religion? The 'Economist' Gets it Wrong." *Breakpoint.* Nov. 28, 2007. http://www.breakpoint.org/bpcommentaries/entry/13/10586

9 Neuhaus, *The Naked Public Square: Religion and Democracy in America* (Grand Rapids, Mich.: Wm. B. Eerdmans, 1984), 23–26.

10 Neuhaus, *The Naked Public Square*, 86.

11 Neuhaus, *The Naked Public Square*, 60, 76. "Sacred canopy" was a term introduced by sociologist Peter L. Berger in the 1960s.

12 Charles Haynes, a noted scholar at the First Amendment Center, attests to this trend. "The big picture," he states in 2005, "is that there's more religion now in public schools than ever in modern history . . . so you can go to many public schools today and kids will be giving each other religious literature, they will be sharing their faith." Quoted by Michelle Goldberg. "How the secular humanist grinch didn't steal Christmas." *Salon.com News.* Nov. 21, 2005. http://www.salon.com/news/feature/2005/11/21/christmas/print.html

13 Neuhaus, *The Naked Public Square*, 76, 122–123.

14 Neuhaus, *The Naked Public Square*, 145, 202–203.

15 Neuhaus, *The Naked Public Square*, 221.

16 Neuhaus, *The Naked Public Square*, 78.

17 Alexis de Tocqueville, *Democracy in America*, transl. & eds. Harvey Mansfield & Delba Winthrop (Chicago: University of Chicago Press, 2000), 278.

18 Tocqueville, *Democracy*, 285.

19 I am indebted to George Lakoff for illustrating the importance of framing in political discourse. See George Lakoff, *Don't Think of an Elephant! Know Your Values and Frame the Debate* (White River Junction, Vt.:Chelsea Green Publishing, 2004).

Index

abortion:
Catholic approach to, 31–32, 33
Christian Right and, 17–18, 24, 31–35
evangelical approach to, 31–32, 33
Schaeffer on, 18, 31, 34, 124
tactics of anti-abortion movement, 32-35
violent resistance to, 34–36, 213–214
Ahmanson, Howard, 118
Alabama Textbook Case, 154
American Vision, 96, 118
America's Providential History (Beliles & McDowell), 175, 184
amillennialism, 238n.6
Angle, Sharron, 185
anti-statism, 72–73, 97–98, 101, 104, 185–188
antithesis:
Baader as early formulator of, 235n.32
as tenet of Christian Worldview, 58, 71, 79, 84, 137, 142, 149, 156
Kuyper on, 71, 73
Van Til on, 76, 79
See also culture war; dualism; spiritual warfare
apologetics, 45, 46, 76–81, 91, 92
Arminianism, 61, 99
Army of God, 36
Augustine, 62, 64, 98
Austrian School of Economics, 113
autonomy:
Baader and, 235n.32
Christian Worldview critique of, 63, 169
Christian Reconstructionists on, 89, 97–105, 115, 194
democracy as expression of, 101–102
environmentalism as expression of, 199
false presuppositions as basis of, 78, 80
humanism as expression of, 104, 146
in philosophy (Kant), 99–101
as rebellion against God, 63, 97
in religion, 98–99
science as expression of, 99, 103–104
social reform as expression of, 102–103
statism as expression of, 97, 101–102, 104, 186
Van Til on, 78, 80
viewed positively, 97, 156, 201, 218

Baader, Franz, 235n.32
Babel, Tower of, 72, 98, 110, 186
Bachmann, Michele, 133, 183
Bahnsen, Greg, 90–92, 96, 107–108
Barton, David, 130, 133, 175, 176, 177, 178, 181, 182, 183, 189, 204
Battle for the Mind, The (LaHaye), 20, 146
Bauer, Gary, 24, 25, 131
Beck, Glenn, 186
Beisner, E. Calvin, 195, 198–200
Beliles, Mark A., 175, 176
Berlet, Chip, 126, 143, 247n.22
Berman, Harold J., 264–265n.48
Bible:
abortion and, 32, 229n.50
Christian Worldview and, 1, 3, 9, 49,

55, 81
economics and, 87, 110–114, 192–195, 199–200
evangelicals and, 14, 152
evidence and, 169–170
law and, 105–109, 119, 125, 129, 202, 205, 208
presuppositionalism and, 75, 76, 79, 81, 89, 122, 158–160
as used by Reconstructionists, 83, 105–114, 119
responsibility and, 193–195
U.S. Founders and, 177, 179–180, 181, 205
Bible references:
Genesis (1:26–28), 37, 72, 125–126, 193
Romans (1:18–20), 79, 158
Romans (1:18–32), 65–66. 71, 97, 108, 138, 142, 170, 234n.19
Romans (13:1–7), 66–67, 110, 203
biblical economics. *See under* Bible; economics
Billings, Robert, 13–14, 116
Blackstone, William, 130, 205
Bray, Michael, 36
Brewer, David, 182, 259n.82 & 260n.83
Bright, Bill, 41–42, 44
Brown v. Board of Education of Topeka, 16
Buchanan, Pat, 142, 150
Bush, George H. W., 22, 187
Bush, George W., 25, 26–28, 200

Calvin, John, 56, 59–68, 84, 86, 97, 98, 108, 121, 137. *See also* Calvinism
Calvinism:
adversarial aspect of, 65–66
authoritarian tendencies of, 63, 68
Christian Reconstruction and, 83–84
as basis for Christian Worldview, 56, 63–64, 65–66
on civil government, 66–67, 72
on cognitive aspect of sin, 64
on *divinitatis sensum* (sense of the divine) , 65
on divine will, 62–64
as logical system of divinity, 59
Madison's views and, 181
as modified by Kuyper, 71–74
on predestination, 59–60, 61, 62, 99
rigor and rectitude of, 57, 59–61
welfare policy and, 196
Campus Crusade for Christ, 41–42, 43
case method, 205, 265n.55
Catholics, Catholicism, 17–18, 21, 31–34, 54, 60–61, 64, 98, 152.
cell groups, 41–44
Center for the Renewal of Science and Culture (CRSC), 163–164
Chalcedon Foundation, 89, 95, 118
Chalcedon Report, 89, 90, 94, 96
charismatics:
as distinct type of evangelical, 15, 226n.7
susceptibility to dominionist influence, 117, 127, 137
Chilton, David, 90, 128
Christian Coalition, 22–25, 189
Christian constitutionalists. *See* Regent constitutionalists
Christian Identity, 244n.94
Christian Manifesto, A (Schaeffer), 20, 53, 122, 124, 125
Christian nation & nationhood, 130, 133, 177, 178, 179, 180, 181, 182, 183, 184, 190
Christian Reconstructionism:
on autonomy, 97–105
Christian Worldview and, 83–84, 118–119, 128, 144
conflict with Reformed community, 91, 94, 95–96, 108
conflict with premillennialists, 95–96
on conspiracy, 144–145
decline in activity, 96
on dominionism, 125–126
influence on Religious Right, 96, 117–119, 121–122, 125–126, 128, 133, 135, 137
on model economy, 111–114
on model government and society, 109–111, 114–115
on model law order, 105–109
origins and rise of, 83–84, 89–90
orthodox Presbyterianism and, 84–85
postmillennialism and, 85–86

Christian Reconstructionism *(cont'd)*
resistance to by religious rightists, 108, 118, 134–135
rifts within, 91, 94–95
right-wing populism and, 86–87
scanty media coverage of, 116
scenario for victory of, 115–116
Christian revisionist history:
in federal legislation, 183
lack of rules of evidence, 177
as morality lesson, 176–177
practitioners of, 130, 175–176, 257n.56
as providential, 174–176, 257n.56
public impact of, 183–184
in school curricula, 182
treatment of U.S. founding, 179–182
See also history
Christian Right:
abortion and, 31–36
anti-statism of, 185–186, 189–91
aptitude and assets of, 47
Bush administration and, 26–28
challenges presented by, 216–218
conspiracy theory and, 145–149
defense against critics, 213–215
definition of, 8
dominionism and, 125–130
efforts to change the culture, 37–47
emergence of, 13–20
free market capitalism and, 191–193
Reagan Administration and, 20–21
Reconstructionism and, 96, 117–119, 121–122, 125, 128, 133, 135, 137
Republican Party and, 23–26
Christian View of God and the World, The (Orr), 54, 55
Christian Worldview:
anti-statism of, 58, 190
antithesis & dualism as basis for, 4, 48, 66, 71, 142, 153, 212
authoritarianism of, 63–64, 68, 208–209
blending of sacred & secular in, 66, 68, 135, 213
Calvinism as basis for, 56, 57, 63–64, 66, 67–68
Christian Reconstructionism and, 83–84, 118–119, 128, 144
Christianity and, 48, 212
comparison with radical Islamism, 212–213
conspiracism of, 144
core ideas of, 1, 3, 48, 58, 137–138
different interpretations of, 5–6
economics and, 128–129, 192
as ideology, 5–6, 49, 57, 217
instructional approaches to, 2, 131–137
Kuyper as key shaper of, 56–57, 71
origins of, 54–57
presuppositionalism as basis for, 71, 75, 76, 81, 158, 170
as response to modernism and secularism, 1, 3–4, 48, 53–55, 69–71, 212
science and, 162, 163
Christianity, traditional:
in American history, 178–182
as compared with Christian Worldview, 48, 212
no longer dominant, 54–55, 69
in the public square, 214–215
sectarian conflict in, 69, 101, 153
spiritual warfare and, 141
Tocqueville on, 215–216
truth important for, 157
church-state separation, principle of:
Christian Right's opposition to, 7, 130, 133, 202-203, 206
under threat, 207–209
circular reasoning. *See* reasoning
civil disobedience, 7, 124
Clarkson, Frederick, 14, 116, 129, 151, 154, 247–248n.22
Coalition on Revival (COR), 125, 128–129, 189, 198
Colson, Chuck, 2, 7, 28, 118, 124, 132, 133, 134–135, 213
Commentaries on the Laws of England (Blackstone), 205, 266n.57
common grace. *See* grace
common law:
Blackstone and, 130, 205
theory of its Christian origins, 264–265n.48

Index

"compassionate conservatism," 27
conspiracism, 143–144, 149
Constitution, U.S., 30, 95, 102, 106, 130, 173, 179–181, 202, 203, 204, 207, 209
Constitution Party. *See* U.S. Taxpayers Party
Constitution Restoration Act, 30, 207–208, 229n.47
constitutionalists, Christian. *See* Regent constitutionalists
Cornwall Alliance for the Stewardship of Creation, 198–199, 200, 263n.35
Council of Chalcedon, 89, 98
court stripping, 30, 207, 229n.47
courts. *See* federal judiciary
covenant, 85, 106, 110, 112, 115, 238n.5
creationism, 134, 164, 169
Cultural Mandate. *See* Dominion Mandate
culture, biblical concept of, 37
culture war, 65, 142–143, 150–156, 218
Culture Wars: The Struggle to Define America (Hunter), 142, 150–151

Darwin on Trial (Johnson), 163, 166, 169
Darwinism:
  campaign against, 134, 147–148, 162, 163, 165, 168, 169, 170, 212
  Christian Reconstructionists on, 103–104, 147, 242n.67, 255n.24
  perceived ramifications of, 69, 147–148
  See also evolution
Dawkins, Richard, 166, 167
Declaration of Independence, 7, 130, 180, 206
deism, 99, 180
DeMar, Gary, 96, 110, 115, 118, 128, 176, 182
DeMint, Jim, 133, 186
demonization, 143–144, 149, 212
Dershowitz, Alan, 180
Diamond, Sara, 116, 247–248n.22
divine command theory, 63. *See also* voluntarism
divinitatis sensum (awareness of the divine), 65, 170
Dobson, James, 2, 25, 26, 29, 38, 44, 108, 118, 124, 131, 135, 136
Dominion Mandate:
  Christian Worldview and, 126–127
  culture building and, 37
  dominionism and, 125–126
  economic endeavors and, 111–112, 193, 199
  as linked to Jesus' Great Commission, 126, 133, 135
  main human social functions condoned by, 72
dominion theology. *See* dominionism
dominionism, 116, 118, 119, 125–130, 131, 133, 135, 136–137, 187, 189, 247–248n.22
Dooyeweerd, Herman, 57, 74–75, 112, 236n.42
Dover evolution trial. *See Kitzmiller et al. v. Dover Areas School District*
dualism (cognitive inconsistency), 75, 159
dualism (concept of good versus evil), 4, 65, 152–153, 155. *See also* antithesis; culture war; spiritual warfare

economics:
  biblical, 93, 111–114, 119, 192–195
  biblical responsibility and, 193–195
  Christian Worldview and, 128–129, 192
  Dominion Mandate and, 111–112, 193, 199
  the invisible hand and, 191–192
education:
  "Christian Worldview" universities and law schools, 44–46
  "classical and Christian schools," 45
  home schooling, 39–40
  public schools, 16, 39, 103, 147–148, 154, 171
  secular universities, 46
  traditional Christian colleges, 44
  traditional Christian private academies, 16–17, 44
Eidsmoe, John, 130, 176, 264–265n.48

environment:
biblical model and, 198–200
Dominion Mandate and, 198–199
global warming and, 199–200
eschatology, 85–86, 129
evangelicals:
abortion and, 17–18, 31–32, 33
Catholics and, 17–18, 31
Christian Reconstructionism and, 90, 94, 96, 116
definition of, 14–15
diversity of, 15
grievances of, 16–17
military and, 42
millennial beliefs of, 15, 85–86
moderate, 5, 198, 217
politicization of, 14–20
Republican Party and, 13–14
evidence:
Christian revisionist historians' handling of, 177–178
documentary, 177, 182
ID advocates' handling of, 169–170
presuppositions and, 77–78, 81
scientific versus legal approach to, 165–167
second-hand, 182
supernatural, 167, 169
evidentialism, 77
evolution, 16, 119, 148. *See also* Darwinism
eye for an eye. *See lex talionis*

facts:
brute, 158, 176
presuppositions and, 77-78, 179
theistic, 78, 158
faith-based initiative, 27–28, 228n.37
Falwell, Jerry, 13–14, 18, 20, 21–22, 45, 117, 124, 215
Family, The, 43, 231–232n.87
Family Research Council, 25
Farris, Michael, 39, 45
federal judiciary, 29–30, 188, 206–207
Federal Marriage Amendment, 29
Federalist Papers, 179, 181
First Amendment, 30, 106, 123, 181, 188, 202, 207–208
Focus on the Family (FOF), 2, 38–39, 136
Forbes, Randy, 183
Foundation for Economic Education (FEE), 87
Frame, John, 77, 237n.65
framing issues:
courtroom approach, 165–166
in culture war terms, 150–156, 253n.62
redefining words, 97, 105, 160, 217–218
use of metaphor, 214–215, 218
use of postmodernist critique, 168–169
in worldview terms, 53, 79, 81, 138, 145
French Revolution, 69, 72, 101
fundamentalists & fundamentalism, 2, 15–16, 21, 33, 34, 40, 42, 43, 44, 47, 128, 148, 164, 212–213, 226n.7. *See also* Islamic fundamentalism

Gandhi, Mohandas, 105, 216
gay marriage. *See* marriage equality
Genesis. *See under* Bible references
Gingrich, Newt, 24, 133, 183, 195
Glassroth v. Moore, 201–202, 206
God:
as arbitrary or embodying will, 62–64, 100–101, 107, 109, 171, 208–209, 213
as ordainer of government, 67, 135, 203
as providential, 103, 174–175, 194, 213
as sovereign, 7, 59, 62, 70, 72, 78, 83, 97, 104, 119, 125, 129, 138, 174, 202, 203, 204
as vengeful, 33, 36, 63, 109, 208–209
government:
Calvin on, 66–67, 72
Christian Reconstructionist approach to, 109–111, 113, 114–115, 119
as competitor of God, 186, 194, 261n.5
as counter to God's purposes, 194,

196, 199
as expressive of autonomy, 97, 199
Kuyper on, 72–73
as biblically ordained by God, 67, 135, 203
as properly minimal, 110–113, 185–191
grace, 73–74
Great Commission, 126, 133, 135
Grimstead, Jay, 117, 125, 128
Groen van Prinsterer, 235–236n.38

Hall, Verna, 176, 178
Hayek, Friedrich, 87, 93
Hegel, Georg Wilhelm Frederick, 70
history:
Neuhaus' treatment of U.S., 215
Rushdoony on "humanistic," 176
Rushdoony on conspiracy in, 144
Rushdoony's treatment of U.S., 102–103
Schaeffer's treatment of U.S., 123.
See also Christian revisionist history
Hofstadter, Richard, 143
homeschooling, 39–40
Home School Legal Defense Association, 39–40
How Now Shall We Live? (Colson and Pearcey), 3, 134, 135
Howse, Brannon, 1–2
Huckabee, Mike, 133, 183
Human Life Statute, 21
humanism:
as an expression of autonomy, 97
as a conspiracy, 146–147
as an ideology, 145, 154
as a philosophical movement, 146
as a religion, 99, 115, 146, 154
secular, 146, 154, 251n.23
the state and, 20, 83, 103, 112, 190
as a worldview, 19, 53, 146
Humanist Manifesto (I & II), 146
Hunter, James Davison, 142, 150–156

ideology:
Calvinism and, 59, 68
Christian Worldview as, 5, 48–49, 57, 74, 119, 130–131, 211–213, 217, 218
dictionary meaning of, 5
humanism as, 145, 154
radical Islam as, 212–213
Inhofe, James, 200
Institute for Christian Economics, 95
Institute on Religion and Democracy (IRD), 40
Institutes of Biblical Law, The (Rushdoony), 90
Institutes of the Christian Religion (Calvin), 60, 64, 90, 108
intelligent design (ID):
at Baylor University, 46
circularity of, 81
in the court of public opinion, 165–166
creationism and, 164
as an example of "theistic realism," 162, 164, 169–170
goals of advocates, 162–164
presuppositionalism and, 81
the religious basis of, 164
in schools, 171–172
as supportive of Christian complacency, 200
"invisible hand," 191–192
Islam, 141–142, 212
Islamic fundamentalism:
compared with Christian fundamentalism, 212–213
on jihad, 141, 212
presuppositionalism and, 213
relationship to Islam, 212
on secularism, 212

Jackson, Jesse, 197
Jacobs, Cindy, 136–137
jihad, 141, 212
John Birch Society, 86–87, 144
Johnson, Phillip, 161–171, 177
Jubilee Law, 114
judiciary. *See* federal judiciary

Kant, Immanuel, 99–101
Kennedy, D. James, 45, 117, 124, 128, 132–133, 148

King, Martin Luther, 32, 215, 216
Kingdom Now, 127–128, 136
Kitzmiller et al. v. Dover Areas School District, 171
Koop, C. Everett, 18, 34
Kuhn, Thomas, 93, 167–168
Kuyper, Abraham:
  anti-statism of, 72–73, 74, 190
  antithesis and, 71, 74, 84, 142, 149, 153
  background of, 69–70
  Calvinism and, 56–57, 59, 62, 70, 74
  Christian Worldview and, 56–58, 71, 72, 74
  on common grace, 73–74
  on Darwinism, 147
  on economics, 112
  influence of, 56–58, 84, 89, 131–132, 133, 137
  on modernism, 56, 69, 71–72
  Neo-Calvinism and, 56, 74
  as philosophical idealist, 70–71
  on presuppositions, 70–71, 76
  as providentialist, 175
  on "sphere sovereignty," 72–73

LaHaye, Beverly, 124, 128
LaHaye, Tim, 20, 85, 124, 128, 129, 146–147
Lakoff, George, 253n.62
Latter Rain, 127–128, 136, 248n.32
law:
  biblical, 105–109, 119, 125, 129
  common, 130, 202, 205, 264–265n.48
  God's (higher), 7, 34, 35, 109, 135, 229n.55
  human law, 7, 34, 35, 36, 205–206
  natural, 31, 33, 99, 100
  of nature, 205
Lawrence v. Texas, 29
Lectures on Calvinism (Kuyper), 57
lex talionis (eye for an eye, tooth for a tooth), 107, 243n.83
libertarianism, 114, 188
Liberty University, 26, 45
Liberty University Law School, 46
Logos School, 45
Luther, Martin, 54, 60
Lutz, Donald, 179
Lyons, Matthew, 126, 143

Machen, J. Gresham, 76
Madison, James, 178, 181
Mann, Horace, 103
marriage equality, 29, 143
Martin, Michael, 237n.65
McCain, John, 183
McCartney, Bill, 44
McDowell, Josh, 128
McDowell, Stephen K., 175, 176
"messianism," 89, 97, 101, 103, 111
Michael Polanyi Center, 46
Military Ministry, 42
Military Religious Freedom Foundation, 42
Mises, Ludwig von, 87, 93, 188
modernism:
  Christian Worldview and, 8, 58, 212
  Hunter on, 152, 155
  Islamic fundamentalism and, 212
  Kuyper on, 56, 68, 69, 70, 72
  as "modern spirit," 152, 155, 212
  as paradigm in crisis, 93
  Pearcey on, 134, 159
  Schaeffer on, 53, 123, 159
  as worldview, 145
Moore, Roy, 201–203, 206–207
Moral Majority, 13–14, 18, 21–22, 117, 187
Morecraft, Joseph, 118, 187
Morris, Benjamin F., 174, 178
Moyers, Bill, 116
Moynihan, Patrick, 197

"naked public square," 214–215
National Coordinating Council (NCC), 129
National Reform Association (NRA), 204
National Right to Life Committee, 32
natural law. *See under* law
naturalism. *See* scientific naturalism
Naugle, David, 4, 66
Neo-Calvinism, 56, 68, 74, 83, 89, 133. *See also under* Kuyper, Abraham
neo-evangelicals, 15, 226n.7

Index

Neuhaus, Richard:
  on Martin Luther King, 215-216
  on the "naked public square," 214–215
  on a "sacred canopy," 214–215
  on Tocqueville, 215–216
New Age philosophy, 17, 148–149
New Apostolic Reformation (NAR), 136–137, 149
Newton, Isaac, 99, 241n.45
Noebel, David, 132
North, Gary:
  as aide to Ron Paul, 188–189
  aspirations of, 92–93
  on Christian Reconstruction, 83, 117
  Christian Worldview and, 128
  on conspiracy, 144–145
  on Darwinism, 104, 242n.67, 255n.24
  on dominion, 126
  on economics, 92–93, 111, 112–114, 192
  on political strategy, 115–116
  on political rights, 115
  as providential historian, 175
  Rushdoony and, 90, 92–93, 94–95
  sources of funding, 240–241n.37
  style of leadership of, 95

Obama, Barack, 185, 186
O'Keefe, John, 32
Olasky, Marvin, 27, 195–197, 200
Operation Rescue, 34–35
original sin, 64, 181, 196
Orr, James, 54–56, 59
Orthodox Presbyterian Church (OPC), 77, 84, 88–89, 91, 94–95, 238n.4, 239n.12

Palin, Sarah, 133, 183, 187
pantheism, 99
"patriarchalism," 95
Patrick Henry College, 26, 45
Paul, Ron, 187, 188–189
Paulk, Earl, 127–128, 136
Peacocke, Dennis, 128
Pearcey, Nancy, 7, 37, 124, 133, 134–135, 147, 159–160, 161, 162, 171, 249n.46
Pennock, Robert, 165, 167, 169
Pentecostals, 15, 117, 127–128, 133, 136–137, 149, 226n.7. *See also* charismatics
Perry, Rick, 183, 185
Personal Responsibility and Work Reconciliation Act, 197
Phillips, Howard, 13, 186–187, 205, 261n.7
pietism, 70
Planned Parenthood, 32,
pluralism, 8, 138, 157, 209, 218
postmillennialism, 85–86, 115
postmodernism, 168–169
predestination, 59–60, 62, 99, 104
premillennialism, 15, 85–86, 95–96, 149
Presbyterianism, Anglo-Scottish, 84–85
Presbyterian Church of America (PCA), 84, 133, 238n.4
presuppositionalism, 71, 75, 76–82, 84, 92, 93, 96, 119, 121–122, 156, 158, 160, 166, 169–170, 177, 179, 237n.65. *See also under* Kuyper; Schaeffer; Van Til
Princeton Theological Seminary, 57
Pro-Life Action Network, 33
Promise Keepers, 44
Protestant Christianity, 19, 182
Protestants, mainline, 5, 40
Protestant Reformation, 8, 49, 54, 60, 98, 102, 123, 153, 161
providence. *See under* God; history
Puritans, 61, 85, 174, 195–196, 203, 238n.5

Qutb, Sayyid, 212

Reagan, Ronald, 14, 20–21, 127
reason:
  autonomous, 78, 80, 98–99
  primacy of will over, 62–63
  sinful, 64
  target of fundamentalists, 212–213
reasoning:
  "analogical," 78
  "autonomous," 78, 80

reasoning *(cont'd)*
circular, 79–80, 81, 237n.57, 237n.59, 237n.65
Scripture as model for, 78–79
Reconstructionism. *See* Christian Reconstructionism
Reed, Ralph, 22–24
"reform," theological idea of, 37–38
Reformed Christians & Christianity, 15, 60, 61, 69, 70, 73, 84–85, 128, 226n.7
Reformed theologians, 75, 76, 77, 79, 91, 92, 94, 95–96, 108
Regent constitutionalists, 130, 205, 206, 249n.40
Regent University, 22, 26, 45
Regent University Law School, 45, 130, 205
"religion of humanity," 103, 104, 145. *See also* humanism
Religious Right. *See* Christian Right
renewal groups, 40
Republican Party, 6, 13–14, 22–31, 45, 187, 188, 189–190, 195, 197, 200–201, 206–207
responsibility:
biblical, 193–194, 195, 196
collective, 194, 197
confined view of, 104–105, 194, 201
environmental policy and, 198–200
personal, 112, 194–195, 197
"presumptuous," 104–105, 194, 201
social policy and, 195–198
revisionist history. *See* Christian revisionist history
rights, 72, 115, 127, 155–156, 215, 216, 217
Robertson, Pat, 19, 22–24, 28, 44, 45, 117, 124, 125, 127, 145, 148, 154, 205
Roe v. Wade, 17–18, 31, 253n.61
Romans. *See under* Bible references
Rothbard, Murray, 87
Rushdoony, Rousas John:
on American history, 102–103
on autonomy, 97–105
on biblical law, 106, 107, 109
on Calvin, 239n.12, 243–244n.85
Christian Worldview and, 57, 128, 153
on conspiracy, 86–87, 144–145
on Darwinism and evolution, 103–104, 147, 255n.24
on democracy, 101–102
on divine and human order, 98
on Dominion Mandate, 126
early career of, 88
as founder of Reconstructionism, 83, 89–91
on history, 144, 176
on libertarianism, 114–115
North and, 90, 92–93, 94–95
"patriarchalism" and, 94–95
public exposure of, 116
religious background of, 88–89
on responsibility, 194
Schaeffer and, 121–122
on the state, 97–98, 101, 104
on theocracy, 110, 114–115
on truth, 158–159
on Unitarianism, 102–103
on the United Nations, 104
on universal morality, 100, 104–105
Rutherford, Samuel, 123, 247n.12
Ryan, John, 33

"sacred canopy," 214–215
same-sex marriage. *See* marriage equality
Sanger, Margaret, 32
saving grace. *See* grace
Schaeffer, Edith, 128
Schaeffer, Frank, 128
Schaeffer, Francis:
abortion and, 18, 31, 34, 36, 124
background of, 18–19, 121
Christian Reconstruction and, 108, 122
Christian Worldview and, 53–54, 57, 121, 128, 131, 133, 153
on civil disobedience, 7, 124
on Darwinism, 147
Dooyeweerd and, 75, 254n.15
on humanism, 53, 146
inconsistencies of, 122–123

Index

Neo-Calvinism and, 121
on presuppositionalism, 121–122
scholarly naïveté of, 123
on theocracy, 7, 122–123
on truth and knowledge, 159, 161, 162, 169, 254n.12, 254n.16
Scheidler, Joseph, 33–34
Schiavo, Terri, 29, 142–43
Schlafly, Phyllis, 17
schools. *See* education
Schweitzer, Albert, 104–105
science:
as form of autonomy, 99, 103–104
concepts hijacked by critics, 160
approach to evidence of, 165
Kuhn and, 167–168
as form of naturalism, 161–162
presuppositions and, 160, 166
public skepticism and, 172
as religion, 167
school curriculum and, 171–172
as target for Christian & Islamic fundamentalists, 212–213
Wedge movement's attack on, 162–164
as worldview, 147, 166
scientific naturalism:
distinction between metaphysical and methodological, 167
Johnson on, 166–167, 256n.36
Scopes Monkey Trial, 16
Second American Revolution, The (Whitehead), 20, 125
Secret Kingdom, The (Robertson), 125
secular humanism, 146, 154. *See also* humanism
secularism:
as target for Christian & Islamic fundamentalists, 212
as threat to Christianity, 1, 48, 53, 121, 142–143, 188, 212, 214, 218
as worldview, 1, 53, 150
separation of church and state. *See* church-state separation, principle of
Sharlet, Jeff, 43
shepherding, 231n.75
Sire, James, 5, 132
Smith, Adam, 191–192
social gospel, 15
sphere sovereignty, 73, 110, 129, 133
spiritual warfare, 4, 19, 48, 71, 142–143, 149, 212. *See also* antithesis; culture war; dualism
state. *See* government
Supreme Court. *See* federal judiciary
Structure of Scientific Revolutions, The (Kuhn), 93, 167–168

Tea Party Movement, 185, 190
Ten Commandments:
as authoritarian, 208–209
as purported basis of American law, 202, 205, 264–265n.48
in *Glassroth v. Moore*, 201–202
religious role of, 105–106
Ten Commandments Case. *See Glassroth v. Moore*
Terry, Randall, 32, 33–35, 124, 128, 187
Texas Republican Party, 133, 189–190
"theistic realism":
as alternative to mainstream science, 162, 169–170
as reflective of presuppositionalism, 169–170
theocracy, 6–7, 110, 114, 122–123, 135, 208–209
theonomy, 91, 105–109
Theonomy in Christian Ethics (Bahnsen), 91
Thoreau, Henry David, 216
Tiller, Dr. George, 36, 213–214
Titus, Herb, 45–46, 118, 130, 205–206, 207, 208, 264–265n.48
Tocqueville, Alexis de, 215–216
Total Truth: Liberating Christianity from its Cultural Captivity (Pearcey), 134
Tragedy of American Compassion, The (Olasky), 195
truth:
as all or nothing, 165, 170
as approached in the empirical sciences, 165, 170
as central to culture war concept, 151–153

truth *(cont'd)*
in Christian tradition, 157
correct presuppositions seen as basis for, 76, 78–79, 158, 169–170
as focus of Christian & Islamic fundamentalists, 213
as God-interpreted, 78–79, 158–159
theistic realism and, 162, 169–170
as totalistic concept, 159–160
Truth Project, 2, 136
Tyler, Texas, 94, 95
Tyndale, John, 238n.5

Understanding the Times: The Religious Worldviews of Our Day and the Search for Truth (Noebel), 132
"unified field of knowledge," 159, 169
Unitarianism, 102–103
United Nations, 104, 144, 190
Universe Next Door, The (Sire), 132
U.S. Taxpayers Party, 186–187, 205, 261n.6

Value Action Teams, 26
Van Til, Cornelius:
on autonomy, 78, 80, 97, 99–100
Christian Worldview and, 57, 84
circular reasoning of, 79–80, 237n.57
debate strategy of, 80–81
influence of, 89, 91, 93, 121–122
intellectual isolation of, 77
presuppositionalism and, 76–82, 169
on truth, 78, 158
Viguerie, Richard, 13
Volker Fund. *See* William Volker Fund
voluntarism:
defined in philosophical terms, 62
as expressed in divine arbitrariness, 62–63, 99, 100–101, 107, 109, 208–209
as argued against by Plato, 233–234n.10

Wagner, C. Peter, 136–137
Walton, Rus, 187
War on Christmas, 143
Warren, Rick, 135–136
Weber, Max, 59, 112
Wedge Document, 163–164
wedge issues, 142, 163–164
Wedge movement:
public impact, 171–172
strategy of, 163–164
Wells, Ronald, 123
Westminster Academy, 45
Westminster Confession, 64, 84, 108
Westminster Theological Seminary, 76, 77, 91, 92, 93, 94, 121
Weyrich, Paul, 13, 16, 22
Whatever Happened to the Human Race? (Schaeffer & Koop), 18, 34, 124
Whitehead, John, 20, 125, 130
Wildmon, Don, 128, 129
Will, George, 197–198
William Volker Fund, 87
Wilson, Douglas, 45
Wise Use Movement, 200
Wolters, Albert, 5
worldview:
conflict and, 4, 19, 53, 71, 151–153
degree of rigidity of, 4–5
derivation of term, 55
as ideology, 5
religious assumptions and, 1, 71, 152–153
truth and, 3–4, 54, 55, 71, 151–153
Worldview Weekend, 2
Wu, John C. H., 264–265n.48